Scripta Series in Geography

Series Editors:

Richard E. Lonsdale, University of Nebraska
Antony R. Orme, University of California
Theodore Shabad, Columbia University
James O. Wheeler, University of Georgia

Other titles in the series:

W. A. Dando: The Geography of Famine
G. A. Klee: World Systems of Traditional Resource Management
F. C. F. Earney: Petroleum and Hard Minerals from the Sea
M. H. Yeates: North American Urban Patterns
S. D. Brunn/J. O. Wheeler: The American Metropolitan System: Present and Future
R. H. Jackson: Land Use in America
J. E. Oliver: Climatology: Selected Applications

The Geography of Housing

Larry S. Bourne

Director of the Centre for Urban and Community Studies and
Professor of Geography, University of Toronto

A HALSTED PRESS BOOK

 V. H. Winston & Sons

John Wiley & Sons
New York

Copyright © V. H. Winston & Sons 1981

First published 1981 by
Edward Arnold (Publishers) Ltd.
41 Bedford Square, London WC1B 3DQ
and distributed in the United States of America by Halsted Press, a division of John Wiley &
Sons Inc.

British Library Cataloguing in Publication Data

Bourne, Larry S
    Geography of housing. – (Scripta series in geography).
    1. Housing
    2. Cities and towns
    I. Title
    301.5'4'091732   HD7287.5

    ISBN 0-7131-6300-3
    ISBN 0-7131-6340-2 pbk

Library of Congress Data Cataloguing in Publication Data

Bourne, Larry S
    Geography of housing.
    (Scripta series in geography)
    "A Halsted Press book."
    Bibliography: P.
    Includes index.
    1. Housing.   I. Title.   II. Series.
HD7287.B67 1981   363.5   80-19908

ISBN 0-470-27058-6
ISBN 0-470-27059-4 (pbk.)

Typeset in the United States of America by
Marie Maddalena of V. H. Winston & Sons
Printed in Canada by Hunter Rose.

Contents

For Paula

Acknowledgements

Although the origins of this book lie in my long-standing interest in urban structure and residential change, the most recent stimulus was my participation in a research program on Urban Housing Markets administered by the Centre for Urban and Community Studies at the University of Toronto. This program was supported by a grant from the Connaught Fund. The book was written in draft form while I was in residence at the Centre for Environmental Studies (CES) in London during 1978-79 under a Sabbatical Leave Fellowship from the Social Sciences and Humanities Research Council of Canada (SSHRCC). I wish to thank SSHRCC and the University of Toronto for their generous support and CES for providing both necessary services and an appropriately stimulating intellectual environment. None of these organizations bears any responsibility whatever for the failures of the final product.

Many individuals, in widely scattered locations, have contributed to the content and orientation of this book—often without their knowledge or consent. The staff of the Centre for Urban and Community Studies provided the home base and the trans-Atlantic support services which proved to be essential. Bev Thompson typed portions of the initial draft, while Catherine Morrissey typed the final draft and the bibliography. Jennifer Wilcox and the cartography office in the Department of Geography at the University of Toronto, under Geoff Matthews, redrew the illustrations with their usual finesse and efficiency.

More difficult to acknowledge are those whose research I have drawn on liberally and whose ideas appear throughout the text. Some of these are former students at the University of Toronto—Toni Andreae, Joe Berridge, Conrad Biernacki, Simon Chamberlain, Chris Maher, Peter Moore, Phil Morrison, Jeremy Rudin, Chris Sharpe,

Katherine Willson; others are faculty colleagues—Barry Cullingworth, John Hitchcock, Bill Michelson, John Miron, David Nowlan, Jim Simmons, and Barry Wellman. Several others also offered useful criticisms of the initial outline or of portions of the text—Kazimierz Dziewonski, Phil Morrison, Ray Struyk, Christine Whitehead, and Maurice Yeates. Unfortunately, none of these people saw the entire manuscript in draft form and so their critical talents were not adequately employed. Of course they too are free from any association with errors or omissions in the text.

Finally, I owe an immense debt to my wife Paula and children David and Alexandra who put up with a sabbatical year dominated by my frequent travels and by the incessant clattering of an old portable typewriter. Without their support it would not have been possible to write this book, nor would it have been worth doing.

L. S. Bourne
Toronto, January, 1980

Chapter 1

Introduction

Housing, at one and the same time, is both a simple and extremely complex term. It is simple because in its everyday sense we all know, or at least think we know, what the term refers to. Housing is a real, physical artifact. It is easily visible, a central component in our daily lives, and vitally important to us all as shelter. In its broader social context, however, housing is immensely diverse and complex, and intimately interrelated with its socioeconomic, political, and neighborhood environment—almost to the point of posing an intractable task for research and planning, for both researchers and policy makers.

This book undertakes to provide a modest introduction to the geography of housing which is also a synthesis of the diverse perspectives on what housing is. Written primarily for those interested in housing in a contemporary urban context, it emphasizes the processes through which housing is produced and then distributed (allocated) among people and places; how patterns in the use of housing have changed over time and within cities; who benefits through these changes; and their implications for public policy.

Housing in Context: History, Society, and Politics

Housing has been a concern of individual families, groups, and at least some governments since the dawn of urban civilization. It is only since the industrial revolution, however, and particularly since the late 19th century, that housing conditions have risen to prominence as a major societal issue and political concern. In fact, the awareness of and societal action on housing problems dates effectively from—and is part of—the social reform movements of the late 19th century. These movements not only crystallized public interest in the appalling condition of the "built" environment within which the majority of working class urban dwellers lived, but articulated a sense of responsibility for society in general to intervene in order to improve those conditions. These movements also resulted in the establishment of explicit minimum standards of housing quality and they initiated a process of government intervention, in what was at that time largely a private market mechanism for the supply and distribution of housing, which has continued to the present day.

One outcome of these historical precedents is that housing is now so firmly embedded in the social, economic, and political fabric of all developed countries that it cannot be studied in isolation. Housing is so obviously important because it provides one of the basic needs of all members of society—shelter. In terms of the living expenses facing households and families, housing ranks second only to food, and for homeowners it is by far the largest single purchase decision most will make in their life-time. Housing is also of immense *psychological importance* since it is an integral part of our definition of what is a desirable quality of life and social status. That is, from the use of housing flow a variety of services to the household—satisfaction, status, privacy, security and equity as well as shelter—and services to the original builders and a host of other agents.

Housing also plays other very different roles in our society. It is an immense element in the national inheritance and a source of personal wealth. It is a major (but by no means the largest) sector in the national economy, a substantial consumer of investment funds, and a large (although volatile) source of employment within the construction and building industries. For local governments, housing and residential land use are the largest consumers of urban space and the principal preoccupation of civic administrators. Housing is not only a source of tax revenue, but more important it and its occupants are the clients for most of the social and physical services provided by local government. In terms of planning, the quantity, type, and quality of housing built in each part of an urban area effectively determine the form and fabric of that area and the patterns of social relations and types of communities which result.

Some of the unique attributes of housing as an economic commodity, social good, and a public service add further complexity to the task of defining the context for a geography of housing. We know that housing is expensive to build, difficult to modify, and generally long standing. Consequently, what we observe when we examine the standing stock of housing in a city at any given time is a layering of houses built at different times, by different hands, and often under very different political and economic conditions. Each layer of new building is in part superimposed on and selectively modifies what has gone before. Within a city this layering is usually most obvious in the geographic zonation of housing by age, style, and density around the city center.

The obvious fact that urban housing (with the limited exception of mobile homes) is *fixed in location* in turn links the fortunes of that housing inextricably to a particular neighborhood and to the changing spatial structure of the entire urban area. Even the most basic function of housing—shelter—is dependent on the condition of the surrounding neighborhood environment. This mutual interdependence still complicates research on housing, compounds the difficulties and failures of housing policies, and contributes to continued inequalities in living standards. In most parts of the developed world, obtaining the key to a house, flat or apartment also brings with it the right to a given level of public services (police, schools, parks, etc.); it determines one's local tax rate and in turn it delivers a set of benefits (security, etc.) or disbenefits (crime, vandalism, etc.) to both the individual household and the larger community.

Given these interrelationships, it is not surprising that interpretations of the role of housing and of the priorities attached to housing policy differ so widely between and within modern societies. The principal distinction is between those who see housing strictly as an economic or investment good and those who see it more as a social good or service for which society takes—or should take—a collective responsibility. For the former, the production and consumption of housing, like that of T-shirts, can be left primarily to the private market. There, financiers, builders, and consumers jointly determine how much housing is supplied at what location, who receives it, and at what price. Since we do not have a national policy for the distribution of T-shirts, they argue, why should we have one for housing. The second view, in contrast, argues that housing is more of a social service which, like education, is to be provided to all members of society, at least up to an acceptable level of quality and quantity.

Clearly housing serves both roles simultaneously in almost all developed economies. It is not strictly a free market good even in the most laissez-faire and capitalist economic systems. In such systems housing is now so entangled in a myriad of government regulations, from those of national governments to those of local authorities and quasi-public financial institutions, that it is difficult to say where the market begins and ends. Moreover, only a small proportion of all new housing in western countries is now without some form of public subsidy, direct or indirect. Nor is housing entirely a social or collective good even in those socialist societies with the most centrally-planned and publicly-owned economies.

Thus, to understand how housing is allocated in any society one must also know something about the systems of government taxation, land tenure, and financial controls within which housing has been and is currently produced. The complex, dynamic housing markets we observe in our large cities are relatively recent creations. For example, in most of Europe up to the 19th century it was difficult to shift housing and land from a rental (leasehold) to an owned (freehold) status. Leases were short and capital was scarce. There were few institutions to extend credit so property exchanges were less frequent, often based on accumulated personal wealth. Only in the last century has it become possible for millions of urban dwellers to purchase their own homes and to buy their own land.

The fact that housing is now in most cases jointly produced and allocated by public and private mechanisms leads inevitably to social and political *conflict*. This conflict has several expressions: between different levels of government, such as between national governments who usually set the basic conditions of housing supply, and local governments who largely determine what housing is actually built and where. Other conflicts arise between social groups and classes, such as between those who own housing and those who do not; between political-geographic areas (the central city vs. the suburbs); and between individual needs and preferences (e.g., for privacy and security) and collective community needs and preferences (e.g., for greater social integration and mixed neighborhoods).

Not all of these conflicts are necessarily bad, although they often have their dark side. Some are a necessary or unavoidable element in resolving diverse social needs (e.g., for efficiency and equity) and competing aspirations regarding housing. Others are real conflicts for which an unbiased arbitrator is required; still others are creations of the particular systems we have devised for producing and distributing housing. Our *challenge* as students of housing is to identify the origins of these conflicts and to distinguish between those which are inevitable but potentially constructive and those which are artificial and/or socially destructive.

One of the consequences of these conflicts, and of the immense importance attached to housing in our society, is that approaches to and debates on housing research and policy have become highly politicized. Of course, the provision of housing has always been, at least since the last century, in part a political process. The recent growth of this political component is evident not only in the increasingly complex overlay of housing and land use legislation but also in the very diverse political philosophies or *ideologies* which shape housing policies.

We must also not forget that housing is, in the final analysis, for people. The often-quoted expression "houses do not make homes" is a simple reminder of the necessity of looking at housing units as dwelling units, as places for living, and as bricks in building and maintaining a social order, not simply as a means of satisfaction for architects, builders, governments, or researchers. All too frequently housing becomes a source of gratification for designers and planners; politicians play a "numbers" game in terms of how many new units were built under their regime, often with little regard for the needs of those people who are to live in those units. Any discussion of housing is incomplete without this social dimension, and without a sense of collective social responsibility.

Objectives: What the Book Is and Is not

The intention is to provide an introduction to housing set within the broad context outlined above. It emphasizes six major themes: (1) the immense diversity and complexity of housing within different neighborhoods, cities, and countries, and the difficulties of generalizing from one political system to another; (2) geographical variability in those factors influencing the supply and demand for housing; (3) the processes by which housing is allocated to households, in both the public and private sectors; (4) the social and spatial outcomes which result from this allocation; (5) the problems and policy responses which these outcomes generate; and (6) the relationships between housing policy and other dimensions of urban structure and public policy. The unifying theme is the attempt to relate each of these areas of concern to the changing patterns and uses of the housing stock as they appear "on the ground."

The enormous breadth of the literature on housing necessitates that any such review be highly selective, in terms of topics chosen for review and the depth of coverage of each topic. This book is no exception. The discussion is limited primarily, but not exclusively, to the housing conditions and policy experience of western developed economies, and to the private market mechanism of allocating housing, especially as it operates in the English-speaking world, notably the United States, Britain, and Canada. One chapter, however, is devoted to alternative housing systems, emphasizing the socialist world, and another to public sector housing.

The geographical focus as noted is on housing in urban areas, particularly the larger metropolitan areas. This focus requires that we bring together the literature on residential land use, neighborhood change, household mobility, and the processes of land conversion and development at the local level, with the more traditionally-defined housing literature. It is argued here that only within such a broad framework can we understand how and why housing production and consumption vary between different geographic areas. Much of the literature on housing has focussed on the national level or on specific local areas or problems, with relatively little attempt to link the two scales within a dynamic context.

The emphasis on urban areas here is not meant to imply, however, that small towns and rural areas do not have serious housing problems. Clearly they do. Instead, it is a recognition of the overwhelming dominance of the urban housing stock (75 to 80%) in most national housing inventories, and of the unique set of pressures to which urban housing is subjected. The latter pressures include: (1) intense *competition* from other land uses in the urban real estate market; (2) mutual *interdependence*, through close geographical proximity, neighborhood effects, and spatial externalities; (3) tighter public *regulation*, through rigid building, servicing, and planning controls; (4) greater *instability*, in terms of the rapidly changing social demands placed on urban housing and the frequent pressures for rezoning and redevelopment; and (5) more marked *differentiation*, in terms of the scale, density and intensity of spatial segregation of the urban housing stock by age, type, and quality. Some of these pressures are evident in rural areas, but not all in combination.

The other major emphasis is on providing, in today's jargon, conceptual frameworks to assist in interpreting housing trends and relationships. Empirical examples are intentionally limited, for rather obvious reasons. To display the full complexity and diversity of spatial and aspatial patterns and processes of change within what is called the housing "system"[1] of a single metropolitan area would in itself require a book of at least this length. Most empirical evidence is "place-specific"; i.e., it tells us more about the city in question than about housing processes in general. Here selected examples from particular cities are included where they serve to clarify conceptual issues, or to add flavor or a note of realism to the discussions, and where they can be easily described. Readers are encouraged to provide the reality or empirical flesh for these conceptual skeletons with examples drawn from their own local communities.

Nor does this volume pretend to be a thorough review of the housing literature, even of that which has an explicit geographical focus. The literature is now so vast and disparate that any such attempt would not only be superficial, but a mind-numbing exercise. There is also now a number of specialized texts and readings volumes available to serve this purpose. The reader is referred to these sources at various points in the text, and an extensive bibliography is also provided. Although there are few general texts on the geography of housing, there is a considerable literature on closely related areas on which this volume draws heavily. These areas include the study of residential land use and urban ecology (Johnston, 1971; Berry and Kasarda, 1977), social areas in cities (Robson, 1975; Herbert and Johnston, 1976), residential mobility (Moore, 1972, 1973), residential segregation and social injustices (Harvey, 1973; Lee, 1977), and social conflict within cities (Cox, 1978).

The result is a book which presents a personal view of housing and housing issues, with all of the advantages and disadvantages which that implies. It is comprehensive to the extent that constraints of time and limited space allow, and subject of course to the author's restricted knowledge and personal inclinations.

On the Scale, Complexity, and Diversity of Housing

At the outset we should again stress the immense diversity of housing, between countries as well as within countries, and the sheer scale of synthesis and analysis which are necessary. It is also extremely difficult to generalize across national boundaries where the inherited housing stock, and the political and financial environments within which policies are formulated, are so different.

Consider the scale problem when looking at a single urban area of say 1 million population. That area would likely contain about 350,000 households and slightly more dwelling units within perhaps 250,000 separate residential buildings. Of the 350,000 occupied units, some 125,000 might be rental units, in a typical North American city, and from 30,000 to 50,000 of these might be in new high-rise structures. House prices could vary from effectively zero (derelict housing) to several millions for a stately mansion, while rents could vary from next to nothing to thousands per month. Each unit also differs, if only slightly, in design and obviously in location.

What of changes over time? In an average year some 20,000 new housing units might be added to the housing stock, with a thousand or so units lost through demolition, fire, conversion, or abandonment. During the same period of time, as many as 50,000 units might change hands through sale or renting (some more than once) and a similar number may change their relative position, in the hierarchy of price or quality, upward through rehabilitation and improvement, or conversely downward through a lack of maintenance or conversion. At the same time, almost any change in the urban environment—such as the opening of a new road or transit line, the closure of an industrial plant or racial change—alters the demand for housing and does so to a different extent in various parts of the city. Similarily, household incomes, attitudes, and preferences may change, altering the relative attractiveness of different house types and neighborhoods.

The important point here is that only when all of these attributes of housing are put together can one appreciate the complexity of what we conveniently label "housing." For these reasons, this book begins simply, attempting to develop a common language of terms and benchmarks, for the more detailed discussions to follow.

Organizing Concepts of the Book

As the preceding discussion suggests, an introductory book on housing could be organized in several ways. One approach would be to being with current housing problems—such as high prices, segregation, deterioration, credit restrictions, or more generally the unequal distribution of housing among types or classes of households. As attractive and stimulating as this approach might be, policy problems do not transport well over time, or from region to region and country to country. Housing problems are not the same in Los Angeles as in rural Mississippi; nor are they the same in Britain, the U.S., and eastern Europe, although as we see there are some important common denominators.

A second approach might take a more behavioral perspective, beginning with the actors—or agents of change—involved in the production, distribution, and consumption of housing. This approach has considerable appeal since it directs our attention to those who make the decisions, and on what criteria, and to the links between decisions made at each stage in the process of housing provision and use. The major disadvantage of this approach is that it acts to direct attention away from the larger arena—the economic, social, and political systems—in which the actors are operating. A second and more pragmatic drawback is that there are far too many actors involved in housing, many of whom are unknown, or unavailable, to enable one to deal with all aspects of housing in sufficient detail in one volume.

A third approach, which we might call a "process-oriented" approach, looks at the actual mechanisms of housing production and consumption. How is housing produced and then distributed to people of different income, race, and class, living in different geographical areas? Here there are two alternative perspectives. The first looks at the *distribution* or *allocation* of housing as a process of *exchange*—of buying, selling, or renting—operating primarily through the mechanism of price (or rent) as established in a more or less competitive economic market. The second looks to the role of government—the "state" and its agencies—in producing and allocating housing based primarily on social needs. As previously noted, both processes coexist in almost all countries, but in widely varying combinations. In those with largely market-based economies, such as the U.S., Australia, or Canada, the former process overwhelmingly dominates. From this point there is a continuum of increasing public control over housing from those societies with more mixed (Britain) or quasi-market economies (Sweden), to the centrally-planned socialist economies in which a private market may still flourish (e.g., Poland) to those in which there is little apparent role for a market mechanism (e.g., USSR).

In this volume the dominant organizing concepts are drawn primarily from the second and third of the above approaches. Housing problems in turn are introduced as outcomes or failures of the market mechanism we use for producing and distributing housing. The organizing focus is the process of *housing allocation*. This focus allows for the integration of aggregate (or aspatial) perspectives on housing with those concerned with housing at a local or disaggregate level within urban areas. It also provides a convenient conceptual umbrella which embraces both public sector housing provision as well as that in the private sector. Attention is also given to the behavioral bases of the allocation process in terms of the diversity of individual and corporate actors—and their roles and aspirations—involved. It is these actors who translate housing supply and demand at the national level into occupied housing and neighborhoods at the local level.

The Arrangement of Chapters

The organization of the text follows from these general themes (Fig. 1.1). This chapter and the next elaborate on the above themes, providing a sense of the content and context of the geography of urban housing. Chapter 2 outlines basic concepts and definitions of terms relating to what housing is, the unique attributes of the housing stock and how that stock changes over time, the matching of households to housing units and their relationship to urban real estate markets and neighborhood change. It also looks at the quantity and quality of housing information and the requirements for monitoring market changes in an urban area. Chapter 3 breaks away from the development of concepts to document the changing composition, structural conditions, and spatial patterns of housing among and within various countries and cities. Chapter 4 describes in more detail the process of housing allocation—with emphasis on how urban housing markets work and who is involved.

Given this conceptual and empirical background, the emphasis in the next four chapters shifts to more detailed analyses of the components and processes of change in an urban housing "system." The sequence is traditional. Chapter 5 examines processes of housing supply and mortgage finance, while Chapter 6 examines housing demand, household relocation and mobility, and demographic change. In both cases, the review starts with an aggregate (national) perspective and then proceeds to look at conditions and determinants of change within urban areas. Chapter 7 provides an overview of some actual mechanisms of change in housing and neighborhoods, such as filtering, and the spatial outcomes of those mechanisms—*i.e., who gets what kind of housing, where, and at what price.* Chapter 8 then selects examples of current housing problems for more detailed discussion; physical decay, segregation, discrimination, abandonment, price escalation—problems which may be seen either as failures of the private market mechanism to operate efficiently or as inevitable injustices deriving from that mechanism.

In the next two chapters attention shifts to a review of housing policies (Chapter 9) and the role of government as landlord (Chapter 10) in western societies. This review must of necessity be cursory and selective since housing policies are not only complex but subject to frequent change and because they differ so widely among countries. Few people even know what our overall housing policy really is, let alone what its impact has been in social and geographical terms. The policy discussions in Chapter 9 are limited to the experiences of the U.S. and U.K.[2]

The inclusion in Chapter 11 of brief discussions of housing conditions and policies in societies other than those from which this book primarily derives is important in its own right, but it also offers a different and at times a very challenging perspective on our own housing problems. Examples from the Socialist world are particularly valuable in this regard. The Third World, although in detail beyond the scope of this book, provides quite a different set of examples; here

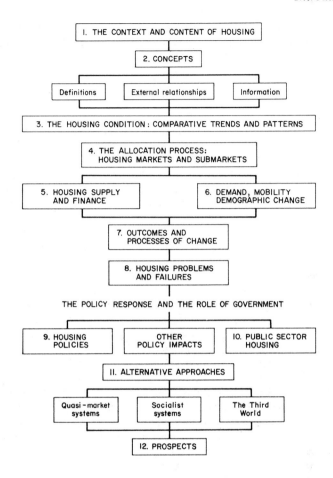

Fig. 1.1. Organization of chapters.

are the vast bulk of the world's urban housing problems and the arena in which what Abrams (1964) called man's continual struggle for adequate shelter will be won or lost.

Housing as an Area of Study

Clearly, the study of housing does not fall neatly into the province of any one of the traditional academic disciplines or professional groups. Nor does the housing "problem" submit to any single political, ideological, or research paradigm. At the same time, housing cannot be divorced from the legal systems and social structures which influence its production and use, or from the neighborhoods in which it is located. The latter renders a geographical perspective on housing as imperative.

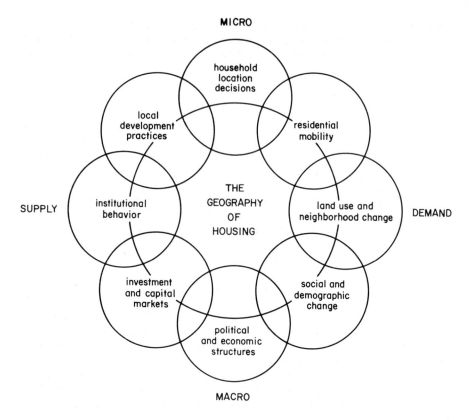

Fig. 1.2. The literature context for studies of the geography of housing.

Figure 1.2 attempts to convey an image of the many established areas of re-search which directly contribute to an understanding of housing in contemporary urban environments. In this example eight distinctive areas of research are shown, although more could easily be added. These areas vary in scale (macro, micro) and in subject matter (demand, supply, policy) as well as in their philosophy and methodology. On the demand side, the most relevant areas here vary from the literature on residential location models and decision-making at the local level to the societal-level context of social values, attitudes, and political structures. On the supply side, the relevant areas include the study of national housing and capital markets (the housing sector), government, institutions, and the corporate actors and property regulations which shape patterns of land development and housing supply at the local level.

Thus, to study housing effectively involves the analysis of a major sector of the national economy, a plethora of institutions and agencies, demographic change, migration and social preferences and constraints on the freedom of choice; in other words, virtually the entire spectrum of our living and working environments. In addition, one must weave through a bewildering array of government policies and programs, many of which have no stated relevance to housing, but which, as we will see, have substantial impacts.

Why this Book at this Time?

Few authors would admit that their book is not timely. Yet many students of housing might well feel that this is not the time for another book on housing, even if to date there has not been a single major treatment of the geography of housing. They might argue that, after all, the major historical problem of an absolute housing shortage has been largely removed, that housing quality has improved substantially, and that housing problems have slipped as a policy priority for most governments in the face of the economic recession, high inflation, political uncertainties, fiscal problems, and energy shortages which have characterized the 1970s.

Although these assertions are generally correct, this kind of book may be most timely for exactly the same reasons. It seems clear that we are now entering a period in which housing issues, at least in highly industrialized western societies, will be rather different from those of the past two or three decades. Although the improvement in housing conditions noted above has reduced the severity of housing problems at the national level, it has also increased the relative importance of those problems facing particular disadvantaged groups in society and those concentrated in specific locations. Even in those countries or urban areas in which there are more housing units than households, problems of housing quality, finance, maintenance, price escalation and perhaps most critically, of the unequal distribution of a nation's housing resources among people and places, remain serious social concerns.

Other recent trends have also altered the nature of our future housing problems. Slower rates of population growth, dramatic changes in the demographic structure of that population, a continuing out-migration of people and jobs from the cities, as well as higher energy costs and inflation, indicate that the volume and type of housing required will change as will the locations at which that demand is expressed. Indeed, in some areas the emerging problem is one of a housing surplus and thus of maintaining the quality of the existing stock in the face of continued new construction and, perhaps, declining demand. As the pendulum of public and government thinking turns to conservation and the reuse of older housing, a new and different set of questions arises for policy-makers and researchers.

Despite the fact that the literature and empirical evidence on which this book depends derive largely from the 1960s and early 1970s, a period of rapid urban growth, an attempt is made to place both the concepts and the evidence in a framework which is applicable to the 1980s. This is not, as the reader will recognize, easy to do. We are all prisoners of our intellectual heritage; our concepts do reflect the conditions under which they were formulated. The task here is to continually reassess our interpretations in light of emerging trends and evolving attitudes. If this book assists in doing so, it will be both timely and worth reading.

Level of Difficulty

As an introduction to housing, this book takes little for granted in terms of background. Concepts are developed slowly and, as noted above, considerable attention is given to defining terms, supported by graphic and tabular materials. In an area as complex as housing, it is often the absence of common agreement on terminology, methods, and concepts which adds confusion and handicaps our ability to deal with real problems. The beginning student of housing (like the author) will want to progress slowly through the text. Frequent reference will be made to materials in other chapters or to more general texts in economics, geography, political science, sociology, planning or urban studies.

It will also be obvious that some concepts and empirical examples require more background than do others. There is simply no way one can avoid complex concepts and techniques in the study of housing. Economic concepts such as indifference curves or elasticities, sociopsychological concepts such as life cycle, and spatial concepts such as place utility are useful tools. Similarly, while mathematical notations and analyses are kept to an absolute minimum, they too cannot and should not be avoided. Finally, some awareness of different political ideologies and research paradigms is taken for granted. In all cases, however, the level of difficulty is not such as to preclude use of the book by the interested layman.

NOTES

[1]The term "housing system" is used here, as a typically vague but convenient shorthand expression, to encompass the full range of interrelationships between all of the actors (individual and corporate), housing units and institutions involved in the production, consumption, and regulation of housing. It is thus a much broader term than the housing market or sector.

[2]Throughout the following text, the terms United Kingdom (U.K.) and (Great) Britain are used interchangeably, although the latter excludes Northern Ireland. Some of the statistical tables refer to the U.K., others to Britain, and still others to England and Wales only. This confusion seems unavoidable. Similar difficulties arise, on a smaller scale, in terms of whether U.S. statistics include Alaska and offshore islands.

Chapter 2

Concepts, Context
and Information

What exactly is housing? What is meant by such terms as the housing sector, the housing market, the housing inventory, and the standing stock? What attributes may be used to measure housing, and which of these are unique? How can we measure the diverse benefits which housing produces when that housing varies from shacks to mansions? More specifically, what kinds of benefits, or services does the occupancy and/or purchase of housing convey to its residents? Finally we ask, what sources of information are available for the study of housing and housing policy? How does this information relate to those research and policy issues which are perceived as important? These questions provide the structure for this chapter.

WHAT IS HOUSING?

There are, then, two major sources of confusion in the literature on housing: one of conceptualization the other of measurement. As outlined in the introduction, housing, at its most basic level, is certainly "shelter," but it is equally clearly much more than that. It is both a physical entity, a social artifact, an economic good, a capital stock, a status symbol, and at times a political "hot-potato." We in turn must be precise as to what aspects of this "multi-dimensional" thing we mean when we refer to "housing."

Definitions of Housing

At least six common definitions of housing appear in the literature:

as a *physical facility* unit or structure,[1] which provides shelter to its occupants, but which also consumes land and demands the provision of physical services such as water and sewerage as well as social services to households;[2]

as an *economic good or commodity*, a consumer durable good, which is traded or exchanged in a market and as an "investment" good which returns equity to its owner;

as a *social or collective good*, as an element in the social fabric and in that society's set of social relations, and which is provided to everyone just as it attempts to do in education, food and, in most cases, health care;

as a *package or bundle of services*—a view which recognizes that the occupancy of housing involves the consumption of neighborhood services (parks, schools), a location (accessibility to jobs and amenities) and the proximity of certain types of neighbors (a social environment);

as a *sector of the economy*, a component of fixed capital stock, a means of producing wealth, and a tool of governments in regulating economic growth.

Housing is clearly all of these at the same time. Each concept is also applicable to particular aspects of housing and is relevant for specific purposes. This listing of definitions does not, however, help us in its present form. It separates and confuses several related but different dimensions of housing—and mixes a concern for what housing is with what it might be. It also does not clearly differentiate between what we put into housing and what we get out of it, including the critical question of location. It may be possible to clarify these distinctions by recombining them through the concept of housing "services."

The Concept of Housing Services

As is by now obvious, housing production brings together a variety of "inputs," while occupancy of that housing provides a series of "outputs." These inputs and outputs in turn can be conceived as representing *housing services*, i.e., as benefits (or disbenefits), for builders, owners, and renters. Clearly, different kinds of housing, in different locations, require very different inputs *and* deliver very different services to those who own or occupy it. It is the role of the market, the housing agency, or whatever system of allocating housing is used to match these inputs and outputs.

Drawing on the preceding definitions, the types of services which housing delivers can be summarized in the form of a schematic flow diagram (Fig. 2.1). Housing supply on the ground represents the combination of a set of inputs: a physical facility (materials), capital, land and labor (including entrepreneurial ability)—the standard "factors" of production which reflect the particular set of relationships in the means of production in that country—combined with location (accessibility) and a local environment or neighborhood.[3] From these inputs flow a series of services as outputs: these include (1) *shelter*—a place to live and protection from the elements; (2) *equity*,[4] for owners at least, in terms of the financial return on a major asset in their personal investment portfolios (and a tax-free asset at that for owner-occupiers); (3) *satisfaction and status*, in that the consumption of housing (preferably comfortable housing in an attractive location) provides a degree of social satisfaction and for some is clearly an important component in

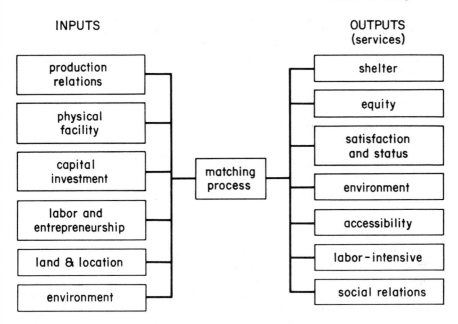

Fig. 2.1. The flow of housing services.

establishing and visibly publicizing their social status; (4) a set of *environmental* attributes and services which arise as externalities (effects external to but impacting on the house itself);[5] and (5) a level of *accessibility* to places of work, shopping, friends, and leisure pursuits.

More broadly, the occupancy of housing in part contributes to defining a set of *social relations*, to identifying a household's position in the social and spatial structure of a local community and a city. This in turn influences the occupants' life style as well as their personal commitment to the status quo in a neighborhood, a city, and the social system generally.

Although the list of services flowing from housing could easily be extended, it will suffice here to add one other, *labor-intensive* services. Isler (1970) defines this component as including maintenance, custodial and protective (i.e., security) services, as these terms are commonly used in reference to rental accommodation. Such services are commonly paid for either in rent, when they are the responsibility of landlords, or in property taxes (or rates) when performed by local government. In the case of owner-occupied housing, these services are generally overlooked; but they should not be. The first two services, maintenance and custodial, are usually performed by the owner personally, but eventually they return income to that owner in the form of capital gains (price increases) or increased status and satisfaction.

Measuring the Flow of Housing Services

Differentiating among these types of housing services is critical for several reasons. First it stresses that housing consists of a mix of attributes, what we term the *housing package or bundle*, some of which are external to the physical structure itself, but each of which delivers its own output. A second reason is that the concept of a flow of services from housing removes the typically sharp distinction between the producers and consumers of housing, except in reference to the rental market and the public sector. Owner-occupants, by this definition, become producers as well as consumers because of their labor inputs and the equity they can accumulate. Third is the explicit recognition given to neighborhood and locational factors. Services deriving from these external sources stress the importance of analyzing housing in terms of environmental or spatial externalities, and in terms of the different values attached to each service by households of different incomes and tastes. Interestingly, discussions of housing supply (see Chapter 5) usually refer to the physical stock of dwellings, while studies of demand refer more frequently to the demand for housing services in general (Quigley, 1978). Not surprisingly, the two approaches do not produce compatible results.

Although it is relatively easy to conceptualize what housing services are, it is quite another matter to measure the magnitude and flow of these services. As a result, most reserachers retreat in the face of the task and rely instead on selective single measures such as average price or rent, or some composite measure which treats housing services as a homogeneous bundle available at a single price. Others, notably in microeconomics, have used techniques similar to regression analysis for attaching "implicit" prices to each component (e.g., number of bathrooms, presence of garage, etc.) in the bundle of housing attributes (Berry and Bednarz, 1975; Goodman, 1978; Rosen, 1978). These techniques produce what are referred to as "hedonic" price estimates, which in turn can be equated with the flow of services from each attribute of the housing stock (see Chapter 7). A very different approach, based on survey research methods, actually explores how people use housing in their daily activities and what "values" they derive from that use (Michelson, 1977; Morris and Winter, 1978).

Clearly some combination of these research techniques is necessary if the nature and flow of housing services is to be measured in any kind of realistic form. In most cases we substitute for measures of housing services the analysis of "bundles" of standard housing attributes, such as house size, price, style, as well as neighborhood and locational attributes. Even defining what that bundle is can become complicated, however (see Chapter 3). For example, Kain and Quigley (1970) used 39 variables relating to the physical, social, and visual qualities of housing in a study of St. Louis. They also varied the spatial scale at which these variables were analyzed from the individual dwelling, and groups of adjacent properties to the residential block front and finally, census tracts. Whatever the measurement or spatial scales used, however, it should be stressed that no single scale will capture the full interdependence of housing consumption and occupancy patterns in an urban environment.

Unique Attributes of Housing

In addition to the conventional definitions of housing as a physical facility, and as an economic good exchanged through a market, housing also has a number of relatively unique attributes which should be explicitly restated. Although there is still a considerable difference of opinion on the relative importance and degree of uniqueness, the following attributes are particularly relevant here:

fixed location (or immobility): generally occupants move, houses do not (except for some mobile homes);

durability: as a physical facility, as well as an investment, housing has a long life-span;

limited adaptability: as a result of the above attributes, the housing stock is relatively slow to respond to changing demands, although the flow of services from that stock can change rapidly over short periods of time;

inhomogeneity: i.e., the complexity and diversity of the housing stock and the services it produces, as well as the large number and diversity of buyers and sellers;

exogeneous influences: housing is highly sensitive to changes which are external to local markets;

policy overlay: housing is also subjected to a multitude of institutional regulations imposed by various levels of government; and

externalities: as recognized in the concept of the housing bundle, spatial externalities—particularly those relating the character of the immediate neighborhood environment—exert a powerful influence on what happens to any single housing unit or group of units.

Many of these attributes are in fact shared by other types of urban real estate, such as industrial and commercial land uses. However, the size and diversity of the housing stock and of its occupants, as well as the strength of local neighborhood effects or externalities, are different in degree if not in kind. Nonetheless, perhaps only in terms of its social and political importance is housing truly unique in the context of urban real estate markets.

The implications of the above attributes are in large part obvious, but are worth stressing. One effect of the immobility and physical durability of housing is to limit the degree of substitution possible between different types and styles of housing. This feature, which is explored in more detail in the next two chapters, can lead to the "segmentation" of the urban housing stock and the operation of distinct subdivisions or sub-markets in housing, which inevitably restricts the choices open to some consumers of housing.

In aggregate, the housing stock is difficult to adapt or modify in response to changes in demand in the short term, particularly since new construction usually amounts to only 1 to 3% of the existing stock in a given year. Yet the flexibility of supply provided within that stock is often underestimated. Most structures initially built for single family use can be converted into multi-family structures or for commercial, institutional, and, at times, even industrial uses. Moreover, multi-family structures can be altered to change the number of dwelling units provided, or they too can be converted to other uses. An examination of almost any inner city neighborhood will reveal a wide range of activities taking place in what are or were formerly residential structures.

In many cases, however, these same attributes, augmented by institutional constraints such as zoning, tend to discourage adaptation and reuse of the housing stock. The existence of spatial externalities again implies that one cannot look at housing conditions, or evaluate housing needs, without examining the character of the immediate environment. The openness of housing markets to external influence and control also means that one cannot understand changes in a local market area without examining the larger social and political context of which that area is a part.

The Concept of Housing Status

Viewed from the perspective of the individual household, the outcome of the flow of services from housing as described above effectively designates the *housing status* of that household. The term housing status is defined by W. F. Smith (1970, p. 23) to represent the entire flow of services, i.e., shelter, public utilities, amenities, accessibility, and access to an environment which comes from occupying housing of particular kinds in specific neighborhoods.

The creation of this status in turn sets the stage for a series of "second-order" effects. These include the rights and obligations attached to the occupancy of housing, including the elements of security (financial and physical) and satisfaction, the right to exclude others from that property, as well as the patterns of use and behavioral activities conditioned by that unit and the objective standards of the housing which is occupied. The latter, in turn, influence the level of satisfaction and external environment of that household's immediate neighbors and the broader community of which it is an integral part.

The value of this conceptualization is that it focusses our interest in the flow of housing services on the rights, obligations, and uses to which housing is put. Housing status then becomes defined as the degree of "control" over one's personal housing environment in relation to the control exerted by others.

Access to Housing and Housing Classes

The concept of housing status can also be defined in terms of "classes" in society and the conflict between those classes. Housing classes arise whenever people enjoy differential "access" to housing, which is of course true in all societies. Thus, according to Rex (1971), there are as many housing classes as there are kinds of access to housing. He identified the following *housing situations* as typifying differential access and thus giving rise to class differences:

(1) outright owner of a house (no mortgage);
(2) owner of a house under a mortgage;
(3) public sector tenant (differentiating between those in buildings with a long life expectancy and those awaiting demolition);
(4) tenant of a house owned by an absentee landlord;

(5) owner of a house bought with short-term loans who is thus compelled to rent rooms; and

(6) tenant in a rooming house.

To the author, this list also represents a scaling of access to housing in terms of descending desirability, as well as an implicit spatial ordering from new suburbs (2), to older suburbs (1 and 5), to the inner city (3, 4, and 6).

This concept is useful here in that it explicitly introduces tenure and credit (mortgage) conditions as components in defining housing status. But it is not without criticism. Clearly the above classification is not exhaustive. For example, it ignores contemporary housing forms—notably multi-family rental and cooperative housing—and the intense contrasts and diversity which can appear within each class. It has been criticized precisely because it extends the concept of class conflict far too broadly. Lambert, Paris and Blackaby (1978) argue that in so doing it obscures the real conflicts which do occur, such as those between landlord and tenant and between institutions and credit-burdened homeowners. These are issues for later discussion.

HOUSING IN SPATIAL CONTEXT

In many ways the study of housing in its spatial context is subsumed under other areas of urban research (see Fig. 1.2). Housing is an implicit, if not explicit, focus of research in at least the following important sub-fields: (1) residential land use and urban real estate; (2) migration and residential mobility; (3) neighborhood change; and (4) social area analysis and urban ecology.

Housing is the building "stock" equivalent of residential land use; in effect it adds the third dimension to such studies (location and site size being the other two), and it is the major component in urban real estate markets. Housing is also the "built" environment for, and the major determinant of, intraurban migration and mobility. Housing is also one of the principal mechanisms through which urban neighborhoods change, and one of the stimulants for such change. Housing "space" is one of the components by which social areas and communities in the city are created and either maintained or lost. In all of these cases, the relationships are circular and cumulative—*housing is both cause and effect.*

As all four of these topics are well covered in almost all basic urban texts, we need not undertake here to summarize each in detail as a separate entity. Instead, discussions of the basic concepts in these areas is dispersed throughout this book when and if they assist in the analysis of housing per se.

Residential Land Use

Residential land use—i.e., the geographic area occupied by or assigned to housing—has been the principal concern of most researchers and planners concerned with urban land use and spatial structure. Although it occupies from 35 to 45% of the land area of most cities, housing must still compete with other uses in the *urban land market* (Alonso, 1964). In theory these uses compete for accessibility and space, and are sorted out spatially in terms of their ability and willingness to pay the costs of locating nearer the city center. Each use has its own schedule of rents or prices it is willing to bid for each location (Fig. 2.2a). The highest bids are by those uses—high density offices, institutional, and commerical uses—which place the highest premium on accessibility and proximity to other uses within the city center. These uses tend to occupy the closest locations, with other uses distributed at increasingly further distances from the center.

The result of this sorting process is the traditional pattern of concentric zones of homogeneous land uses radiating outward from the city center (Fig. 2.2b). Depending on the size of the relative bids, the numbers of uses considered, housing would occupy perhaps three distinctly different zones within this idealized city. One is a high density zone (B-C) immediately surrounding the commercial center, much of which might consist of town-housing or high-rise apartment towers. The second zone is the broad middle band of lower density suburban housing located between older and newer industrial (C-D and E-F) districts. A third zone not usually included in most traditional descriptions of urban land use, but of growing importance, is that of exurban residential development. In such areas, housing (including second homes, retirement cottages, and recreational properties) increasingly competes with and out-bids agricultural land uses. The result is the emergence of an *urban field* around our major urban centers in which urban residential activities may extend up to 100 kilometers beyond the continuously built-up land use boundary (F and beyond).

This simplified concentric zonation, of course, seriously distorts the extensive mixing of housing with other land uses which we observe at all distances from the city center. Yet it does provide the broad spatial framework within which we examine the complex operation of a market—or what is defined in the next chapter as an allocation process—for housing space and housing services. Relatively few households or housing units, however, are directly affected by competition from nonresidential land uses, and for this reason we subsequently emphasis competition *within* the residential sector. Nevertheless, the extent to which competition from other urban land uses influences the aggregate amount, price, and location of land available for housing does set broad guidelines for the operation of the allocation process for housing itself.

Housing and Neighborhood Change

We have already acknowledged that it is impossible to separate the urban housing stock from its location and neighborhood context. Nor would one want to. The importance of the external relationships—the spatial externalities—which link the fortunes of any dwelling unit or set of units to those of its neighbor is such that any study of the housing stock must be paralleled by one which examines change in the broader neighborhood context.

There are almost as many ways to articulate the processes of neighborhood changes as there are people who have studied the subject. Johnston (1971), Herbert (1972), and Jones and Eyles (1977) offer comprehensive surveys of the

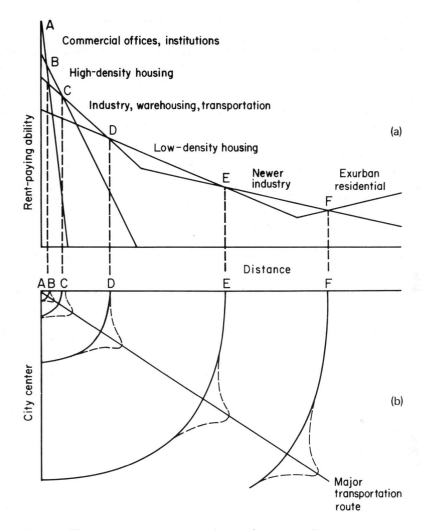

Fig. 2.2. Housing in a competitive urban real estate market.

literature and concepts of the social geography of urban areas. These approaches include the traditional ecological approach (Park, Burgess, and McKenzie, 1925), and its many variants (see Berry and Kasarda, 1977); models based on the residential filtering process (Hoyt, 1939; Lowry, 1960; Grigsby, 1963); other formulations based on the role of institutions and social conflict (Harvey, 1973, 1977; Cox, 1978); more formal economic models (Kain and Quigley, 1975); gaming and probabilistic models (Gilbert, 1972); statistical accounting frameworks (Moore and Clatworthy, 1978); and the changing patterns of social relations (Cybriwsky,

1978). Each of these approaches, in varying degrees, provides some direct (or indirect) role for the housing stock and its changing patterns of occupancy.

Perhaps the most persuasive of the above approaches to date has been the ecological approach, dominated by the Chicago school of sociology of the 1920s. Although widely criticized, these concepts still provide a useful descriptive framework for studies of the dynamics of housing in cities. In their view, neighborhoods change through a process of *invasion and succession* in which new institutions and populations gradually penetrate (invade) areas occupied by other groups and eventually come to dominate those areas by displacing members of the initial groups (succession). Spatially, the outcome of the process is the same concentric zones radiating out from the city center as in the competitive bidding process for land outlined above, except that each zone contains groups of increasing social status.

Underlying this concept or model of neighborhood change are several stringent assumptions, or what the ecologists called "conditioning factors," at least three of which relate to housing. They assumed the existence of a rapidly growing city, with an industrial economic base, a steady inflow of migrants of mixed ethnicity and generally low incomes and almost ubiquitous improvements in transportation (e.g., Chicago as it was in the early 1900s). The ecological argument also assumed that (1) housing becomes socially obsolescent through aging; (2) new housing is primarily constructed on the outer margins of the city; (3) the opportunity to improve one's housing situation is extensively promoted by a large real estate industry; and (4) people prefer new housing over old.

These assumptions are not without some validity, as evidenced by their persistence in much of the literature to this date; however, they clearly overstate the case. The geographical outcomes which result—displayed in every urban text as the classical ecological model of concentric zonation—comprise an inner "transition" zone of low-quality housing near the city center, followed by a zone of "working-man's" housing and an ethnic ghetto, and extending to better-class housing on the urban periphery. These patterns are but logical consequences of the above assumptions.

Hoyt (1939) provided perhaps the most explicit link between housing and neighborhood change in his classic study of American cities for the U.S. Federal Housing Administration (FHA). His focus was the effect of residential growth (and decline) on the homeowner and on the risk facing the investor in residential mortgages. His conclusions are well known and widely documented and need only be briefly summarized here as they relate to housing.

Hoyt concluded that changes in urban residential patterns followed systematic directions or paths, shaped by the location of areas of residences of "the leaders of society." Once established, these high-status areas tended to persist and to expand outward from the city center in well-defined sectors parallel to the fastest transport routes and towards areas with the most environmental amenities. Their outward movement was encouraged by the physical growth of the city, by the tendency to construct new high-class housing on the urban periphery, and by the consequent deterioration of older housing. The sectoral form reflected the attractiveness of accessibility, and the tendency for the growth of adjacent areas of intermediate value housing to limit the lateral expansion of high status areas. In this description, one can see many of the ingredients of subsequent models of filtering and residential change (Chapter 7).

Numerous modifications and extensions have been made to this "sector" model, some by Hoyt himself. Firey's (1947) well-known criticisms of the Hoyt model in fact act to broaden and deepen—rather than refute—that model. Firey insisted on the need to include the importance of the historically "contingent" character of land uses (and housing) in a city and the role of social values and sentiments—the cultural ecology—in shaping patterns of residential change. Rodwin (1950) also argued for an extension of Hoyt's emphasis on the attractiveness of high-status residential areas to include a more refined analysis of "class" structure and to stress the importance of rising incomes and aspirations in encouraging all households to improve their housing conditions by moving. Subsequent work in social area analysis (Herbert and Johnston, 1976) has brought these various contributions and empirical models together to provide a composite description of the urban ecological base. This includes a concentric zonation of certain household attributes, such as family size and housing stock characteristics (e.g., age, density, and structure type), and an overlay of sectoral variations in household occupation, income, and housing value. Superimposed on both of these patterns are localized ethnic communities.

In all cases, recent trends have distorted, although not destroyed, these classical patterns. Widespread highway construction in the city and suburbs, a massive decentralization of jobs, rapid racial transition, the boom in apartment buildings throughout the urban area, and the rehabilitation of housing in selective older areas of the inner city have made contemporary housing and neighborhood patterns far more variable and complex. For this reason, the student of housing must look beyond the valuable but restricted context provided by studies in urban ecology and residential land use. On the other hand, it is necessary to keep in mind the diverse origins and directions of neighborhood change envisaged in the classical ecological model and its many derivations.

One extension to this literature has been the attempt to conceptualize temporal sequences or stages of neighborhood change (Birch, 1971). Table 2.1 provides one example of what these stages might look like. They should not be interpreted as "inevitable" stages, but more as expressions of the attributes which might typify particular neighborhoods as they evolve over time (their life cycle). The utility of this example for our subsequent discussions is that it stresses the fact that neighborhood change is the composite result of a series of changes in housing, occupancy patterns, demographic structure, social composition, and land use. All of these components are interrelated, but each has its own momentum or life cycle. Housing, then, acts as both a determinant and a consequence of neighborhood change.

Housing and Household Activity Patterns

At the level of the individual household, housing—or more accurately the "home"—also plays a central role in the daily activity patterns of the household. The home is the major focus and haven for, and the base location from which most

Table 2.1. Summary of Neighborhood and Housing Life Cycles

Sequence (stage)	Housing and physical attributes			Social attributes			Other
	Dwelling type (predominate additions) and tenure	Level of construction activity	Population density	Household & family structure	Class, social status, income	Turnover, migration, mobility	Other characteristics
Suburbanization (new growth) "homogeneity"	single-family (low-density multiple), owner-occupied	high	low (but increasing)	young families, small children, large households	high (increasing)	high net in-migration, high mobility turnover	initial development stage; cluster development; large scale projects.
In-filling (on vacant land)	multi-family, rental	low decreasing	medium (increasing slowly or stable)	aging families, older children, more mixing	high (stable)	low net in-migration, low mobility turnover	first transition stage—less homogeneity in age, class, housing; first apts.
Downgrading (stability and decline)	conversions of existing dwellings to multifamily; rental	very low	medium (increasing slowly) population total down	older families, fewer children	medium (declining)	low net out-migration, high turnover	long period of depreciation and stagnation, some non-residential succession
Thinning out	non-residential construction—demolition of existing units	low increasing	declining (net densities may be increasing)	older families, few children, non-family households	declining	higher net out-migration, high turnover	selective non-resid. succession
Renewal	(a) public housing; rental	high	increasing (net)	young families, many children	declining	high net in-migration, high turnover	the second transition stage; may take either of two forms depending on conditions
or	(b) luxury high-rise apt. & townhouse	high	increasing (net)	mixed	increasing	medium	
Rehabilitation	conversions	medium	decreasing	few	increasing	low	

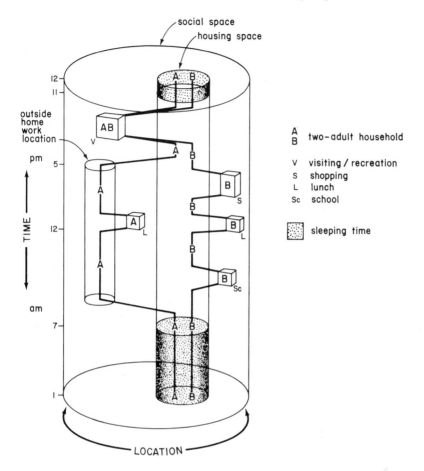

Fig. 2.3. Housing in the daily prism (time-space mapping) of household activity patterns (after Hägerstrand).

households pursue their day-to-day activities—their daily cycle. The type and location of that housing, combined with the attitudes of households toward their housing situation, in turn condition those activity patterns (Chapin, 1976). Only the most regular and recurring of those activities, however—the journey to work is one example—are eventually recorded in the aggregate, longer-term patterns of housing and neighborhood change.

This daily rhythm of social behavior can be illustrated by reference to the concept of "time-space" mapping, based on Hägerstrand's formulation of the *daily prism*. Figure 2.3 illustrates this concept by outlining the typical movements of a couple (A B) through space and time as they carry out their daily routines of working, visiting, shopping, traveling, and home-based activities. Of course the actual patterns will differ for each household, depending on its age, composition, life-style, and income, and for each location of residence, but with the home remaining as the common base. Although the principal emphasis in this volume is with those activities which are less frequent and more dramatic (e.g., moving house), and with those activities which are mirrored in the behavioral patterns of aggregates of households, it is important that we do not overlook the fact that housing shapes, and is shaped by, many individual human activities which are not evident at the aggregate scale.

HOW THE HOUSING STOCK CHANGES

In addition to defining what is commonly meant by the term housing, and what is involved in such concepts as housing services, attributes, and status, it is also essential that we indicate what forms or types of changes can take place within the housing stock itself. Here the term housing stock or *the standing stock of housing* is defined as the inventory of residential structures or individual dwelling units currently occupied or available for occupancy. Bringing together at this early point different forms of change in that stock provides an essential background of concepts and a common vocabulary for subsequent discussions.

Sources of Change in the Housing Stock

The total number of housing units changes over time in response to the net balance of adjustments in the different components of supply. This balance can be summarized succinctly as follows:

| Total housing supply (units) time t + 1 | = | Total supply time t | + | New construction time t → t + 1 | + | Subdivisions of existing units − mergers of existing units net conversions t → t + 1 | − | demolitions, other removals t → t + 1 |

or symbolically as:

$$H_{t+1} = H_t + NC_{t, t+1} + Cnet_{t, t+1} - D_{t, t+1}$$

assuming that vacancies are contained in H. The total housing inventory is therefore the inherited stock or supply from previous periods plus (or minus) the net balance of new construction and conversions less removals from the stock.

To illustrate the relative size of these components of change we can refer briefly to the changes in the U.S. housing inventory between 1970 and 1976.[6] During this period, the total 1970 inventory (H_t) of 70,184,000 dwelling units increased by 10,697,000 or 15.2%, based on the addition of 13,222,000 units through new construction ($NC_{t, t+1}$), less 4,686,000 units lost or removed ($D_{t, t+1}$), plus a net addition of 2,161,000 units from unspecified sources. Unfortunately, there are no specific estimates available of the number of units added or lost through conversion, although those units presumably are contained in the unspecified category.

This simplified breakdown can be extended, however, to include both a much wider range of changes in the housing stock and the diverse spatial and temporal expressions of these changes within cities. We are here not only interested in changes in housing supply, but in the flow of housing services that derive from sources other than alterations to the number of units. Such changes include those in the quality, tenure, and price of housing supplied, the locations within the city at which these changes take place, and their subsequent impact on neighborhood change and social welfare.

Figure 2.4 undertakes to summarize the full range of modifications which can take place in the composition and spatial pattern of a housing inventory within an urban area. Most of these are obvious kinds of changes, but seldom are they brought together and made explicit in the housing literature. Housing units can be added to the inventory as part of three structural processes: (1) as new units built on previously undeveloped land, (2) through modifications in the form and usage of the existing stock, or (3) by replacement of existing units with new construction. Each of these three processes may also take very different forms, depending on the location (as extensions to the built-up area or infilling), the scale and nature of the development (in price, occupancy, tenure, size, and design), and in the origin of the investment decisions involved (public or private). This range of inventory adjustments, in turn, conforms roughly to a time scale (from initial construction, through modifications, to eventual replacement) and to a spatial scale (moving from redevelopment in the city center to the extension of the built-up urban periphery). Each expression of adjustment in housing supply can also be measured at different levels of spatial aggregation: varying from the individual dwelling unit, building, or site, to aggregate statistics for entire city blocks, neighborhoods, or socioeconomic regions within an urban area.

Perhaps the most complex changes, and certainly the most difficult to observe and measure, take place within the existing stock itself. Here four such changes are recognized: (1) shifts in the relative *quality* or value of housing units or groups of units within the housing inventory (the filtering process); (2) changes in the *intensity* with which housing is occupied (leading to systematic changes in occupancy and population density); (3) shifts in the *tenure* of occupancy (from owner-occupied to rental and vice versa); and (4) changes in the *number* and *size* of dwellings and the type of use. The latter includes the conversion of residential structures to nonresidential uses and, although less frequent, the conversion of nonresidential structures to residential use, as well as residential conversion whereby existing housing units are subdivided or merged without a change in tenure.

The process of subdivision and merger, as defined above, is the principal mechanism through which new units may be created from the existing stock, or the size of existing units altered in the short term. Often, but not necessarily, it is accompanied

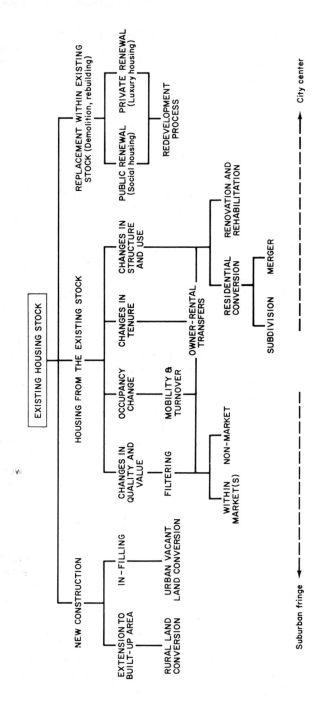

Fig. 2.4. Types and processes of change in an urban housing stock.

by a change in housing quality and tenure. Similarly, the filtering process is the principal mechanism, at least in Grigsby's (1963) view, by which housing units of different quality are released from the existing stock. We examine both of these concepts in more detail in Chapters 5 and 7.

Temporal Changes: The Aging Process

One of the few attributes of housing which can be measured with any degree of certainty is its age. The aging process is one of the underlying dynamics of the housing stock, much as it is in the demographic structure. The age of housing also tells us a great deal about the conditions under which it was financed, built, and occupied, about the character of the residential areas which result—as depicted in the ecological model above—as well as about the changing supply of housing of different styles and periods or "vintages." Thus one tends to speak of, for example, 19th century brownstones in New York and Boston, of 1950 bungalows such as in Daly City, California, or of Victorian suburbs in London and Manchester.

The most important single attribute of new housing, on the other hand, is precisely that it is new. It is obvious that the number of old residential structures, such as Victorian terrace houses or 19th century brownstones, built during past periods, cannot now be increased—although the number of dwelling units and the flow of services from those structures can be altered, as shown above. One also knows that even if nothing else changes, the addition of new housing irreversibly alters the market and the relative attractiveness of all older housing.

Once housing is built, the subsequent process of aging not only tells us something about the changing character and composition of housing, but about the pressures on the stock. Most housing is considered to have a *finite life-span*, depending primarily on two factors: the quality of initial construction and the level of subsequent maintenance. Although that life-span may, in physical terms, be several hundred years, in economic terms 50 to 60 years is considered in most instances to be a reasonable life expectancy. In North America, however, the tendency has been to accelerate this process, discarding old housing far too quickly in relation to its physical usefulness, in preference for what is new and perhaps cheaper to run. At the same time, recall that land as such does not usually deteriorate, leading to a continually changing balance of building values and site values over time.

In any case, the aging process alters the mix of housing types with each passing decade and to the extent that aging brings depreciation, changes the "quality" mix of the existing stock. Each decade also takes its toll, reducing the number of units through fire, natural disaster, redevelopment, slum clearance, conversion, and abandonment. The result is displayed schematically in Figure 2.5, which illustrates the changing age profile and life expectancy curve of a given 10-year stock of housing. If we were to overlay a series of these curves, often called housing *depreciation curves* (Grigsby, 1963), for the housing stock built in several successive decades, we could see the inherently dynamic nature of that stock, as well as the changing composition of housing inherited from past periods.

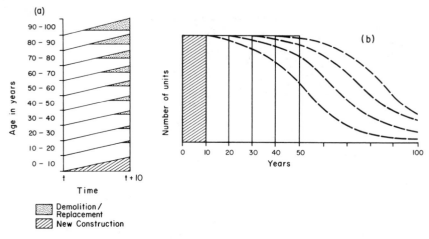

Fig. 2.5. The changing age profile of housing.

Note that this does not necessarily mean that housing quality declines consistently or even inevitably with age. On both points there is a long and detailed debate (Grebler et al., 1956; Grigsby, 1963; Needleman, 1965; Wolfe, 1969; Nutt, Walker, Holliday, and Sears, 1976; Kirby, 1979), which is still unresolved. The point is that the relative distribution of housing quality does shift and this in turn solicits different responses by households and builders.

The Spatial Imprint of Supply Changes

The period of housing construction also has a direct spatial impression. Since, as is obvious from the above, most new housing is built on the edges of cities, a ·map of average housing age at any given time would show a series of roughly concentric rings radiating outward over time from the city center (Adams, 1970). A series of cross sections of a hypothetical city over time such as Figure 2.6, would show a wave-like pattern of building activity, the crest of which shifts outward with each decade. As the peak of new building moves further from the center, a smaller wave of rebuilding emerges near the center, although usually not until several decades after initial construction, and it too continues to move outward over time.

Although these patterns are obvious to anyone who looks at a city, perhaps less obvious is the relationship of each building phase to external factors: to long swings in the building cycle and to sudden technological innovations, particularly in urban transport, but also to changes in building design, consumer tastes, and public policy. Figure 2.7 illustrates how the rate of buildings and the predominant mode of urban transport interact to produce spatial rings of urban development of very different size, within which the housing supplied differs in age, density, design, tenure, and price as well as location. These patterns serve as underlying

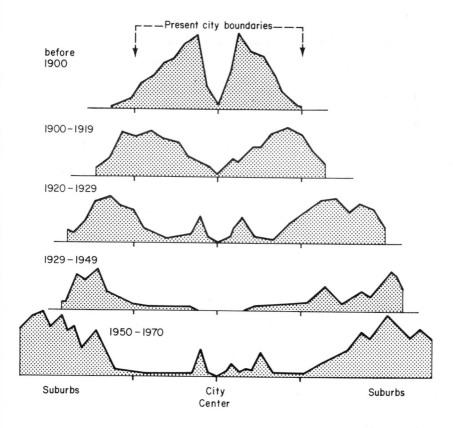

Fig. 2.6. Spatial cross section of building patterns and age of housing in a typical city.

components for our examination in subsequent chapters of the working out of supply and demand in a contemporary urban context.

INFORMATION ON HOUSING AND REAL ESTATE

Perhaps in no other field of social and economic research does the issue of basic information produce as much debate and wringing of hands as in the case of housing. We are confronted with an apparent contradiction between the image of a vertible flood of housing statistics on the one hand and repeated calls in the literature for more accurate, comprehensive, and useful data on the other hand. The obvious explanation for this real contradiction is that the multidimensional nature of housing (as an economic good, an investment asset, and a social service) raises

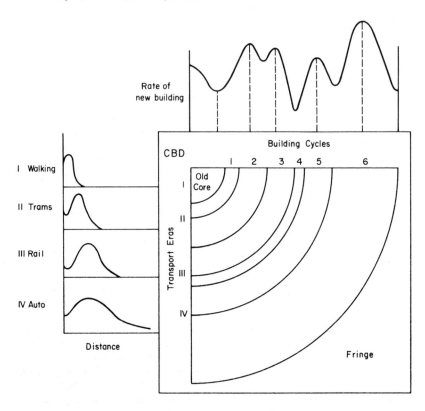

Fig. 2.7. The impact of building cycles and transport innovations on the spatial structure of housing.

questions of a far broader scope than existing sources of information could possibly hope to satisfy. The difficulty of measuring housing services noted above is a case in point.

Equally important, in far too many cases we have gathered information on housing without knowing what we wanted that information for. Other valuable sources of information, such as local property records, which exist for different purposes (setting taxes or rates), are seldom in a form which is convenient for use in housing research, while other records are soon destroyed. Still other sources are often intentionally secret, either by law (e.g., taxes) or through the self interest of participants in the housing market (e.g., estate agents).

Types and Sources of Information

Table 2.2 provides a check list of some of the potential sources of basic data on the housing stock, its occupants, and on the operation of housing markets.

Table 2.2. Some Sources and Types of Information on Housing and Real Estate

Scale	Sources	Examples of types of information
International	U.N., UNESCO OECD, World Bank	Comparative trends in investment, housing stock and housing needs
National level	Decennial census	Nature of the housing stock and its occupants; residential migration and intraurban mobility, new household formation, immigration
	Housing departments	Housing starts, completions, vacancies, improvements, financing; public sector starts, sales, rents, subsidies and occupant characteristics
	Banks, lending associations and building societies	Mortgage lending, interest rates, purchaser characteristics, sources of financing, types of subsidies
	Treasury, commerce, employment and labor departments	Investment levels, construction activity and housing costs, employment levels and building manpower needs, household furnishing and facilities
	Welfare and social security dept.	Housing needs, household budgets, rent-to-income levels, poverty and housing-related social pathologies
	Real estate and building associations	Volume and composition of market transactions, prices and rents, land costs, turnover rates, vacancies
	Special surveys	National and regional housing needs, preferences and user satisfaction
Local level	Property depts., taxation and assessment roles	Detailed records on individual properties: physical attributes of size, land area, housing quality, etc.; taxes, tenancy changes
	Local housing agencies, registry offices, local building associations and societies	Detailed property listings, market prices and rents, sales; local sources of financing; ownership patterns and land transfers; local public sector tenant characteristics
	Home builders, real estate associations	Location of new construction, local building costs, asking prices, attributes of different neighborhoods
	Local businesses and private consultants	Indices of location of residential change (e.g., telephone connections, newspaper delivery), area-based market assessments and data co-ordination
	Local welfare and social services, school boards	Specific areas of housing need, supporting services, monitoring local demographic change (e.g., school children)
	Special surveys	Local community housing needs, specific groups (e.g., elderly, homeless, transients) user preferences and satisfaction

The principal distinctions here are (1) the *scale of the information source*—national or state government agencies or associations and local governments and associations, and (2) the *level of aggregation*. The latter differentiates between aggregate data on groups of households or housing units or geographic areas, and individual-level data on single households or housing units.

For the spatial analyst, there are several important questions relating to both of these attributes. What is the potential for and suitability of spatial disaggregation—nationally by sector or within urban areas—of aggregate housing data? What is the appropriate *spatial referencing system* for individual property records? In the latter case, for example, records on individual households or units for a given city may not even specify their location within that city, as in the case of some national surveys, or the spatial units used may be arbitrary and have little or no geographic meaning. Finally, how can data from different sources, and at varying levels of aggregation, be linked?

Note that we are referring here to information *on* all housing market activity rather than information available to participants who are actively *in* the market (see Chapter 4). It should also be noted that questions of the quality of information on housing are not only of academic interest. Those public agencies which must seek to anticipate changing conditions in an urban housing market, as the basis for policy initiatives (e.g., for schools), and those businesses which depend for their existence on accurate assessments of market trends (e.g., retail firms), are equally concerned with both the nature and quality of housing data (Forrest, 1976). All would benefit by improvements in *urban data systems* relating to housing and residential change, and to the operation of urban real estate markets in general.[7]

Although the emphasis in this volume is on numeric or quantitative data, we should not loose sight of the fact that much of the important information we rely on is non-numeric or qualitative. Of particular interest are the perceptions that people, governments, and firms hold of what types of housing and environments are preferred and why, and how these perceptions in turn influence their behavior. In this context there is also a growing and relevant literature in geography, sociology, planning, psychology, and related fields (Peterson, 1967; Michelson, 1974, 1977; Morris and Winter, 1978; Clark and Moore, 1978).

One additional question we must consider in looking to sources of information on housing is their ability to "tract" or *monitor* changes accurately over relatively short periods of time. Only in this way can important "signals," which act as forerunners of major changes to come, be detected in time for policy makers to respond. Figure 2.8 provides, schematically, a sample of several of the more important variables (time series) which might be monitored in an urban housing market. These measures include the volume and composition of new construction (starts and completions), the percent of new units occupied (the absorption rate), frequencies of sales and rentals (occupancy turnover rates), the average prices of both new and resale units, household formation and demographic change, and adjustments to the existing stock. In addition, we want to know the changing cost components in housing construction and repair, and various ratios of income and costs for different income groups by family status and type of tenure. Ideally,

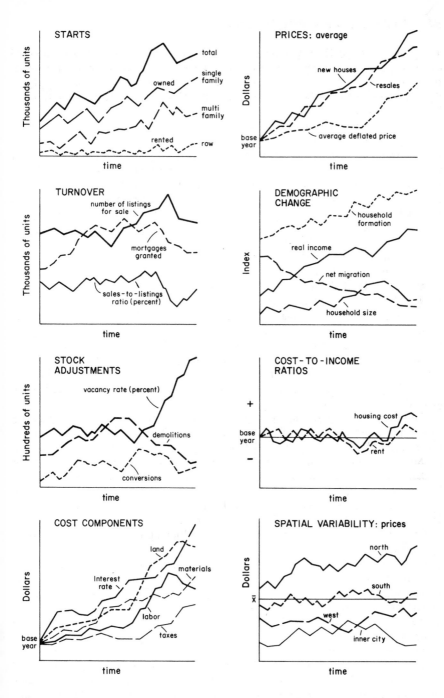

Fig. 2.8. Some elements in monitoring an urban housing market.

35

most of these indices should also be available for the same spatial units within the city. A tall order, indeed, but an information system worth striving for.

On the Quality of Information

Whatever the source, the researcher must undertake a series of evaluations of quality in total and for each specific purpose for which the data are to be used (see W. F. Smith, 1970; Morrison, 1977). At least five basic indices of quality stand out, based, of course, on the assumption that we already know the purpose for which the information is to be used:

> *accuracy:* whether the information available is or is not a reliable and consistent description of the real world (e.g., measures of the structural quality of housing are notoriously inaccurate and inconsistent);
>
> *comprehensiveness:* the degree to which the measures used, and the spatial delimitation of the housing market, are sufficiently broad for the problems under study;
>
> *representativeness:* since many sources of numerical data on housing derive from samples, including much of the census and special surveys on market transactions, it is essential that we know what the sampling error or "bias" is;
>
> *continuity:* the length of a consistent time series of information; and
>
> *compatibility:* the ability to link any single housing data source with other sources of relevant information.

The question of comprehensiveness in a spatial context in turn raises the question of *what is an appropriate geographic area for studies of urban markets.* If we view housing transactions as being interrelated across an entire urban area, as part of one big market, or a series of linked sub-market as defined in Chapter 4, then the information source must encompass the entire urban region. This region would extend outward to include far-flung suburban and exurban developments, as well as areas of retirement and second homes. Few existing sources do so.

A similar problem of bias emerges in the case of data representativeness, i.e., *representative bias.* This bias arises in part because only a small proportion of houses and households are in the market during any given time period. Not only does that proportion vary depending on market conditions, but so too does the composition of both households and housing units. Thus any study of changes in housing market transactions over time must consider what part of those changes are attributable to market trends and which simply reflect a *composition effect* in terms of the changing distribution of housing units involved.

There are, of course, numerous other problems associated with particular measures of the housing stock, demand, and needs—far too many to reference here. What, for example, is the appropriate measure of household income as a determinant of demand? Is it current income or long-term (permanent) income, or as Bossons (1978) argues, some measure of household *wealth* (i.e., assets)? How should housing needs be assessed, especially when housing standards tend to change with social attitudes and market conditions?

Further, how does one measure the total demand for housing within a defined geographic area? Does it include only those households who are there now? Or does it include the potential population who could be there in the future, assuming that developable land is built on at roughly the same rate as in previous periods? This is the conventional means by which local-area demand and supply are estimated. What about measures of supply and demand within already built-up areas? The point here is that by spatially disaggregating our analyses of housing demand and supply we add an immense element of complexity and uncertainty to those studies.

Recent trends in housing construction, demographic structure, and government subsidies have also further complicated the compilation and use of housing information. For example, traditional housing classifications were once relatively straightforward. Single-family units could be equated with home-ownership and lower densities, rental units tended to mean private rental and higher densities, and apartments and flats were (with the exception of large cities) primarily rented and, if new, were often high-rise. Now there is an increasing degree of mixing of these traditional types through such changes as variable forms of ownership (condominia, private and nonprofit cooperatives), structure types (stacked town-houses), and such a proliferation of housing subsidies and allowances that the traditional public-private dichotomy has lost much of its previous meaning.

NOTES

[1] A housing unit (or dwelling unit) for present purposes refers to a single house, apartment (flat), or a single room or group of rooms occupied or intended to be occupied as separate living quarters. Generally a dwelling unit is considered to be separate if it has either or both of (a) direct access from outside or from a common hallway, rather than through some other persons living area; or (b) complete kitchen facilities for exclusive use by the occupants. A housing structure is a physically separate building, containing one or more units, and which is managed as one structure.

[2] A household may be defined as one or more individuals who occupy a single dwelling unit. The principal distinction is between "family" households, in which individuals are related by blood, marriage or adoption, and "non-family" households which are any combination of individuals living together. Note that this definition links the number of households and dwelling units to such an extent that separate definitions are impossible.

[3] The term neighborhood is used here in its traditional definition as a relatively homogeneous area of physical (land use), housing, and social characteristics within which social and land use interrelationships are stronger than those outside that area.

[4] Equity in economic terms is the value of an owner's interest in a property in excess of outstanding claims or liens on that property. For a homeowner this would normally be the difference between the market value of a house and the amount of outstanding mortgage debt.

[5] The term externality as used here refers to a situation in which the use of a particular housing unit or parcel of land has a direct impact on the costs or benefits of occupying other units nearby, but for which the initial occupant does not pay, or benefit.

[6] Detailed statistics on the U.S. housing inventory in 1970 and 1976 are contained in the six volume series (H-150-76) of the *Annual Housing Survey, 1976* (see U.S. Department of Commerce, 1978).

[7]An interesting overview of the importance of micro-level urban data systems, with a unique application to geographical changes in housing occupancy, is provided in Moore and Clatworthy (1978).

Chapter 3

The Housing Condition: Indices and Patterns

At least since Engels' (1844) classic study of housing conditions of the urban working class in 19th century industrial England, there has been an almost universal concern for improving housing conditions. This chapter undertakes to provide a review of current housing conditions and recent trends in selected countries as a descriptive background for the discussions to follow. First, it examines and displays aggregate indices and trends in housing supply, demand and quality, the changing mix of housing tenure, building forms and occupancy, and housing costs and expenditures. Second, it examines the spatial patterns and variability of such indices within urban areas. Detailed discussions of specific determinants and processes of change, however, are left to subsequent chapters on the housing market (Chapter 4), spatial outcomes (Chapter 7), and problems (Chapter 8).

AGGREGATE TRENDS AND INDICES

Diversity and Change: An International Comparison

The first and perhaps most obvious point to stress, and one cited in the introduction, is the immense diversity of housing supply and quality between countries and among cities within the same country. How, in fact, does one generalize about housing conditions which vary from the tar-paper shack in Selma to the mansion in Memphis and the Fifth Avenue apartment, or from the back-to-back in Leeds to the country house in Surrey, let alone across national boundaries? The answer is that one does so only at an aggregate level and with extreme caution.

Table 3.1. Aggregate Indices of Housing Conditions in Selected
Western Countries[a]

Housing index	U.S.	U.K.[b]	Canada	Sweden
Population (1976) in millions	215.1	56.0	23.1	8.2
Population increase (% change 1966–76)	0.9	0.2	1.4	1.5
Residential construction as % of Gross Fixed Capital Investment (1976)	3.9	3.8	6.0	4.0
Total stock of dwellings (1976) in 000s	79,089	20,607	7,567	3,530
% dwellings owner-occupied	64	53	61	35
% dwellings in public rental[c]	2	31	3	36
% dwellings in private rental	35	16	36	29
Median no. of rooms per dwelling (1976)	5.1	3.9	5.0	4.1
Average no. of persons per room (1971)	0.56	0.58	0.61	0.68
Persons per household (1976)	2.9	2.8	3.1	2.7
% older dwellings built before . . . (as of 1976)	34 (1940)	31 (1919)	31 (1945)	32 (1940)
% dwellings lacking one or more basic facilities (1976)[d]	3.1	9.0	2.8	7.0
Average sale price of urban new house (1978)	$54,000	£20,530	$54,186	200,000 Skr (1975)
New housing construction (average annual starts in 000s)	1,530 (1960–76)	357 (1966–76)	245 (1971–76)	90 (1968–77)
% starts in multi-family (1976)	24.4	21.0	42.3	25.3
Vacancy rate %: owned	1.2	na	1.0	1.3
(1976) rented	5.6	na	1.8	4.5

Notes: [a]There are variations among countries in the definitions used; [b]Figures generally refer to England, Wales and Scotland; [c]State governments, local authorities, new towns, housing associations; [d]Full plumbing facilities, heating and/or structural quality; na = not available.

To illustrate such diversity, Table 3.1 provides a series of indices on the relative size, character, and rates of change in housing and occupancy patterns in individual western countries. Given the very wide differences in definitions employed, however, as well as in the methods of collecting national housing data, these figures should only be interpreted as crude indices. Nonetheless, it is immediately obvious that housing stocks, and the demands placed on those stocks, do differ considerably between countries. In part this diversity reflects the cumulative legacy of housing inherited from the past and in part it reflects current, or at least recent, changes in housing policies, social attitudes, and political priorities. Yet there are some common denominators, particularly in terms of levels of capital investment in housing, demographic structure, and in occupancy ratios, which appear to be more or less typical of highly developed, western, and capitalist societies.

The housing stock inherited from the past is perhaps the first and principal source of diversity. In terms of the age of the stock, note in Table 3.1 that some 34.7% (in 1976) of the U.S. stock was built before 1940. In Canada and Australia the stock was somewhat younger. In Britain, on the other hand, roughly 49% of the stock pre-dates WWII and nearly 31% was built before 1919. In all cases, urban housing stocks tend to be somewhat younger than their rural counterparts.

The source of this differential accumulation of housing from past periods is evident in the historical building record. Figures 3.1 and 3.2 trace the path of new housing construction in the U.K. (from 1920) and the U.S. (from 1890), respectively. The summation of this series of annual totals, discounted by the aging process and structural adjustments described in Chapter 2, comprises todays housing stock. Note first that these two historical profiles exhibit a number of important dissimilarities. The U.S., for example, went through a relative boom in

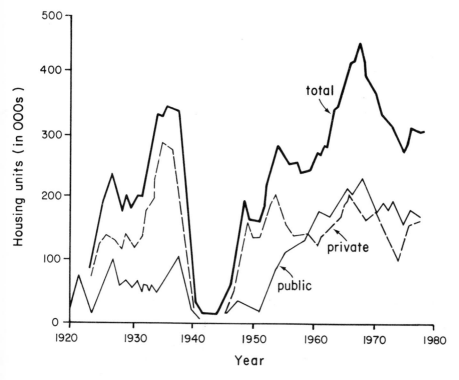

Fig. 3.1. New housing construction, U.K., 1920-76.

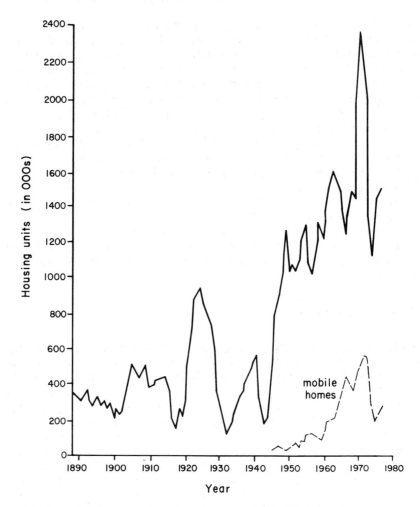

Fig. 3.2. Private, nonfarm housing starts, U.S., 1890–1976.

housing construction in the 1920s, followed by a severe slump during the depression of the 1930s. In contrast, the U.K. witnessed rather low levels of construction during the 1920s, in the aftermath of WWI, followed by a boom in the 1930s. The latter was fed by the extension of low interest loans and mortgages to the private sector, but particularly by the first large-scale production of public (or local authority council) housing. This latter stock of housing is still evident in the British urban landscape, an obvious contrast with North American cities. During WWII, both countries, as did most other developed nations, witnessed very little housing construction, but then came the government-induced postwar explosion.

By 1945 there was an enormous pent-up demand for housing following the war and, at least in the U.S. and Canada, after nearly two full decades of minimal house-building. Governments introduced massive incentives to stimulate private construction and to create jobs (see Chapter 9). The building response took new housing starts to over 1.0 million units annually in the U.S. before 1950 and to over 2.3 million in 1971. The U.K., with extensive war-time housing damage (in which over 400,000 houses were destroyed and nearly 1.0 million damaged) and an older housing stock requiring extensive modernization, faced even more severe and rather different demand pressures and political constraints. These pressures called for, and again received, greater direct government participation in the form of public sector building by local councils (especially as part of the new town development schemes). Note that the relatively strong postwar performance of the private sector in the U.S. also reflects the much higher population growth rates there in comparison to the U.K.

Whatever their source, these booms and busts in house building are the aggregate trends which we see mirrored in the differentiation of housing by age, style, and price within urban areas. They are also the source of many of our contemporary housing problems.

The Tenure Transformation

Perhaps the most pervasive trend contained within this building record has been the increasing rate of homeownership (Fig. 3.3). Most western countries have shared in this transition: during the 1960s and 1970s the rate increased in France from 35 to 45%, in Italy from 40 to 50%, and in the Netherlands from 33 to 43%. Among the developed countries, the proportions of homeownership tend to be highest in the more recently settled and English-speaking countries— Australia (70%), U.S. (64%), and Canada (61%) where tastes, tradition, available space, and building styles have encouraged individual ownership of land and housing.

High ownership rates are not universal, however, even in high-income countries. In West Germany (34%) and Sweden (35%), for example, as well as in much of central and Southern Europe, the proportion of homeownership has remained relatively low (although it is now increasing—see Kemeny, 1979 on Sweden). In part this is a reflection of the heavy emphasis during the postwar period on apartment construction, which tends to be rental, and on publically-owned or cooperative housing. But it is also a reflection that in these countries other forms of tenure have continued to be attractive substitutes for homeownership.

Viewed historically, this trend toward widespread homeownership is considered by some authors to be the greatest single transformation in housing, aside from the absolute quantity of new housing provided (Pawley, 1978). In the U.S., the homeownership rate in 1900 was 46.7 (out of 15.9 million units). It remained roughly stable during the first two decades of the century, declined slightly in the late 1930s (to 43%), then increased rapidly after 1945, particularly during the 1950s. The rental sector during the same period declined from 53.3% in 1900 to 35.4% in 1976. For blacks and other minority groups, the percentage has

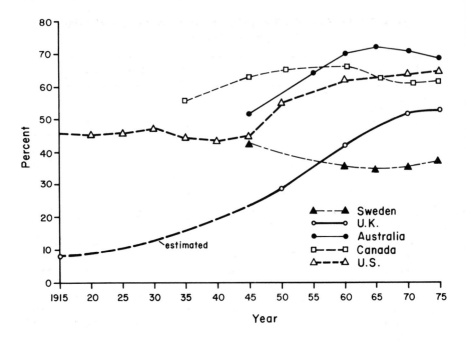

Fig. 3.3. Trends in homeownership rates, selected countries, 1915-1975.

remained well below that for whites (at 43.8%), but the rate of increase was substantially greater (Table 3.2).

In these figures one can see the combined effects of several different factors: (1) the evolution from a rural to an urban or metropolitan society, in which homeownership rates might initially go down; (2) the vast postwar increase in personal disposable wealth; (3) the resurgence of the single-family building form (which is predominantly owner-occupied); (4) the favorable status attached to homeownership in our tax systems; and (5) the increasing role of governments and financial agencies in extending credit (mortgages) for homeownership. The latter has been a deliberate policy objective since at least WWII.

In the U.K. the tenure transformation has been more startling. At the end of the last century, only about 10% of the housing stock was owner-occupied while nearly 90% was in private rental and related forms of tenure. After 1919, and especially after WWII, the homeownership rate increased steadily from 29% in 1950 to 42% in 1960 and 54% in 1977. Unlike the U.S., Canada, or Australia, however, public sector housing also grew proportionally during the same period, from virtually nothing to 26% of the stock in 1950 and over 31% in 1976 (see Chapter 10). This has left a rump of private rental housing of just 16%. Effectively, the private rental sector in Britain is being erased, in part due to deliberate government policy—including the early success of public sector house-building—and in part as an unfortunate side effect of other policies.

Table 3.2. The Changing Size and Composition of the U.S. Housing
Inventory, 1900–76

Index	1900	1920	1940	1960	1970	1976[a]
No. of occupied dwellings (000s)	15,964	24,352	43,855	53,024	63,450	72,523
% owner-occupied: total	46.7	45.9	43.6	61.9	62.9	64.6
Whites	49.8	48.2	45.7	64.4	65.4	67.4
Blacks and others	23.6	23.9	23.6	38.4	42.0	43.8
Farm	64.4	58.1	53.2	73.8	80.5	81.5
Non-farm	36.9	40.8	41.1	61.0	62.0	64.0
No. of vacant, seasonal and migratory units (000s)	na	na	na	1,742	973	1,534
% of units mortgaged[b]	38.3	39.8	45.3	56.8	60.3	63.0
Population/occupied units	4.8	4.3	3.8	3.3	3.1	2.9
% units with: telephone	na	na	na	78.5	87.0	90.1
air conditioning	na	na	na	12.4	36.7	50.6
dishwashers	na	na	na	7.1	26.5	39.6
% units in buildings with:						
one unit[c]	na	na	na	76.1	74.2	72.0
2 to 4 units	na	na	na	12.9	13.8	10.0
5 units or more	na	na	na	11.0	12.1	18.0
% units in metropolitan[d] areas: total SMSAs	na	na	na	66.2	67.4	67.1
in central cities	na	na	na	35.0	32.9	30.7

Notes: [a]In a few instances the figures relate to 1975; [b]For 1970 and 1976 figures refer to properties with one housing unit only; [c]Excludes mobile homes; [d]Refers to 243 standard metropolitan areas as defined in the 1970 Census. na = not available.

In almost all western countries the private rental sector is now coming under similar pressures. Increased government regulation, including rent control, tenant security legislation, building code enforcement, and inadequate depreciation allowances, has rendered investment in private residential rental less attractive to both landlords and investors. In addition, the rising costs of construction, management and maintenance of rental accommodation, and social displeasure with some landlord practices, have discouraged builders from adding to the existing stock.

Sweden, on the other hand, has to date provided a rather different model (Duncan, 1978; Headey, 1978; Kemeny, 1978). The proportion of owner-occupied units remained roughly stable throughout much of this century, despite rapid industrialization, a massive shift of population from rural to urban areas, and the country's emergence as a world leader in per capita income and social welfare. Successive governments have encouraged a variety of tenure forms, notably non-profit and cooperative developments and a competitive public sector. The resulting patterns of housing occupancy are also very different.

Structural Forms: High-Rise and Low-Rise

Closely interrelated with changes in tenure, as both cause and effect, are shifts in the type of housing built. This again is a complex subject and one which is difficult to convey here in all its complexity. The principal features of this century and of the postwar period in particular have been the increase in single-unit structures (especially the detached single-family unit) and the boom during the 1960s in apartments and flats (notably in high-rise buildings). Figure 3.4 outlines the growth and subsequent decline of multi-family housing since 1960 in the U.S., Canada, and Australia, most of which is privately-built, rental, and high-rise.[1] In the U.K., on the other hand, almost all high-rise flats have been built by local authorities as public-rental housing, but these have never exceeded 20% of all housing starts. In many continental European countries, the percentage of new housing in high-rise structures has been somewhat higher than in the U.K., but again predominantly in the public sector, and often as part of large and unfortunately homogeneous suburban estates.

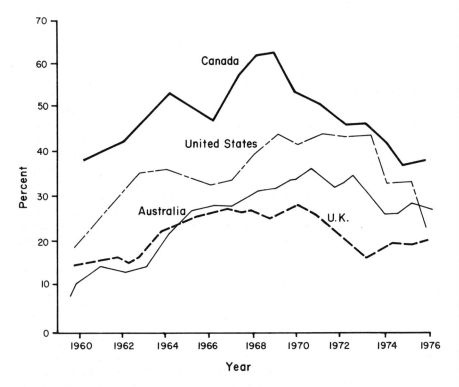

Fig. 3.4. Multi-family housing construction as a proportion of total starts, 1960–76, selected countries.

The postwar boom in high-rise construction derives from many and diverse sources, with the mix depending on the country involved and whether one is talking of the public or private sector. Not the least important reason for the growth of public sector high rises has been the desire of architects and planners to design and test monumental structures, in line with the misplaced architectural fashions of the time. Private builders and developers also anticipated greater cost efficiency, as well as higher densities and profits, in high-rise building compared to low-rise building. In North America, the relative growth of apartments in the private sector also followed from more liberal municipal regulations on private redevelopment, the provision of government tax incentives (tax shelters and subsidies), a real increase in the demand for rental accommodation from young and small households, and by rising urban land costs (Bourne, 1969).

In both the U.S. and Canada, high-rise, multi-family housing construction peaked in the late 1960s (at 44% of all starts in the former and 64% in the latter) and has declined steadily in absolute and relative terms since then.[2] The reasons for the decline are similar in reverse to those cited above for its initial expansion; also, new factors have discouraged the construction of all types of rental units: these include tightening planning and rent controls, slower growth and demographic change, a squeeze on profit levels and community resistence. It should be stressed, however, that one must be careful to identify those factors which apply specifically to multi-family, and particularly to high-rise construction, and those which apply to rental accommodation in general.

In the public sector, high-rise residential construction has now all but ceased in preference for lower-rise but still high-density housing. Dissatisfaction with high-rise living, especially on the part of households who have no choice in housing, those with small children, or both, combined with often inadequate construction, poor maintenance, and vandalism, finally culminated in a dramatic shift in public sector housing policy during the 1970s (see Chapters 9 and 10). Moreover, the geographical concentration of so many disadvantaged families in unfamiliar and often inhospitable living environments inevitably led to social conflicts, malaise, and, in some instances, widespread physical destruction. These conditions in turn intensified what is a long-standing and unresolved debate on the merits and demerits of high-rise living (Sutcliffe, 1974). In subsequent chapters we examine this debate more closely, asking what is wrong with public sector high-rise buildings and why so many planning and design objectives turned out to be so mistaken.

Other recent trends: Alternative forms of building design and tenure have emerged recently in both North America and Europe to further complicate our summary. Some of these forms are relatively new (mobile homes, stacked townhouses) while others are a return to earlier forms (semi-detached, linked, and row housing). Tenure in turn has become more mixed—notably in terms of the relative growth of cooperatives (co-ops) and condominiums.[3] The latter tenure form, involving the common ownership of facilities external to the dwelling units, have traditionally been more common in Europe than in North America. Condominiums in fact were only identified separately in U.S. building statistics in 1973, when some 240,000 units were constructed (about three-quarters in multi-family structures).

Since then, however, the number of condominium units built has steadily declined, in part because of initial legal and management difficulties and in part because of an apparent lack of consumer acceptance. Such units have to date served primarily only two disparate groups: the lowest income owner occupier category and the wealthiest. Ironically, an increasing number of rental units within the existing housing stock have been converted to condominiums, in both North America and Europe, often in large cities or recreational communities, as owners seek to shed operating costs and to recapture their equity during a period of financial (cash-flow) stringency. Still, condominiums now represent only 2 or 3% of the U.S. housing stock.

Another and perhaps uniquely American trend has been the extensive use of mobile homes for year-round accommodation. Mobile home construction, which is counted in the above statistics on housing starts, has during the 1960s and 1970s accounted for from 13 to 22% of all private housing starts in the U.S. and as much as 33% of all single-family starts. Despite the use of the term mobile, however, the major advantages of such units appear to be those of lower purchase price and

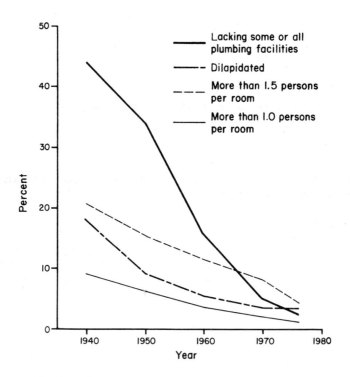

Fig. 3.5. Trends in selected housing quality indices, U.S., 1940–76.

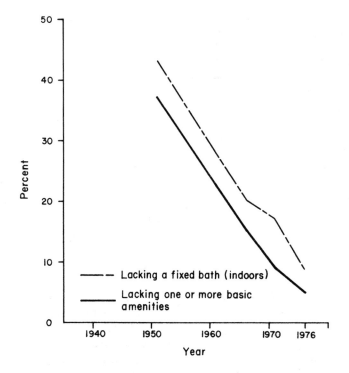

Fig. 3.6. Trends in housing quality and amenities, U.K., 1950–76.

operating costs, including lower property taxes, and the speed with which they can be set up in an area of new housing need.

Quality Measures

By almost any yardstick one cares to use, the overall quality of the housing we consume has increased substantially since WWI. Figures 3.5 and 3.6 plot a selection of indices of trends in aggregate housing quality for the U.S. and U.K., respectively. The indices include the proportion of housing units lacking one or more basic plumbing facilities, or those in which households do not have the exclusive use of such facilities; the proportion of housing units classified as dilapidated or structurally unfit; and the relative degree of overcrowding. Similar graphs could be reproduced for most western countries and would show similar trends.

Even allowing for definitional changes over time, the sharp declines in all of these indices of housing deficiencies are self-evident. In the U.S., by 1976, most such traditional indices now identify less than 5% of the housing stock as deficient.

They might then be described as identifying problems of decreasing social significance, at least in national terms. In the U.K., the decline in the proportion of
housing defined as inadequate has if anything been faster, although the lack of
amenities remains relatively more serious. These trends have been accompanied
by immense quality improvements in the existing stock, through the addition of
basic facilities such as bathrooms, new kitchens, central heating and air-conditioning
(see Table 3.2), as well as through a vast increase in household appliances and
furnishings. In the U.S., for example, the number of new single-family units with
two or more bathrooms increased from 58 to 77% in the short period 1970-76.

Note that this overall improvement does not necessarily mean that the absolute
number of units with structural deficiencies has declined, although in most countries this is indeed the case.[4] Note also that increases in housing quality take place
as much through the construction of new units, which tend to be at higher quality
levels than is the average for the existing stock, as by the improvement or removal
of existing substandard units. In fact, the trend to increasingly higher standards
for new construction has, over the postwar period, virtually swamped the average
quality indices for the older stock. These standards, in turn, have created some of
our subsequent problems of providing sufficient numbers of "affordable" housing
for lower-income households, (W. F. Smith, 1970; Stegman, 1972; Struyk et al.,
1979). Nor does the sharp drop in substandardness mean that quality problems
within the existing stock are no longer serious for certain groups of households
and in certain locations. Ironically, the disparity between those in adequate and
those in inadequate housing has likely increased, and become more apparent, due
in part to the numerical decline of the latter.

Housing Expenditures, Prices, and Costs

At the same time as average housing quality has improved, and as noted partly
as a result of these improvements, the relative costs of housing have increased.
Here precise data are extremely difficult to obtain, in suitably detailed and constant terms, and are even more difficult to interpret once obtained. As crude
indices, we could examine the ratio of prices or rents to average incomes, or compare the level of expenditures on shelter with some standard index of what is
deemed to be socially acceptable. Both are useful. There are, however, two problems with such indices: one is separating those households who have chosen to
spend more of their income on housing than is the standard (say 25%) from those
who are forced by circumstances to spend more; and similarly identifying those
who consume less housing (in quality) by choice than is permitted by current
housing standards. Second, we must distinguish between increases in housing
costs over time which are attributable to building larger and better quality units
from those which represent increases in the per unit costs of housing services.

In general, the proportion of household income spent on housing tends to
decline with increasing income. In the U.S., in 1976, housing expenditures declined as a proportion of all personal consumption expenditures from 40% for
those households earning under $2,000 annually to 18% for those earning over
$15,000. The median for all income groups was 27.5%. In the U.K., in 1976, the

the proportion spent on housing declined in a similar fashion from 39% for those making less than £15 per week to 16% for those earning over £100 per week, with an average of 20.1%.

Over time, the average proportions of household expenditures assigned to housing have increased, although slightly, but here again measurements of cost are particularly difficult. Americans spent about 26% of their total consumption expenditures on housing in 1960, compared to 27.0 in 1970 and 27.5 in 1976. In the U.K., housing expenditures (including fuel and light) increased from just under 16% in 1963 to 17.5 in 1970 and, as noted, 20.1 in 1976.[5] The situation is considerably more severe for households who are renting privately, and their situation appears to have deteriorated. Between 1960 and 1970, average rent-to-income ratios increased for households in all income groups, but especially for those earning less than $5,000 (U.S., HUD, 1973). For minority group households who are renting, the situation is usually much worse (see Chapter 8). Homeowners, on the other hand, tend to be shielded from much of this increase in costs because of tax deductions for mortgage interest payments and (in the U.S.) for state and local taxes, and because of the untaxed value of inputed rent (the rent they do not pay) and their equity accumulation in homeownership.

Statistics on actual changes in house prices and rents are voluminous but also inconsistent. Rates of change vary widely depending on the length of the time period involved and the specific index of prices used as a basis of comparison. Since house prices and rents in the private market tend to increase in spurts, more so than does income, one can produce quite different impressions by simply altering the time interval under study. The only meaningful measure overall is that of relative house prices and rents, relative to the consumer price index (CPI) or as ratios of incomes (as above) or wealth, averaged over several periods.

Over the longer term, it appears clear that house prices have not increased relative to income, for the same quantity and quality of housing services. During the 1970s, however, prices have increased in most western countries in real terms (discounting for inflation and income growth). Table 3.3 summarizes recent price trends in four western countries. Each country would, of course, show a different path of price and rent increases over time, depending on national conditions. Even within countries, differentials in price levels and rates of change of over 100% occur between cities and regions (Bourne and Hitchcock, 1978).

The time paths for house prices in the U.K. and U.S.—although not strictly compatible—are illustrated in Figures 3.7 and 3.8, respectively. In the former, house prices exploded relative to the retail price index during 1972 and 1973, rising some 60% over that index. But from 1974 to 1977 they declined dramatically in real terms to a level about 20% above the index, before beginning to climb again in 1978. In the U.S., because of much lower levels of inflation and income growth in the early 1970s, house prices rose more slowly in the first part of the decade, but have increased substantially since 1976 in line with higher inflation and lower levels of new construction.

Changes in the costs of housing production are also contained within these price changes, but not necessarily in a consistent fashion (see Chapter 5). An examination of the cost indices for residential construction reveals that, for the

Table 3.3. Average Annual Increases in Real House Prices

Country	Average rate of inflation in %		Average rate of growth in per capita disposable income in % (1969–75)	Average change in real house prices in % (1971–75)	
	1970–74	1975–76			
United States	5.9	5.8	1.9	4.4[a]	
United Kingdom	10.4	16.5	3.6	6.2[b]	6.5[c]
Canada	6.5	7.5	4.2	3.8[d]	7.8[e]
Australia	8.9	12.4	5.1	7.5	

Notes: [a]Median new house price; [b]Average price, new houses mortgaged with building societies; [c]Average price, all houses mortgaged with building societies; [d]Average cost of new NHA-financed houses; [e]Average price MLS transactions.

Source: Adapted from Scheffman, 1978.

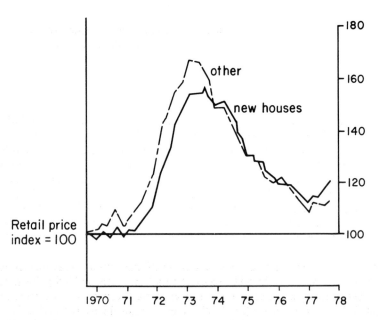

Fig. 3.7. Trends in average house prices, U.K., 1970–78.

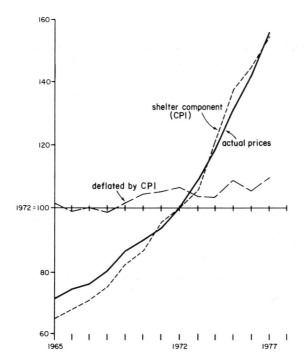

Fig. 3.8. Changing price indices for new single-family homes, and the shelter component of the CPI, U.S., 1965–77.

most part, these indices have increased in parallel with overall price inflation in the economy (Table 3.4). For example, since 1960, in the U.S., average wages in the building trades have increased slightly faster than material costs and house prices. At particular points in time, certain components of cost will lead while at other times the same indices will lag. Recent increases in interest rates and energy costs have also added substantially to production costs; and in North America generally land and carrying costs have risen sharply, often it seems augmented by the costs of cumbersome bureaucratic procedures for approving new residential developments, and by land speculation. Land costs alone rose 12.8% annually between 1972 and 1976.

Between 1970 and 1976, construction costs have been escalating at an increasing rate, although with wide regional variations. Seidel (1978), for instance, quotes figures for cost increases on a representative house as follows: site preparation (up 84%), carrying costs (up 133%), construction financing (up 173%), actual house construction costs (up 50%). In this example, carrying costs include the cost

Table 3.4. Price and Cost Indices of U.S. Construction Industry
1960–76 (1967 = 100)

Index	1960	1965	1970	1972	1976
Median family income	72.3	84.5	122.3	140.0	184.0
Prices: new single-family houses[a]	78.1	93.2	117.4	131.0	191.4
Wages: hourly rates, unionized labor	75.4	90.9	128.8	153.2	200.5
Aggregate building cost[b]	81.9	90.4	122.4	145.8	198.6
Shelter costs: rent[c]	91.7	96.9	110.1	119.2	144.7
Homeownership[c]	86.3	92.7	128.5	140.1	191.7
Fuel oil and coal	89.2	94.6	110.1	118.5	250.8
Effective mortgage rate %[d]	5.9	6.1	7.6	na	9.0

Notes: [a]Median price, houses of constant quality; [b]Boeckh Residential Cost Index
(for small residential structures); [c]C.P.I. series; [d]New houses only; na = not available.
Source: U.S. Bureau of the Census, various yearbooks.

of raw land and site improvements, interest charges, and the length of the planning
and development period. Over the same period, changes in building codes, which in
many areas made such items as smoke detectors, thicker insulation, and other
safety features mandatory, further increased building costs.

On the consumer side note that average shelter costs (where there are also
serious measurement problems) have not increased as fast as most construction
costs, at least through 1976. Note also that rent levels (which are admittedly
underestimated by the CPI) have increased at a much slower rate than homeownership costs. The latter include the costs of home purchase, mortgage interest, taxes,
insurance, and maintenance and repairs. Not surprisingly, the largest single component increases in the overall shelter cost index have been in interest payments
and heating fuel costs. Again, however, the housing analyst is required to sort out
for his or her own geographic area the relative contributions of each of there different components to increased construction and shelter costs before drawing any
conclusions on the determinants of cost changes.

Demographic and Racial Transitions

We have said little to this point about the changing populations which live
inside the preceding housing statistics. After income growth, the most substantial
variable affecting housing demand in the aggregate has been the (most) recent
demographic transition. This transition, the result of a long-term historical trend
of declining birth rates (Westoff, 1978), is directly reflected in the changing

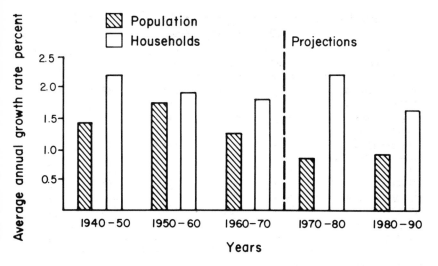

Fig. 3.9. Annual growth of population and households, 1940–76, with projections to 1990, U.S.

composition and size of individual households (Fig. 3.9). The average size of households in the U.S. declined from 3.7 persons in 1940 to 3.3 in 1960 and to 2.8 in 1977. The most dramatic increase has been in one- and two-person households; from 31.9% of all households in 1940 to 51.2 in 1977, and the rate of increase shows no sign of levelling off.[6] In the U.K., average household size also dropped from 4.6 in 1901 to 2.8 in 1976.

These new households are not only much smaller and wealthier than their predecessors, but they are different in make-up, life-style, and housing needs and preferences. Sharply lower fertility rates, reduced family dependency[7] ratios, and higher rates of female participation in the labor force have combined to create a major shift in housing expenditures and occupancy patterns. With an increasing percentage of married women working, and thus of households having two (or more) income earners, the disposable income available to these households has also increased. Thus, it is not surprising that the price of housing in the 1970s has been bid upwards.

In Figure 3.9 one can also see the outline of the very different schedule of housing demands we will face in future decades. Through the 1980s and 1990s, while total population growth slows down, the rate of new household formation will likely continue at a relatively high rate. The level of housing production required will thus remain high, but there will need to be a very different mix of units from that required in the past. One of the more difficult questions facing the housing analyst is precisely to guage the implications of this new household structure on housing demand and the building industry in the future. Existing housing policies (as outlined in Chapter 9) will also have to change.

The additional, and perhaps most visible component of demographic change affecting most urban housing markets in the U.S. has been the rapid growth of minorities–notably blacks and Spanish-speaking populations–in the central cities. The resulting transition of hundreds, if not thousands, of neighborhoods from their initial (and predominantly white) populations to minority group occupance is evident in any published record on American cities (Rose, 1972). Between 1940 and 1978, for example, the proportion of the central cities population which was black increased from 14.2% to over 30%.

The housing implications of this process have also been immense (Downs, 1975; Leven et al., 1976). Because of discrimination and the relatively low incomes of minority groups, neighborhood transition created, or contributed to the creation, of the ghettoes of segregated and often deteriorated housing which characterize so many inner cities (see Chapter 8). It also encouraged large-scale movements of white households and investment capital to the suburbs. In some instances it has led to the creation of *dual housing markets* in many metropolitan areas, one for the majority population and one for the minority (Berry, 1975, 1979). And, it has led to a situation in which the race issue permeates almost all aspects of post-war American housing policy (McKay, 1977; Yinger, Galster, Smith, and Eggers, 1978).

The most rapid period of black in-migration to the cities–the 1950s and 1960s– laid the basis for many of the American urban housing problems (described in later chapters). Yet the rate of net in-migration has dropped recently, and is now negative for many northern cities, thus dramatically altering the demands placed on housing in these dualistic housing markets. One corollary of this decline in in-migration has been the abandonment of housing now common in many older cities in the U.S. The interesting question here for the 1980s is whether the removal of the pressure of heavy black in-migration will in turn alter the process of racial transition in urban neighborhoods and the housing conditions which result.

Such transitions are not, however, unique to U.S. urban areas. In almost all countries with extensive immigration, or continued rural in-migration to the cities of social groups of distinctively different incomes, race, or religion, social segregation and neighborhood transition have ensued. In many, but certainly not all cases, this transition has resulted in the deterioration of housing and subsequent neighborhood decline. Despite these negative aspects, however, such transitions have at the same time often substantially improved the quality of housing available to minority groups, including blacks and chicanos in American and new commonwealth immigrants in British cities, at least in comparison to their previous housing conditions. But, we might ask, at what social cost.

Occupancy Patterns and Profiles

Occupancy patterns within the housing stock also differ markedly between countries, as well as between cities, as the preceding figures on tenure suggest. In North America, Britain, and in most other western countries, the wealthy tend to be owner-occupiers and the poor renters, but not exclusively so. Figures 3.10

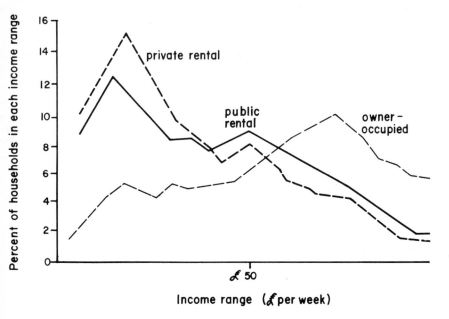

Fig. 3.10. Tenure distribution by income group, U.K., 1976.

and 3.11 plot the distribution of income groups by their tenure status for both Britain and the U.S., respectively, for 1976. For the U.S., the two tenure distributions are almost mirror images of each other, centered on the median income range of $10–15,000. Households below that income are predominantly renters; those above it tend to be owner-occupiers. As noted above, blacks and other minority groups are also more likely to be renters, and in the U.S. at least, only the very poor are in public housing.

In Britain, on the other hand, income groups tend to be more widely distributed across the three major tenure types, although higher income households still tend to be predominantly owners. The public sector in particular has a much wider range of incomes than it does in the U.S. (see Chapter 10), including some households of relatively high incomes, and instead it is the private rental sector which contains the largest proportion of the very poor.

Although the relationship between average income and tenure is well known, the above figures must be interpreted with considerable caution. The relationship is complicated by the fact that housing tenure also varies directly with the composition and age of the household, and the latter in turn varies with income. As Table 3.5 indicates, the proportion of households renting decreases steadily for those households whose head is under 25 through each age cohort until age 65,

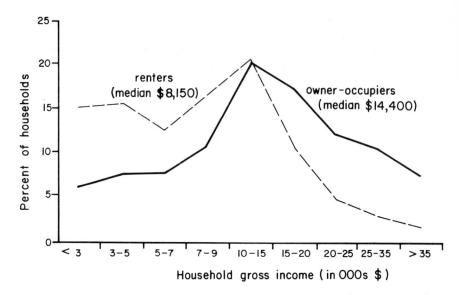

Fig. 3.11. Tenure distribution by income group, U.S., 1976.

Table 3.5. Changing Characteristics of Households and Housing Tenure, by Age and Type of Household, U.S., 1970-75

Type of household	Total households			% who rented in 1970	1970-75 % change in number who:	
	1970	1975	% change 1970-75		Owned	Rented
	(in millions)					
Two-or-more persons	52.3	58.2	11.2	32.8	16.1	1.2
Male head, wife present,	43.6	46.9	7.8	29.4	14.9	-10.2
Under 29 years	7.7	9.0	16.9	63.3	38.2	5.1
30 to 34 years	4.5	5.3	17.1	33.3	30.0	-7.5
35 to 44 years	9.3	9.3	0.0	23.7	5.8	-19.2
45 to 64 years	16.4	17.0	4.1	19.2	10.7	-23.8
65 years and over	5.7	6.4	11.9	21.6	18.0	-10.5
Other male head	2.4	3.1	28.9	27.5	20.5	38.1
Female head	6.3	8.1	28.4	52.0	25.1	31.5
One-person households	11.2	14.4	28.8	57.3	28.2	29.2
Under 65 years	6.2	8.2	32.3	66.4	26.3	35.2
65 years and over	5.0	6.2	24.5	45.9	29.5	18.6
All households	63,446	72,524	14.3	37.4	17.3	8.8

Source: U.S. Bureau of the Census; Annual Housing Survey.

at which point it again increases. At the same time, households headed by females are most likely to rent, as are one-person households in general.

Table 3.5 also reveals the combined impact of changes in demographic structure and shifting patterns of tenure in the U.S. housing stock. Between 1970 and 1975, the number of owners increased twice as fast as the number of renters. In several age cohorts, the numbers of households renting actually declined in absolute terms. The shift to homeownership noted above is then further emphasized when one considers the relatively rapid growth of households in those age cohorts which are considered most likely to rent. If the latter are defined as those cohorts in which the proportion renting was higher than the overall average,[8] there was but a 4% increase in renters in this category between 1970 and 1975, compared to 34% increase in owner-occupiers. What seems to be happening is that the rental sector is becoming socially polarized. Given the pressures on private renting noted earlier, that sector is housing fewer families and a larger proportion of the poor, single-parent and single-person households.

SPATIAL PATTERNS OF HOUSING WITHIN CITIES

The particular "geography" of housing within any urban area is to a considerable extent unique. That geography depends on the particular combination of a diverse set of local as well as national factors. Among the former factors are the city's site, topography, transport system, income level, social heterogeneity, and economic base as well as that city's historically inherited building stock. A city whose economy is based on a few large industrial plants located on the urban periphery will have different housing and journey-to-work patterns than a city dependent on the service sector in which employment is typically located in the CBD. A city whose growth has been recent and rapid, such as Houston or Toronto, will have a different pattern and stock of housing than one whose growth was principally in the last century, such as Baltimore or Manchester. Similarly, housing in a city which is built around attractive hills, an ocean front, or a network of commuter railways will differ in character and distribution from that of cities constructed on a flat plain or under the influence of the automobile. In addition, the degree of control by past and/or present governments will, in turn, alter the geography of housing attributes and opportunities.

Such basic conditions interact to produce urban housing stocks which differ markedly in their physical attributes and spatial patterning. These in turn influence the prevailing types and patterns of tenure, the distribution of land and house prices, the outline of social neighborhoods, the pattern of household mobility, and ultimately influence the networks of social relations in that urban community. Note that we said influence, *not* determine social relations. Housing is but one of the important factors which conditions living conditions and life-styles in an urban area.

Overall Patterns of Housing Stock Attributes

The spatial pattern of urban housing is then a physical expression, overlain with local topographic and transport variations, of the age and economy of the city and the socio-political system in which that housing is produced and consumed. We could not possibly convey here the diversity and complexity of housing stocks or patterns for several different cities. Instead, an attempt is made in the following pages to illustrate this diversity and complexity through a brief display of the housing attributes for only one city—metropolitan Toronto—which the author knows best. Toronto is a relatively new city, a lakeshore city located in a fertile agricultural plain and built around a rectangular road system. It has also grown rapidly in the postwar period (Metro population 2,200,000). Its housing pattern reflects these basic conditions. For other cities, readers are referred to the now voluminous number of urban atlases and statistical abstracts which plot selected housing indices for many individual cities or for groups of cities.

Before turning to the specific analysis, however, we should reiterate that the housing patterns of most western industrial cities do exhibit certain obvious regularities. For example, average age of housing tends to decrease in a regular fashion with increasing distance from the city center, with the oldest stock being in those inner areas which have not undergone extensive redevelopment (see Chapter 2). Housing density, tenure, and structural type also tend to vary with distance from the city center, with the highest densities and greatest concentrations of multi-family and rental housing in older areas. Housing quality and price also tend to be differentiated with respect to distance from the city center, but with the principal distinction being between sectors of different social status. In addition, through the simple expedient of being built at the same time, often by the same builders, most cities tend to exhibit large contiguous tracts of relatively uniform housing types, styles, and prices.

Clearly, however, even these simple regularities have become increasingly blurred over time. Widespread demolition, redevelopment, and rehabilitation have altered the age, quality, and tenure characteristics of housing in many older urban areas. In some areas the initial stock has been obliterated by high-rise building or by middle-class rejuvenation. In other cities, with historically valuable central areas and tight planning controls on redevelopment, older housing areas have been preserved, but are often ringed by a belt of high-rise suburban housing developments. These new estates may be privately-built or publicly-built, expensive or relatively cheap. Moreover, any major change in the transport system, such as a new expressway network or public transit line, can alter the relative accessibility of different neighborhoods and thus the attractiveness of housing in those areas.[9] New housing preferences, immigration, racial transition, and life-style changes, in turn, may shift patterns of occupancy within the stock and values people place on that stock.

As an illustration of the resulting complexity of what is perhaps a "typical" urban housing stock in North America, we undertook a regionalization or grouping of the housing stock of metropolitan Toronto. Some 90 variables descriptive of attributes of the stock (age, tenure, type, price, and size) and of the use of that stock (length of occupancy by age, sex, and previous tenure of the head of household) were subjected to principal components analysis.[10] The spatial heterogeneity of the housing stock was confirmed by the fact that 21 factors were necessary to account for 80% of the variability in the original data set. Moreover, the resulting groups or factor structures varied with the particular methods of analysis used and the subset of variables included.

The four dominant patterns of housing stock variability in Toronto, representing just over 50% of the initial variance among census tracts, are displayed in Figure 3.12 (a, b, c, d). The first factor clearly picks out the older inner city housing stock. This area is characterized not simply by the older age of the housing, but by structural type (row housing, duplexes, semi-detached), higher densities, and higher proportions of rental tenure. This area is differentiated from a broad middle band of more homogeneous, lower-density suburban housing dating from the early postwar period. Interestingly, some of the very recent suburban areas in which a greater variety of housing types (detached, row-housing and apartment buildings) have been provided, also appear as part of the above "inner city" dimension, at least when measured in terms of housing stock attributes.

The second factor contrasts areas of large, single-detached and owner-occupied housing with those containing an overwhelming proportion of apartments. This contrast is evident in *both* old and new areas. Factor 3, in turn, differentiates between areas of higher average house prices and rents, and generous quantities of household appliances, and those of smaller, less expensive but still predominantly owner-occupied housing units. Factor 4 identifies the newest suburban areas which, as noted above, are not only new but have a greater mixture of housing types and prices than do their older postwar suburban counterparts.

A number of other and much smaller factors (not mapped here) reflects the particular unique ingredients of the urban housing landscape under study. These dimensions include areas of (1) smaller, inexpensive rental housing; (2) new high-rise apartments; (3) predominantly first-time house buyers; (4) very expensive private rental units; (5) longer-term tenants; (6) female household heads; (7) owner-occupied apartments (primarily new condominiums); and (8) areas of recent immigrant concentration. Note that public sector housing (which is proportionally small) is not identified separately in the original data set, and thus does not appear in these results.

The four general factors listed above confirm, in their broad outline at least, traditional classifications of the housing stock, i.e., (1) *age* and structural *type*—notably the inner city; (2) *tenure* and *type*—owner-occupied vs. rental, and single-family vs. apartment; (3) *price* and *size*; and (4) *new* housing. Yet this multivariate analysis also illustrates that these attributes are interdependent in various complex ways. Age of housing, for example, is related to building type, tenure, price, and location, but each in a different way. Price, in turn, is interrelated with type, age, tenure, and location, but again through several distinct patterns of association. Thus, the danger of examining only single measures of the housing stock is precisely that it obscures the variety of cross-relationships which more accurately describe the housing conditions of an urban area.

Variability Between Areas: Spatial Concentration

Within these multivariate dimensions, individual attributes of the stock may also exhibit very different patterns of variability across an urban area. As an

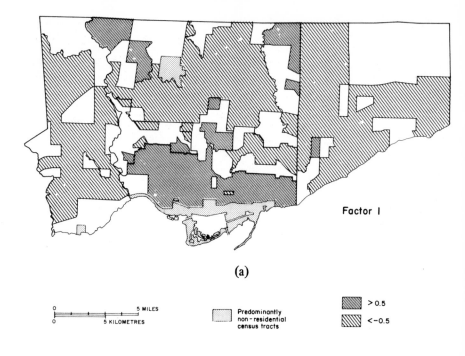

(a)

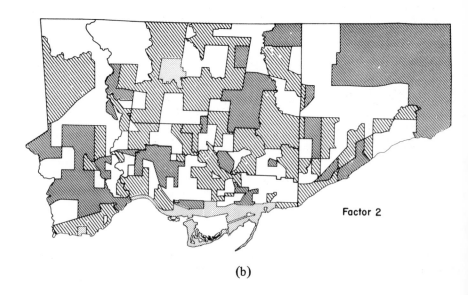

(b)

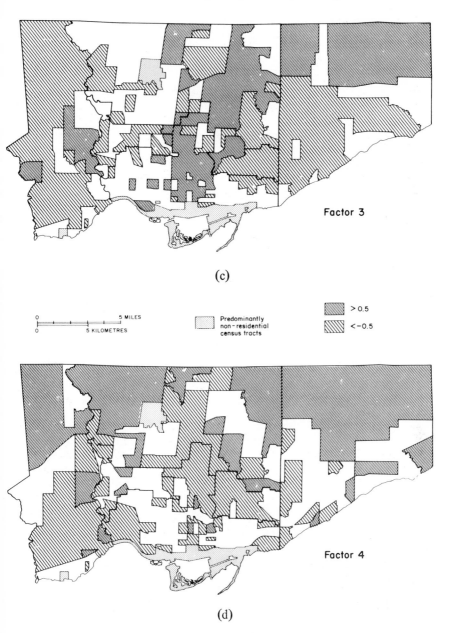

Fig. 3.12. Multivariate dimensions of an urban housing stock: a principal components analysis of housing attributes in metropolitan Toronto.

Table 3.6. Relative Degrees of Spatial Concentration of Individual Attributes of Housing Stock and Occupancy, Metropolitan Toronto (1971 data, by census tract)

Housing stock	Gini Coefficients
Most concentrated	
1. % owner-occupied dwellings in buildings of more than 10 units	0.489
2. % dwellings of value $3000-$7499	0.485
3. % dwellings of value $7500-$12499	0.483
4. % dwellings with value over $62500	0.467
Least concentrated	
1. % rented dwellings with bath or shower	0.043
2. % apartments rented	0.143
3. % owner-occupied dwellings of 5-7 rooms	0.147
4. % dwellings owner-occupied	0.160

Households	Gini Coefficients
Most concentrated	
1. % households with female head under 20 years old	0.494
2. % households with male head under 20 years old	0.492
3. % households with female head 35-44 years old	0.420
4. % tenants with automatic dishwaster	0.415
Least concentrated	
1. % tenants with one autombile	0.114
2. % owner-occupiers who were previously owner-occupiers	0.147
3. % tenants of less than one year occupancy	0.148
4. % tenants of 1-2 years occupancy	0.165

Source: K. Willson, 1978, unpublished M.A. thesis, Department of Geography, University of Toronto.

example, Table 3.6 provides one measure of geographic concentration—the Gini coefficient[11]—for those variables among the set used above which are the most or least concentrated. Recall that this coefficient, like any other measure of spatial form, is very sensitive to the number of observations (e.g., housing units) which have each particular attribute and the size of the spatial units used (e.g., census tracts). The most concentrated attributes thus tend to be those which are relatively infrequent, and those least concentrated are by definition those which are most common.

With this bias in mind, Table 3.6 is nonetheless suggestive of the considerable variability among housing and occupancy attributes within an urban area. The most geographically concentrated housing stock and occupancy attributes are the highest and lowest priced units and those households with young or female heads, or both. The least concentrated attributes are those describing almost ubquitious household facilities (an automobile, bath, and shower), the larger tenure categories (% owner-occupied) and occupancy measures which pick out other-than-first-time home buyers and renters. Although again specific to the urban area under study the results do indicate the necessity for researchers to carefully examine the spatial variability of each housing attribute.

Within-Area Diversity

There is almost as much diversity in housing within the neighborhoods or subareas of a city as there is between those areas. One expression of this diversity can be illustrated by the use of simple frequency distributions of selected attributes of individual housing units within the study area. Figure 3.13 plots the frequency distributions of housing prices and rents for six subareas (in this example, census tracts) in the central city and suburbs of metropolitan Toronto. These are not by any means extreme cases, yet the variability within these areas is both considerable and dissimilar between areas.

Note first that areas with very much the same median house price (or rent) can and do have contrasting frequency distributions of prices around those medians. In some areas this variability is remarkably narrow (e.g., CT 365), as in homogeneous suburban areas. Such homogeneity is typical of suburban areas built at the same time and under restrictive exclusionary zoning. In other areas the distribution of housing values is relatively broad and normally distributed, as in CT 351, or it may be biased (skewed) toward lower-value units (CT 72) or toward higher-value units (CT 129). Still other areas may exhibit a bi-modal distribution, such as CT 47, in which there is a distinctly low-rent sector (<$60/month) and then a separate and more regular distribution centered on the median value of $145 per month.

This illustration serves to stress two points. One is the immense complexity of the housing stock even within small areas, often reflecting the scale and timing of initial construction; the other is that aggregate statistics, such as medians and averages, can conceal very different ranges of local housing characteristics. It is therefore imperative for the student of housing to examine the within-area variability of each housing attribute before using aggregate indices for descriptive or inferential purposes.

Although the preceding results are in detail specific to one urban area, and to the number of subareas and categories of variables employed, the major dimensions of housing patterns are plausible and roughly conform to what we often observe in reality. The results are also suggestive of the challenge task facing the student of urban housing in simply trying to describe and analyze basic patterns of housing attributes at one point in time. When one then undertakes to measure housing quality and user satisfaction as well as changes in these attributes over time, the task becomes more difficult and the need for careful analysis is that much greater. To assist in this task, the following three chapters outline a series of conceptual frameworks within which housing patterns can be interpreted.

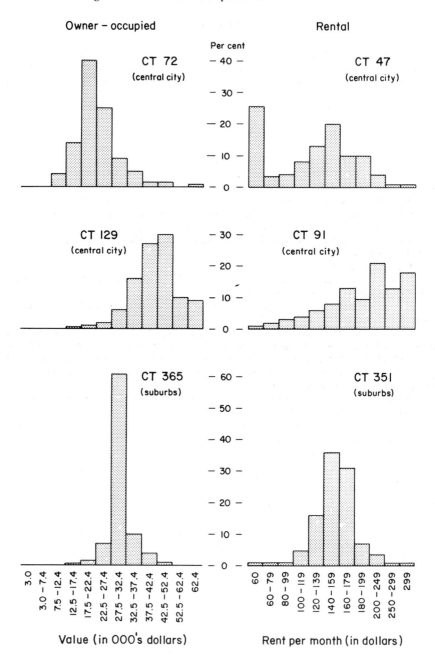

Fig. 3.13. Frequency distributions of housing prices and rents within urban sub-areas, metropolitan Toronto.

NOTES

[1] The rate of multi-family housing construction has been higher in Canada than in the U.S. for a number of reasons: (a) more generous tax and depreciation allowances for rental construction; (b) the absence of tax-deductability for mortgage interest on owner-occupied housing; (c) higher urban land costs; (d) local planning permissions; and (e) the longer traditional of multi-family living in some regions (e.g., Quebec).

[2] In the U.K. public sector, high-rise building (that of 5 stories or more) reached its peak in 1967 and has since declined to a relatively low level. The amount of privately-built high-rise construction, unlike North America, has been insignificant. Low-rise, multi-family construction has, however, continued at roughly 20% of total starts. The relative absence of private sector high-rise housing has contributed to the negative image of such structures in the U.K. as recent versions of the 19th century tenements.

[3] Condominiums are residential buildings in which generally the occupant holds title to his or her own unit, and the right to dispose of that unit as they see fit, as well as a share in the common parts of the structure—the halls, shell, gardens, and physical equipment. In a cooperative the individual household usually holds a share in the co-op itself rather than title to an individual dwelling unit, although the size of the share held may determine the size of the unit occupied.

[4] In 1976 there were over 2.7 million dwelling units in the U.S., and 1.7 million in the U.K., lacking one or more plumbing facilities.

[5] Detailed housing statistics for the U.K. are contained in U.K., Central Statistical Office, *Social Trends*, Vol. 9. London: H.M.S.O.

[6] Other changes in household composition and in "headship" rates are equally dramatic. In the U.S., for example, the number of households headed by women grew by 33% between 1970 and 1976, to 21.8% for white households and 37.6% for black households. In the same period, the number of households consisting of adults alone rose 38% and the number consisting of unrelated individuals rose by 67%.

[7] Defined as the ratio of those persons not in the paid labor force, primarily children and the elderly and housewives, to the total number of persons employed.

[8] Notably those households with heads age 29 years or less, other male-headed households (non-families), and those with female heads.

[9] Goldberg (1977), for example, has argued that part of the differences in average house prices between American and Canadian cities is the latter have tended to rely more heavily on public transit rather than expressway systems.

[10] Using the SPSS sub-program FACTOR with varimax rotation and with all data converted to percentages (see Bourne and Simmons, 1978; Willson, 1978).

[11] The Gini coefficient measures the area between the actual cumulative frequency distribution of a given variable over all units of analysis (census tracts) and a straight line representing an equal distribution. The coefficient varies from zero (observations distributed equally over all areas) to one (observations concentrated in one area).

Chapter 4

The Housing Allocation Process
and Urban Housing Markets

Whatever its ideology or form of government, each society must have some mechanism for allocating investment to housing and then for allocating housing to its population.[1] The former allocation is primarily a question of the division of national income among sectors of the economy, while the latter is primarily a question of the distribution of housing among social groups and households at given locations. This chapter focuses on the latter distributional issue generally, and specifically on the operation of allocation mechanisms for housing with urban areas.

Types of Housing Allocation

There are two principal mechanisms for allocating housing. One is the traditional private "market" which allocates households to housing on a competitive basis in terms of the values people attach to housing and their ability to pay. A second is that of public sector allocation in which governments, housing officials or some other community group, distribute housing according to individual and collective needs and the objectives of the agency involved.

Most countries obviously have some mixture of both forms of housing allocation. The emphasis varies from largely public sector allocation in societies which are centrally-planned to an almost exclusive reliance on the private market mechanism in "laissez-faire" societies. In between are a range of combinations of *quasi-market* or *quasi-public* systems—including those in countries in which a large public housing sector operates within a larger market system and those in which small market sector operates within what is essentially a state-controlled housing system. These distinctions are seldom very clear, however, and, as shown later, they are becoming increasingly less clear.

The actual system of allocating housing differs widely even within the same country. This diversity arises not simply because these are so many different systems, but because of differences in the size, heterogeneity, and fluidity of the housing stock, and in the variable demands which people place on that stock. Not surprisingly, the same system will not produce identical results in all areas.

Objectives and Criteria in Housing Allocation

At the outset, we might assume that the private market and the public sector have contrasting objectives and differing criteria for evaluation of the allocation process. The private market for housing is based on the financial resources of firms and their willingness to produce housing for profit, as well as on the income of households and their willingness to pay for housing services through purchase or rental. In contrast, the public sector operates on the basis of housing needs, as defined by individual households or by society collectively. In both instances, however, the objective of matching housing supply and demand, i.e., the allocation process, is roughly the same.

Although both sectors do share some objectives, each employs somewhat different criteria to evaluate those objectives. Table 4.1 provides examples of what those objectives and criteria might be. In theory, the private market emphasizes efficiency, generally in terms of maximizing output while at the same time minimizing overall levels of excess prices and rents. For the public sector, the paramount objective is greater equity or social welfare, in terms of assuring adequate housing for all according to their needs. Nevertheless, when viewed in aggregate, all public agencies must also have efficiency as one of their objectives—in terms of how they distribute units to households—if they are to achieve maximum use of their resources in meeting social needs. Similarily, the private market must have an element of equity in its operation in that price increases force households to regulate how much housing they consume.

A similar duality emerges when one examines the process of allocation. The overwhelming mechanism in the private housing market, among both producers and consumers of housing is *competition*. Yet competition also appears in the public sector, in terms of defining who is to get housing of what type and where, and among the various agencies involved in housing allocation. Wherever there is competition there is also a countervailing force, which we call simply *cooperation*. This factor is evident in housing allocation not only in such obvious and positive examples as that of housing associations and nonprofit and self-help groups, but in terms of *collusion*. In the private market, the latter might involve individuals and groups acting together to exclude others from living in their neighborhoods, or to set prices or rents, or to restrict mortgages in certain areas of a city. Similar, although perhaps less obvious, collusion occurs within the public sector in attempts to alter the location of public housing or the waiting lists of people trying to secure access to that housing (see Chapter 10).

Note also that the two types of allocation operate at quite different scales. In

Table 4.1. Similarities and Contrasts in Private and Public Housing Allocation

Index	Private market allocation	Public sector allocation
Principal objective	Efficiency	Equity
Criteria of efficiency	Minimizing aggregate housing prices and rents	Maximizing use of existing stock
	Maximizing output and profits,	Minimizing administrative costs
	Maintaining rates of return	Maintaining adequate stock
Criteria of equity	No one can move without making others worse off,	Assuring adequate housing for all
	Price restricts over-consumption	Treating all equally according to their needs
Process of allocation	Competition (ability to pay)	Needs and social priorities
Countervailing process	Collusion, Cooperation	Competition (among agencies and tenants)

the private market, it is usually the individual (household) who is bidding for housing, yet the process does not assign a specific individual (John Doe) to a specific housing unit. Instead, it assigns classes of similar households to a limited range of housing types and locations. In contrast, the public allocation process is in theory a community-based allocation yet it actually involves assigning a specific John Doe to a given housing unit in a unique location. This means that both processes contain the seeds of their own contradiction in that it is seldom the case that individual and community welfare coincide.

Additional Questions

Regardless of the type of allocation system used, however, a number of similar questions can be asked of each. First, how does the allocation mechanism for housing actually function? How are the criteria of allocation—whether they be ability to pay or the identification of need—established? To what extent are the criteria explicit, such as in housing prices, and to what extent are they implicit, as in the case of discrimination?

Second, what mechanisms are used to monitor changes in housing preferences, needs, and supply to ensure that there is a reasonable match between households and the housing stock? What information is needed? How is this information to be collected and distributed, and by whom? The private housing market in theory takes in this information as a matter of course, digests it, and then puts out in the form of "signals," such as changes in vacancy rates and prices or housing deterioration and household relocations. Many of the same signals come to the public agencies involved in housing allocation. More frequently, however, the public sector must rely on other measures: the length and composition of its waiting list, and complaints submitted from existing tenants (sometimes in the form of graffiti).

A third question relates to the implementation of changes indicated by the information received. In a market system people presumably respond directly to economic "cues." If they don't, they find themselves with less housing or pay more for the same housing. In any publicly-controlled system, some combination of the carrot (such as subsidies) and the stick (persuasion or higher rents) may be employed. The nature of the response in the housing system is critical in understanding the spatial outcomes which we document in the following chapter.

THE NATURE OF URBAN HOUSING MARKETS

The market for housing, like that for most other goods and services in our society, is primarily an economic market set within a given political framework. It may be defined as a set of institutions and procedures for bringing together housing supply and demand—buyers and sellers, renters and landlords, builders and consumers—for purposes of exchanging resources. In this example, the resources are housing services. In economic theory, the role of the market is to allocate scarce resources in an efficient manner so as to maximize output, or social well-being, while minimizing costs. The mechanism of allocation, as defined above, is price.

Unlike most other markets, however, the urban housing market deals as much with the exchange of rights to property as it does with a consumption good such as housing. Property is not usually consumed as we consume toothpaste, for example. It cannot, in most instances, by physically moved (excluding mobile homes). Moreover, the use of urban property is often severely restricted (e.g., through zoning and neighboring uses) and even these rights can be withdrawn by public fiat (compulsory purchase or expropriation). It is also true that unlike conventional markets, such as the Sunday morning food market, there is no marketplace, at least no single geographic marketplace, for housing. Instead, buyers move to the goods rather than the reverse.

Types of Housing Markets

The initial distinction which must be made in defining housing markets is one of *scale*. Generally, two distinct scales are recognized: (1) the macroscale, which is concerned with the housing sector of the national economy and the interaction of supply and demand at an aggregate (usually national) level; and (2) the microscale, which focuses on the behavior of individual producers and consumers at a more local level.

At the macro-level, research interest tends to focus on aggregate levels of production and consumption of housing, but with little or no regard for the composition of the stock and its distribution among households and places. The housing market is essentially defined by the relationship between the rate of investment in housing supply and aggregate expenditures by households. As such, housing competes with other sectors (both durable and nondurable goods) in the national market for scarce income and productive resources. Although beyond the scope of this book in any detail, the student of housing must begin with the macro-level housing market since it is primarily at this level that the parameters (or limits) are established for local housing transactions.

At the local or micro-level, we are in fact studying how these national aggregates are reflected in the housing markets of individual regions or urban areas. More specifically, we are concerned with the spatial expression of the matching of supply and demand—i.e., how the housing allocation process actually works on the ground. How is housing produced and exchanged? How are prices and rents determined and how do they vary among types of housing at particular locations? What is the role played by local institutions and governments?

In addition to scale, housing markets can be defined on numerous other criteria. Among these criteria are the location of control (privately or publicly-owned), or more broadly tenure type (rental, owner-occupied, cooperative), age of housing and position in the market (new and resale), and price of quality (derelict units or stately mansions). In almost all cases, however, any disaggregation below the national level (a sectoral definition) or below the scale of an entire urban region (a spatial definition) implies the existence of "sub-markets" for housing. This question is taken up in the last section of this chapter.

Spatial Delimitation

The spatial definition of a housing market then obviously depends on the kind of market one has in mind. At the local level, however, perhaps the only distinguishing feature of a housing market is that it is a limited spatial entity. Even so, defining that entity is by no means straightforward. Generally, an urban housing market may be defined as a contiguous geographic area, more or less clearly bounded, within which it is possible for a household to trade or substitute one dwelling unit for another without also altering its place of work or its pattern of social contacts. In other words, people can change residence without necessarily changing jobs or friends (and vice versa). Identifying the appropriate study area thus depends primarily on determining the spatial extent of substitution in housing. In practice, however, given the difficulties of measuring substitution, we tend to define local housing markets in parallel with local labor markets, where the latter are centered on a major employment concentration, usually the central business district.

It will be immediately evident that neither of these definitions produces discrete spatial boundaries. Instead, given the increasing number of potential work locations, the extensive distances over which commuting to work is possible in the modern metropolis, and the fact that few urban areas are totally isolated geographically, the tendency is for one local housing market to merge into the next. In addition, the increase in second homes, and in the purchase of homes in the rural countryside in anticipation of retirement, has vastly extended the spatial extent of most local housing markets. In the face of this complexity, researchers have tended to fall back on the use of local municipal boundaries, or those of census metropolitan areas, in defining the spatial area of a local housing market. This restriction, however, often leads to serious distortions in the research results reported.

Finally, the spatial delimitation of urban housing markets also varies depending on where one is within the housing allocation process. It is likely, for example, that large builders and developers would view New York and Philadelphia as being in the same housing (supply) market, between which they might easily consider reallocating resources. On the other hand, it is unlikely that the typical consumer would regard the substitution of dwelling units in the two cities as feasible or desirable. More emphatically, the single-parent, with five young children, living on welfare in a high-rise block on the lower east side of Manhattan, would have a very different view of the urban housing market and its geographic extent than would, for example, the young upwardly-mobile executive working for an multi-national corporation. In sum, while we may, in subsequent pages, rely primarily on one method of defining urban housing market areas, we should recognize that this is but one of many possible images.

Components of a Housing Market

Figure 4.1 provides an outline of the components in a typical housing market. The two major components are the housing stock and the inventory of households in a given market area. Recall from Chapter 2 that we are in fact discussing the flow of housing services from the stock and the housing status attained by particular households. The linking mechanism is the market *transaction*—the exchange process—which brings together units from the stock and certain households. Completion of this transaction process in turn produces a set of outcomes, such as changes in the level and locational pattern of vacancies, prices, investment and overcrowding, as well as in occupancy and neighborhood turnover.

The essential ingredient in the market is change; it is clearly a dynamic process. Both the housing stock and the inventory of households change *internally*, such as through the aging process, as well as through *externally-induced* changes. The determinants of external change primarily alter the rate of new housing construction and the size, demographic structure, and income of the population which give rise to the demand for housing. But all of these components—and this is the essence of the market concept—are interrelated. Increases in household income, for instance, will not only raise the demand for housing, it will alter the nature of that demand. It will also attract more in-migrants into that housing market area, it will also stimulate new housing construction and encourage people and institutions to invest in improvements in the existing stock. This, then, in total is what we term the *housing system*.

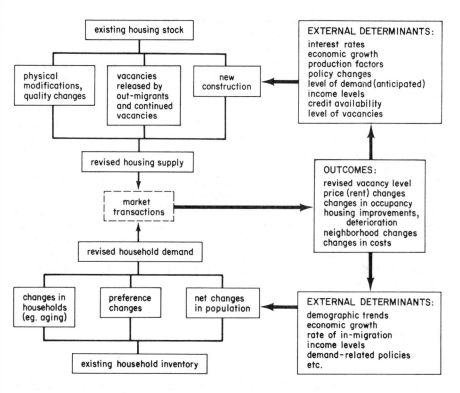

Fig. 4.1. The components of an urban housing market.

HOW THE MARKET WORKS

Even with an agreement on definitions, there is an immense diversity of interpretations of how the housing market actually works. Some researchers conceptualize the market as a perfectly competitive economic market in which households have uniform tastes and complete information, and in which the supply of housing is relatively fixed. Some see the market primarily in terms of the institutions and decision-makers involved, while others see it as a process of social conflict and a continuing element in the class struggle in contemporary capitalist society. Still others look to the normative question of how the market should work rather than how it does work. The views are as different as the definitions of housing itself, summarized in Chapter 2.

Here an attempt is made to integrate elements from several of these approaches into a broader framework. We begin, however, with the concept of a competitive market drawn from micro-economics since the housing market is, at least in basic outline, an economic transaction process and because this is the best-developed part of the literature. The concept is then extended to include the behavior of individual actors and institutions operating within and outside the market, and then to encompass the social structure which influences who in fact has *access* to the market and at what cost.

Micro-economic View: The Market Clearing Solution

The most precise interpretations of how the housing market works derive primarily from the micro-economics literature. One such concept views the matching of households and housing units as essentially an "assignment" problem. It begins, as in Figure 4.2, with a supply matrix of housing units classified by attributes of the dwelling, neighborhood and location, and a demand matrix of households classified by their attributes, preferences, and constraints (e.g., income, mobility, etc.). For simplicity, income is usually taken as an overall index of demand and purchasing power, while dwelling price is taken as an index of the type of housing supply available.

In theory, the economic market allocates housing units to households on the strict basis of the prices of those units and the amounts households are willing to pay for housing. The former are represented in a set of *asking prices* and the latter in a matrix of *bid prices* from households. The allocation proceeds so as to achieve a *market clearing solution*, i.e., one in which all units are allocated and all households are accommodated, in the most efficient way. Efficiency in this case is defined as that allocation which minimizes over (or under) consumption of housing and in which total rents paid (and prices) are at a minimum.[2] Again, in theory, all households are assigned to the housing they prefer and can pay for, after all other households with similar preferences and higher bid prices have been allocated. The assignment is also optimal if, as defined above, no household could be made better off with a different assignment without making other households worse off.

This formulation is not dynamic, however, in the sense that it does not allow for change. Nor does it allow for a diversity of behavior among households or for a persistent disequilibrium in the market, e.g., when supply and demand do not match. Nevertheless, it does identify very simply the basic economic components in the process of market allocation. To embellish the concept, we must initially add concepts relating to the behavior of both the consumers and producers of housing.

Households must initially choose between some quantities of housing (q) and all other goods (z) among which in combination they are equally satisfied and therefore indifferent. These combinations, when ordered systematically, as represented by the curve I′ in Figure 4.3, define the household's *indifference curve*. Their combined expenditures on housing and other goods are in turn subject to an overall budget or income constraint, represented by the budget line BB′. Although the household could choose any one of many possible combinations, such as q_1 units of housing and z_1 units of other goods, the optimal allocation of their resources is at the point T where the budget line BB′ is tangential to the indifference curve. At that point, the household would consume q_2 and z_2 units of housing and other goods, respectively.

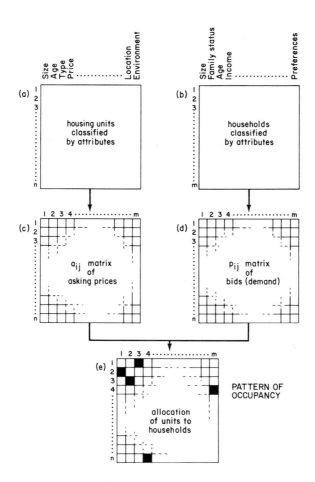

Fig. 4.2. A market clearing model of housing allocation.

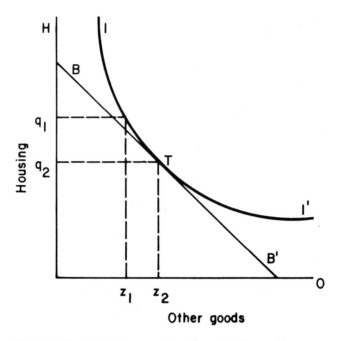

Fig. 4.3. The choice between housing and other goods.

In choosing a particular quantity of housing (services), most households must also choose between a given quantity of housing and a location. The latter, conventionally, is expressed in terms of a *trade-off* between housing costs and accessibility (or commuting costs) to some central workplace (the CBD). In Figure 4.4, we assume two households with roughly similar incomes but dissimilar indifference curves, I_1 and I_2, respectively, regarding desired combinations of housing and accessibility. Their respective income constraints, $B_1 B_1$ and $B_2 B_2$, are tangential to their indifference curves at points T_1 and T_2, respectively. The first household would, therefore, choose a_1 units of accessibility and q_1 units of housing and thus live closer to the city center, while the second household would accept fewer (a_2) units of accessibility to obtain more (q_2) units of housing and thus would locate further from the center.

Furthermore, each household will have a somewhat different preference for each type of housing unit, leaving aside for the moment the additional question of tenure choice. These preferences will be reflected in the prices each household is willing to bid for each unit (Fig. 4.5a). The result, in theory, is a *distribution of bid prices* for each unit in the housing stock. When considering all units together, the result is a matrix of bid prices (as in Fig. 4.2). In this simple illustration, household 1 is willing to bid most for housing unit 2, while household 2 is willing to bid

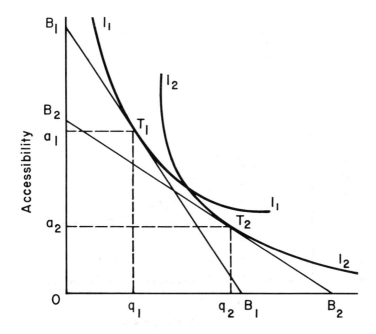

Fig. 4.4. The choice between housing and accessibility.

more for unit 4 than for any other unit. In an optimal allocation, household 1 will occupy unit 2, even if the potential bid of household 2 for that same unit is higher.

Each producer (e.g., landlord, builder, owner-occupier) of housing will have an *asking price* for each unit (or units), based on the initial costs of producing (or replacing) that unit plus a premium which he thinks that households currently in the market will pay (Fig. 4.5b). Although one can think in terms of a matrix of asking prices for each household (as shown in Fig. 4.2), in reality there is usually but one asking price for a given unit, which is lowered or raised based upon the households in the market at that time. When the location variable is added, of course, the asking price varies even when the housing units are equivalent.

These transactions also take place over a period of time. During that time, differences in the perceptions of the market, as reflected in the vendors' (sellers') asking prices and buyers' bid prices, are resolved. Thus, over time, we expect a convergence between asking and bid prices until a final sale price is reached (Fig. 4.5c). This convergence may take only a few hours or days, or it may take weeks or even months, depending on market conditions.[3] In a dynamic or tight market, for example, with few housing vacancies and rising prices, the bid price may finally exceed the initial asking price. In a very slow market, this convergence may not take place at all, and the property could be withdrawn from the market. In any

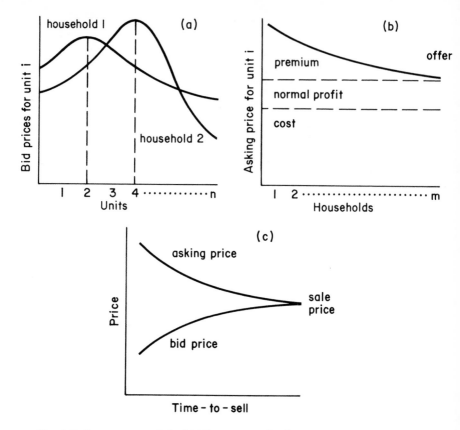

Fig. 4.5. Components of the bidding process for housing.

case, the behavior of buyers and sellers in these two market situations will be very different.[4]

This model can be extended one step further by adding the effects of different production costs facing producers in determining the kinds (and densities) of housing units which are provided. For illustrative purposes, assume that there is a single production function (with constant returns to scale) made up of only two components: inputs of land (L) and non-land (N) inputs, with the latter including the costs of labor, materials, and capital. For each input there is a single set of prices, r for land and n for non-land inputs. In Figure 4.6, we see that where the price of land is low relative to non-land inputs, more land will be consumed per unit of production and the tendency will be to construct low-density, likely single-family houses. Where the ratio of land to non-land prices increases, multi-family higher-density units will be built, and beyond a certain point, $(\frac{r}{n})_2$, only

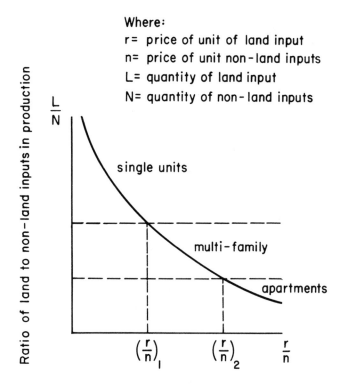

Fig. 4.6. Determinants of the type and density of housing produced.

high-rise buildings will be produced. Figure 4.6 also provides a schematic cross section of the composition of housing types and densities in a typical city extending outward from the center to the suburbs.

The Process of Bidding for Housing

The actual process which buyers and sellers, or landlords and tenants, go through in setting prices (or rents) is not well understood. In contrast to the process of deciding on a specific location for a house (see Chapter 6), we know considerably less about how expectations, prices, and the rules of negotiation involved in housing transfers are established. One can focus on the behavior of either buyer or seller or of both together, perhaps as Cassidy (1975) suggests, as a temporary coalition formed for purposes of exchange.

Whatever the approach, however, it is clear that each household entering the market faces a given set of *entry conditions*. In the private market, these conditions usually include price (rent), the down payment required (or rental deposit), credit availability (mortgages) and cost (the interest rate), and the cost of moving and buying or selling (transaction costs).[5] These may also include the costs and difficulties of modifying the unit to suit their tastes and needs, as well as the possibility of discriminatory charges by the seller, estate agents, or lending institutions. Clearly, to consider all these factors simultaneously is an immensely difficult task; yet millions of ordinary people solve such complex problems all the time whenever they buy or rent a house or apartment.

Most households also have some kind of checklist of what housing they need, where they want to live, and what they can afford. They solve the decision problem in roughly that order. For many households, it is not the *nominal price* of the unit which is important, however, but the monthly carrying costs (mortgage plus taxes, utilities, and maintenance) and the *cash requirement* in terms of down payment. The former bears most directly on the household's current income and the latter on household wealth (e.g., assets). This combination leads to an inevitable trade-off between the size of the down payment and the mortgage. In the new housing market, the relative balance of the two is usually specified a priori, but in the older resale housing market both tend to be up for negotiation more frequently, especially if the vendor is involved in taking back a mortgage, as is often the case in the inner city.

The importance of timing in this transaction process should be stressed. That is, while the distribution of buyers and sellers in the market changes markedly over time, the available stock and, of course, neighborhood and accessibility attributes change much more slowly. The former, then, has a more significant effect on the market in the short term.

Who and What Houses are in the Market?

We also know that the proportions of households and properties actually on the market at any given time is relatively small. Depending on local conditions, perhaps only 5 or 6% of all houses in a city come up for sale or rent during a relatively short period of time (6 months to a year). Similarly, only a small proportion of households are actively seeking a new dwelling or a trade, at any given time. This does not mean, however, as noted in Chapter 2, that all changes are confined to units or households on the market. Others find their situation has changed even though they have remained in place, and not entered the market. This distinction between *market* and *non-market* changes is one we use throughout the following discussions.

Of those houses and households on the market at any given time, a substantial proportion are also new (i.e., newly-built housing or newly-formed households and in-migrants). This proportion, which may be as high as 40%, in turn leads to the question of which sector, the new or existing stock, dominates in setting prices in the market. Generally it is argued that the *existing stock is dominant* (Grigsby, 1963), but there is considerable evidence that either the new or resale markets can dominate at different times.[6]

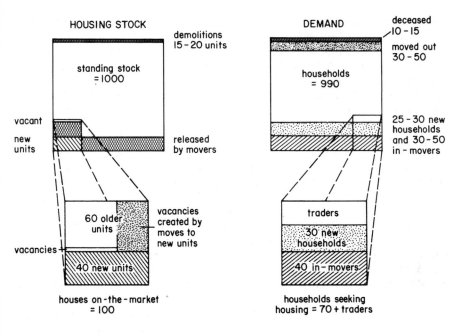

Fig. 4.7. The households and housing units on the market.

To illustrate the changing composition of an urban housing market, consider a simple example of the flows of households and housing units (Fig. 4.7). Assume a hypothetical urban area with a housing inventory of 1,000 units occupied by 990 households, the difference being vacant units. Over a short period of time, say one year, 15 to 20 units might have been demolished or otherwise removed from the stock, and 30 to 50 units would be newly built. On the demand side, perhaps 10 to 15 households would now be deceased or have been dissolved, 25 to 35 new households would have been formed, and 30 to 50 would have moved to other urban areas. Although we are not considering either the price of the units or the income of households at this point, it is evident that housing units tend to be added at higher than average quality and price levels while new households enter at all levels in the income profile.

The housing market at any point in time might then consist of some 100 units available for sale or rent, and from 90 to 110 households looking for housing, depending on local conditions. Of the 100 units on the market, the following composition might be expected:

60 older units, of which on average:
  - 35 would represent units available because of trades between households currently occupying older units, as well as vacancies

  - 25 would represent new vacancies created by the movements of the initial occupants into new units

40 new units, of which on average:
  - 25 would be occupied by older households formerly living elsewhere in that market area
  - 15 would be occupied by new families or in-migrants

At the end of the period of study, the new stock would then consist of 1,025 units (40 new units less 15 demolitions) and approximately 1,010 households.

The most difficult component of these flows to predict is the number of "traders" (e.g., replacement demand); how many people are in the market in search of a more preferred or appropriate housing bundle. In fact, all households are by definition *potential members of the market* in that if conditions were considered favorable they would undertake to purchase (or rent) alternative housing. In practice, however, only a very small percentage do.

The Actors in the Market: The Behavioral and Institutional View

The housing market is obviously even more complex than that outlined above. Not only does the market not work as neatly as economic theory implies, including the observation that it is never in equilibrium, but in addition it is shaped by a multiplicity of decision makers, rules and regulations. A myriad of participants or *actors* are involved in the real-world production and allocation of housing, all of whom operate within an established system of "institutions." Figure 4.8 outlines the components in this view of the structure of the market.

The focus of this approach begins with the identification of the individual decision-making units or agents involved and the manner in which their behavior is linked to the housing market. The central element is again the market "transaction." This might be any decision to construct or renovate a new house or to transfer a mortgage, but in most instances it implies the purchase (or rental) of a dwelling unit. It also culminates a lengthy process through which housing is constructed, financed, marketed, and then eventually occupied.

The institutional context of housing identified in Figure 4.8 contains both individual and corporate actors, such as government agencies, and it also suggests *guidelines* for the behavior of all actors. The latter includes, for example, the legal system which defines property rights, the financial system which determines who gets what credit (and where), the policy system (national and local government policies) which sets out building and land use regulations, as well as the context of societal preferences and precedents regarding the way we "do business." Any housing market transaction requires the tacit approval (or at least the absence of formal disapproval) from these various actors and conformity with established rules and regulations.

Many of these actors have come under close scrutiny by housing researchers. W. F. Smith (1970), for example, provides a careful review of the role of each actor and institution in the housing allocation process. Others have added notes of criticism regarding those roles. Pahl (1976, 1977) refers to the entire spectrum

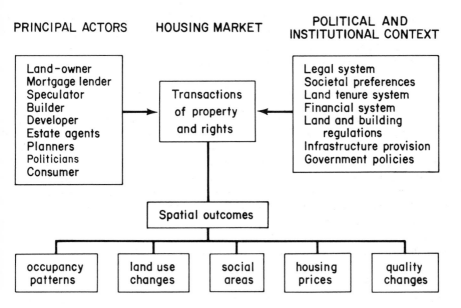

Fig. 4.8. Actors and institutions in the housing market (adapted from W. F. Smith, 1970, p. 42).

of administrators, politicians, and technicians in the housing field as *gate-keepers* who effectively determine who gets what from the housing market and where. Palm (1976, 1979) has examined the role played by real estate agents in shaping the housing choices available to households through their control of market information, and Harvey and Chatterjee (1974) have examined the critical role of mortgage lending institutions in segmenting the operation of housing markets in older parts of the city. Still others have looked at the impact of specific government policies—such as rent control, growth and development controls and fiscal restraint—on housing (see Chapter 9). All form part of the institutional context.

Access to Housing and Housing Conflict

An alternative view interprets the housing allocation process as the result not of a competitive economic market or institutional behavior per se, but of a deeper process of class conflict. Following the earlier classic work of Max Weber, Rex and Moore (1967) argue that housing allocation is a direct function of the class struggle inherent in capitalist societies as well as the central element in understanding the social structure of the city. That structure, they conclude, is the result of "...a class struggle over the use of homes in the city."

That struggle arises, as noted in the previous chapter, when people have *differential means of access* to the housing market. The fundamental cause of such differentials, of course, is the existence of wide differences in income in our society. But, as Castells (1975) and others have argued, it does not stop there. Access to housing, and the very different housing "situations" which this produces, also depends on access to credit, as was noted above. That access, in turn, depends not only on income but on the predictability of the flow of future income. This concept roughly parallels the economists' definition of long-term or permanant income. Income predictability in turn depends on one's career path and occupational status as well as on one's social position and thus one's ability "to use the system."

A person's ability to use the system to gain greater access to housing is further dependent on the ability to gain and use information and social contacts. That ability, as both Harvey (1973) and Castells (1975) argue, is in large part *culturally determined*, particularly with respect to one's familiarity with the cultural values and behavioral norms of the dominant social class (the wealthy and the burgeoisie). To the extent that the poor, the working classes, and new immigrants do not share these same values, or understand or accept the behavioral norms, they are systematically denied a level of access to housing which even their low incomes would allow.

We then conclude that the urban housing market is, at the same time, more than it appears. It is an economic assignment problem, a competitive bidding process, an institutional and behavioral system, and an element in the social conflicts which plague all mature societies.

ONE MARKET OR MANY?:
HOUSING SEGMENTATION AND SPATIAL SUB-MARKETS

Of basic importance in understanding how housing markets work is the question of whether sub-markets exist or not. There are two dimensions to this question. One is whether the stock is partitioned into distinct "segments" in aspatial terms, and the second is whether the urban area is geographically subdivided into "spatial sub-markets." Most students of housing agree that an urban housing market, particularly in a large metropolitan area, does not operate as "one large market" but rather as a series of *linked sub-markets*. But what are sub-markets? How would we know when they are present? What are the links? These questions warrant a relatively extensive treatment here precisely because sub-markets are most likely to arise—and to become socially visible—through the spatial differentiation of an urban area.[7]

Types and Sources of Sub-markets

Sub-markets, as the term implies, may be broadly defined as quasi-independent subdivisions of an urban housing market. Within these subdivisions supply and demand interact to produce homogeneous clusters of housing types or household characteristics in which there is a unique set of prices (or rents) and between which there is little substitution of one unit for another. While it is obvious that houses and households with similar attributes tend to be grouped in identifiable areas of the city, it is quite another question to assess whether this grouping leads to significant differences in the prices paid for a given amount of housing services.

In general, sub-markets might arise for several different reasons: (1) through the sheer *size* and *heterogeneity* of the housing stock; (2) through the *diversity* of demands placed on that stock by households; and (3) because of barriers or *disequilibria* in the market itself. On average, the larger the urban area the greater is the heterogeneity of the stock and of households, and thus the more likely are sub-markets to arise. Moreover, the substitution of housing over long distances is often impractical. By disequilibria we mean primarily constraints on the supply of housing of given types at given locations relative to the demands for such housing. Inevitably the stock changes more slowly than does demand. Such disequilibria become more sharply focused if additional barriers, such as racial discrimination, are also present.

One consequence of these constraints is that a price *premium* (or discount) may be paid for housing in specific areas in comparison to the price of similar housing in other areas. These premiums, sometimes called *quasi-rents*,[8] are assumed to reflect geographic differences in the operation of the market within particular neighborhoods, but also may identify the existence of spatial sub-markets.

An examination of the literature reveals an immense diversity in the definition and use of sub-markets (Table 4.2). The range of criteria used to define those sub-markets, the variable number of sub-markets, and the list of attributes of the geographic areas involved are immense. Sub-markets have been defined simply on the basis of the newly-built and resale housing stock (Maisel, 1963), on areas of changing social status (Maher, 1974), on municipal boundaries (Straszheim, 1975), and on the zones created by the differential behavior of mortgage-lending agencies (Harvey, 1973, 1977a) and real estate agents (Palm, 1978).

Each of these approaches varies in purpose and concept. Some have had the identification of sub-markets as their primary objective. Others have used the definition of sub-markets as a necessary stepping-stone to subsequent analyses, and still others have assumed the existence of sub-markets without really acknowledging what they were doing. Few have actually taken the trouble to test whether their zones are in fact spatial sub-markets.

Alternative Definitions, Criteria, and Tests

The most common use of the term sub-market is perhaps a simple *taxonomic* or classification use. Conventionally, the stock is divided into tenure classes (owner-occupied vs. rental), structure types (apartment, row housing, and single-detached), and value (price), while households are classified by income, family type, and race or ethnic origin. These categories in turn may be subdivided by location within the city (e.g., inner city or suburban), or with reference to work locations. Figure 4.9 provides a summary of these traditional definitions.[9] The limitation of the use of the term sub-market here is that while these criteria do differentiate visible

Table 4.2. The Diversity of Definitions and Applications of Housing Submarkets: Selected Examples

Author	City	Principal criteria for classification	Types	
			Number	Examples
Grigsby (1963)	Philadelphia	location, tenure value race	many	central city/suburban owner occupied/rental high; medium/low price black/white
Needleman (1965)	London	tenure	4	local authority; owner-occupied privately rented (furnished) privately rented (unfurnished)
Maher (1974)	Toronto	social status	5	regions: stable single-family increasing ethnicity increasing social status increasing population and crowding owned/rented; high turnover
Harvey and Chatterjee (1974)	Baltimore	location, income, ethnicity, mortgage financing and turnover rates	12	grouped into 8 areas or general types primarily on the basis of housing prices and finance: e.g., ethnic South Baltimore
Kain and Quigley (1975)	Pittsburgh	density, size quality (age) and tenure	30	basically structural: 15 types cross-classified by interior size, building type, lot size and tenure, for each of two time periods: post 1930 and pre 1930.
Ball and Kirwin (1977)	Bristol	multivariate: socio-economic and stock variables	11	identified as clusters of homogeneous attributes: primarily a social typology; students, affluent, immigrants; and tenure.
Palm (1978)	San Francisco– Oakland	Real estate information– Boards of Realtors districts	7	real estate districts are aggregations of municipal units (e.g., Marin County), defined by a principal components analysis of social, housing and environmental variables.

A) BY HOUSING STOCK

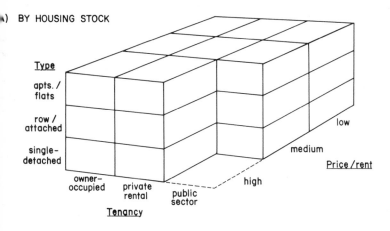

B) BY HOUSEHOLD TYPE

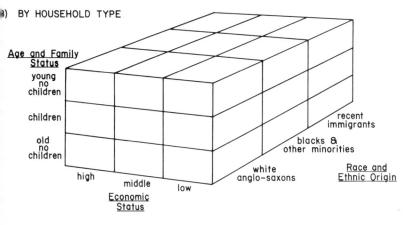

C) BY LOCATIONS / NEIGHBORHOODS

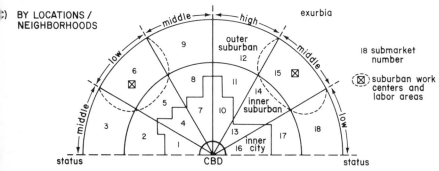

Fig. 4.9. Intra-urban housing sub-markets: traditional definitions.

subdivisions of the stock and its inhabitants, it remains to be proven that they also represent real differences in the behavior of the market.

A second approach makes use of the concept of *substitution* among housing types and locations which we employed earlier in this chapter to delimit the outer boundaries of an urban housing market. Grigsby (1963, p. 34), for example, in his classic study of housing in Philadelphia, defined sub-markets in the following way:

> the test of whether two dwelling units are in the same submarket is whether substitutability is sufficiently great to produce palpable and observable cross-relationships with respect to occupancy, sales, prices and rents . . .

He argued that substitution could be measured empirically by observing the number of movements or *transitions* of households between one sub-market and another. Converting the number of movers into proportions would then provide a matrix of transitions and a direct assessment of how closely linked are housing movements in different areas. Obviously, some movements take place between almost all sub-markets, although the probability of movement declines with the *distance between the sub-markets*, with distance measured in terms of value, social class and structural type as well as geographic distance. The result then is a gradation of movements (or linkages) between sub-markets but with every sub-market linked most closely with those nearest to it. This is what is meant by a series of "linked sub-markets."

A more formal statement of substitution among sub-markets looks to the *cross-linkages* between demand and price. One such measure relates the proportionate change in the consumption of one kind of housing to the proportionate change in the price of other kinds of housing. In symbolic terms:

$$\eta_{ij} = \frac{\Delta q_i}{q_i} \bigg/ \frac{\Delta p_j}{p_j}$$

where q refers to quantity and p to price for two types of housing units, i and j, respectively. If the coefficient η_{ij} is small or zero, then a change in the price of unit j (that is Δp_j) produces little or no effect on the quantity of housing type i consumed. The two units can then be said to be in separate sub-markets. On the other hand, as η_{ij} becomes progressively larger, then it can be assumed that the two types of housing units are good substitutes, and therefore can be considered as being in the same market. In this way it is likely that the demand for expensive, detached single-family houses in the suburbs, to take an extreme example, could be easily separated from that for low-cost, low-quality inner city housing.

A fourth approach actually tests whether the prices paid for similar bundles or attributes of housing are distinctly different in the various parts of an urban area. This might involve the comparison of a series of regression equations, with price as the dependent variable, one fitted for the entire urban housing market area and the others fitted to the same area disaggregated into potential sub-markets.

If the fit of the equation is better for the sub-markets than for the entire urban area, the researcher would conclude that sub-markets exist *and* that they help to "explain" the spatial behavior of house prices. Straszheim (1975) and Palm (1978), for example, found that disaggregating the housing market of the San Francisco Bay area in this way significantly improved their ability to explain variations in house prices. However, Schnare and Struyk (1976) and Ball and Kirwin (1977), in studies of Boston and Bristol, respectively, did not.

Spatial Sub-markets: A Summary

One might then conclude that sub-markets for housing do exist, but that their importance—in terms of influencing market behavior, prices, and the choices open to consumers—remains to be established. In part, the confusion over the use of the concept derives from the obvious fact that the methods of testing for significant differences in house prices seem so far removed from the reality we observe. The ghetto tenement, the suburban box, and the leafy mansion district must be in distinct sub-markets, we ask? They are, of course, but not necessarily in terms of the prices paid for each unit of housing quality, and not if they all respond to essentially the same pressures of supply and demand.

A more fruitful approach perhaps is to focus on those specific constraints in the housing market which one would not expect to appear uniformly across the urban area. As examples, spatial sub-markets might arise as a result of:

> *supply restrictions:* the limited availability of certain kinds of housing which is in demand, but which cannot be easily reproduced (e.g., 19th brown-stones or low-cost older units).
>
> *accessibility restrictions:* some houses may have a unique location, which conveys to them an additional benefit (or liability) in terms of accessibility (i.e., single-family housing within walking distance of the center).
>
> *neighborhood restrictions:* for various reasons, particular small areas can and do become especially attractive (or unattractive), for which entry is limited and people will pay a premium (or discount).
>
> *institutional restrictions:* perhaps the most obvious is the practice of redlining, in which mortgage-lending agencies refuse to lend in certain areas. Other examples include the effects of building codes, zoning and planning regulations.
>
> *racial, ethnic, and class discrimination:* the obvious problem that certain families are limited in their search for and choice of housing because of direct exclusion.
>
> *information restrictions:* some households have differential access to information on housing opportunities, and on how the market works.

The combined result of these restrictions is that the prices paid for certain houses, by certain types of households, will be more (the premium) than might be expected for similar housing in other areas, and that movements of households between areas would be less than one might predict. The important distinction is to discover where these differences in price (or rent) are paid intentionally and where they are paid because people have no choice.

Why Are Sub-markets Important?

Despite its complexity, the sub-markets question is important. First, as in any situation where spatial disaggregation is necessary, the way the urban housing market is subdivided for purposes of research shapes the results and insights obtained. It is preferable that such subdivisions be based on their relationship to the operation of that market. Second, sub-markets are important because the assumption that they exist permeates much of the literature on residential mobility, neighborhood change, ghetto formation, racial segregation and housing deterioration.

The sub-market issue is also relevant to housing policy. Simply put, if independent sub-markets do exist, then policy initiatives must be directed to particular segments of the stock and to specific areas of the city if they are to be most effective. If they do not exist, then policies can be uniformly applied across the entire housing market. Under the latter assumption, that all segments and areas are interdependent, the effects of construction subsidies or housing allowances, for example, will (eventually) work their way through the entire market. The impact of housing policies formulated under these two interpretations will be very different indeed.

Finally, even if it is not possible to empirically identify sub-markets on the precise, but rather narrow, criteria of substitution and independent price schedules, it is important that we identify where price differentials do exist and who pays them. The size of these differentials, and the fact that certain groups in society tend to carry the burden, are sufficient to warrant further investigation. But until the actual market implications of these differentials are assessed, perhaps we should only label the geographic areas involved as "market areas" or housing "regions."

NOTES

[1] Excluded here are those societies and cultures, such as rural subsistence cultures, in which housing is produced and consumed individually or in small groups.

[2] More formally stated, the allocation process might be considered efficient in economic terms if the prices of adjacent residential properties (e.g., single lots for housing) are equal at their boundaries. If they are not equal, a transfer of some portion of that lot would in theory take place resulting in both households being better off than before.

[3] A useful measure of the short-term performance of a housing market, noted in Chapter 2, is the "time-to-sell" or "wait-time." This is the period between the listing of a property and the actual sale.

[4] Note also that the behavior of buyers and sellers will be different simply because each owner-occupier will have a different assessment of their own housing unit than will a buyer. The latter very likely will be indifferent among several similar units currently on the market.

[5] Typical transaction costs for owner-occupied housing include fees for the search and registration of the title or deed to the property, land transfer taxes and fees (if any), insurance, and lawyers fees for conveyence. More broadly defined, transaction costs may also include the physical costs of moving house.

[6]There are very wide differences between urban areas in the proportion of houses on the market which are new, reflecting different rates of population growth and levels of prosperity.

[7]The following discussion draws heavily on previous papers by the author and his associates (Bourne, 1976; Bourne and Simmons, 1978; Bourne and Hitchcock, 1978).

[8]Quasi-rents are a form of economic rent, which refers to the surplus element in charges for the use of land and housing over and above what would be considered as normal rent.

[9]The spatial pattern of sub-markets in Figure 4.9c would, of course, be substantially more complex in the large and multi-centered modern metropolis, particularly with the growth of large employment concentrations in suburban areas.

Chapter 5

Housing Supply, Distribution, and Finance

The first set of processes underlying the inventory of housing conditions and urban housing markets discussed in Chapters 3 and 4, respectively, which we should consider relate to housing supply. In what ways does that supply change in aggregate and within small areas? How is housing produced and by whom? What is the actual sequence of events in housing production and land development?

This chapter examines the supply process and the determinants of change in the housing stock. Initially, discussion focuses on the aggregate or macro-level; the housing sector in the national economy, temporal variability in building activity, and the determinants of new construction and changes within the existing stock. The second section examines how these aggregate relationships translate into patterns of supply on the ground, including the characteristics of the building industry and the various actors which produce that housing. The third section examines the complex subject of housing finance, emphasizing the demand side in terms of home purchase and the spatial variability of mortgage provision within urban areas.

AGGREGATE PERSPECTIVES

Housing in the National Economy

We know from the evidence presented in previous chapters that housing is a small but nonetheless very important sector of the national economy. That importance, typically measured directly in terms of aggregate production (output), or in levels of investment, employment or consumer expenditures, has remained roughly constant over time. As a percentage of gross fixed capital investment in most developed countries, residential construction has varied from 4 to 8%, and in investment terms from 3 to 6% of gross domestic product (see Table 3.1). But these figures understate the importance of the housing sector. The value of services deriving from housing totals as much as 15 to 20% of domestic expenditures by consumers, and an even larger component of national household wealth.

Housing supply is important in the economy for two other reasons: it tends to be used as a *regulatory tool* by national governments and it generates an extensive number of *multiplier effects*. The former arises because housing, at least in North America, is seen to be particularly sensitive to the movement of the economy through "business cycles," and is thus frequently used by governments as a means of "countering" the impact of these cycles (thus the terminology of housing as a counter-cyclical policy instrument). This practice, however, tends to make the housing sector itself even more cyclical than it might otherwise be.

The multiplier effects arise through the obvious external requirements of residential construction. Before housing is in place, it requires, in most urban areas, the provision of substantial capital goods and social services—in the form of roads, transit, schools, sewer and water facilities and other public utilities—most of which are provided by local governments or by the developer or builder on behalf of local government. Once in place, housing requires a substantial production of consumer durable goods, such as household furnishings and equipment, before it can be occupied. Nor do the multiplier effects stop there. As the new housing stock and its residents age, both public and private services have to be maintained and at times improved, generating considerable long-term operating (or "down-stream") costs. These important secondary impacts are the subject of discussion in later chapters.

Temporal Rhythms in Supply: Long and Short Building Cycles

One of the basic and, it seems, almost inevitable properties of housing supply in market-based economies is that of wide fluctuations over time (Lewis, 1965; Thomas, 1973; Gottlieb, 1976). These fluctuations, which often appear in the form of regular building cycles, are important in themselves primarily because of the uncertainty and instability they create, for both producers and the labor force, for which consumers pay a premium in housing costs. They also translate into very different housing patterns on the ground. As demonstrated in Chapter 2, these cycles are intimately interrelated with distinct eras of technological change or innovation, particularly in transport and building systems, as well as with the movements of investment capital. The combination of these rhythms provides the temporal "umbrella" within which local patterns of residential construction, occupancy turnover, and price shifts take place.

In general, there are perhaps three different lengths of cycles evident in historical studies of residential building:

> *long-term* cycles of from 20 years (sometimes called Kusnets cycles) up to as much as 40 to 50 years (called Kondratieff long cycles);

medium-term cycles of from 3 to 7 years (the standard business cycle);

short-term fluctuations varying from a few months to little more than a year, including seasonal variability.

These distinct but overlapping temporal rhythms are demonstrated in schematic form in Figure 5.1 (a, b, c).

Such waves of investment in housing, and in the urban built environment generally, have been the subject of increasing research and policy concern. In terms of long cycles, Thomas (1973), for example, has clearly demonstrated the cyclical nature of capital investment in the north Atlantic economy in the 19th century, and more specifically, that building cycles in Britain and the U.S. were inversely related to each other and to the growth rates of their respective economies. Labor (immigration), and especially capital, shifted back and forth across the Atlantic depending on the respective rates of profit and wages in each country.

Others have looked at cycles of more intermediate length, in terms of residential building (see Firestone, 1951 on Canada; Lewis, 1965 on the U.K.; and Wheaton, 1966 on the U.S.) or in urban development generally (Gottlieb, 1976). The latter, for example, identified a cycle of building activity in 30 urban areas in the U.S. varying from 15 to 25 years in length. Hoyt's (1933) monumental study of 100 years of land values in Chicago also revealed distinct long-run regularities in the rise and fall of the urban real estate market, and Isard (1942) identified the close relationship between building cycles and transport innovations. More recently, Adams (1970) and Whitehand (1972) have shown how these building rhythms impact on the spatial structure of development within U.S. and British cities, respectively. Further, Berry (1976) has illustrated the shorter term (seasonal and annual) fluctuations in the Chicago urban housing market, and argued these form one part of a family of rhythmic changes which characterize any dynamic urban area. These cycles also differ between sectors (black and white) of that dual housing market.

Despite this extensive empirical evidence, however, there seems to be little agreement on the reasons why these temporal regularities occur. In part they reflect the ups and downs of our turbulent international economy. In part they also reflect the durability of the housing stock, the slowness of that stock to respond to new demands, as well as longer term social and demographic changes which are only evident over a generation or two. These cycles also follow the vascillations in capital markets, interest rates, and investment movements over time (Maisel, 1963). More generally, they reflect the particular stage of economic development and level of urbanization in a given country (Burns and Grebler, 1977).

Other observers have reinterpreted this evidence from different ideological positions. Harvey (1978), for example, sees such building cycles arising because of the needs of the capitalist system, at both international and national levels, to continuously accumulate ever larger quantities of capital in order to survive. This capital accumulation is achieved by maximizing the rate of profit through encouraging "uneven" spatial and temporal development in the long term. In the search for higher profits, capital is moved between economic sectors and locations, even across national boundaries, and between residential and nonresidential

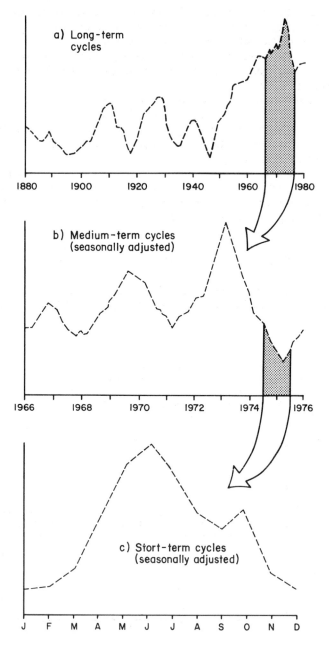

Fig. 5.1. Temporal variations in housing supply and investment (schematic).

sectors, wherever the rate of return is highest. The question still remains, however, of why profits are higher in certain locations for specific periods of time.

Shorter term or business cycle variations are equally complex. There is little doubt, however, that housing supply is particularly responsive to short-term fluctuations in demand. Since most of the demand for housing is supplied by the existing stock in the short run, a proportionally small change in total demand can lead to a significantly greater change in the "flow" of new units. The expectations of buyers and sellers are even more variable over time, in response to their perceptions of future changes in house prices and credit availability (e.g., inflation). Moreover, the often localized nature of housing demand, the geographic fragmentation of sectors of the building industry and the "atomistic" nature of the housing market itself, in which each actor behaves independently, combine to produce an overreaction in supply during periods of boom and an excessive cut-back during periods of decline. Taken together with the inertia of housing institutions, governments, and financial agencies, the existence of such wide temporal fluctuations in supply is then perhaps not surprising.

Aggregate Supply Relationships: The Determinants of New Construction

What factors then determine the actual rate of new construction? Figure 5.2 outlines a simple model of the interrelationships within (and flows of construction

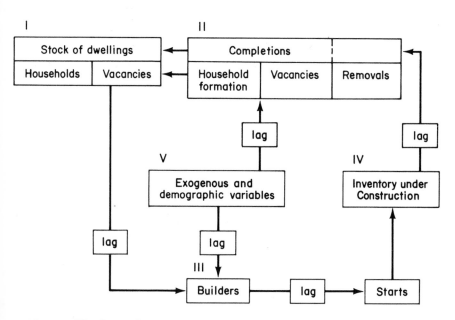

Fig. 5.2. The flows of construction activity in an aggregate housing market (after Maisel, 1963).

activity through) a national housing market. The model begins with a given stock of dwellings, households, and vacancies (as in Chapter 4). The number and kinds of vacancies, again combined with anticipations of changes in exogenous conditions (interest rates, the level of economic growth, etc.) and demographic variables (age, birth rate, household size), induce a response on the part of builders to undertake the construction of new housing. These starts in turn become part of the shifting inventory under construction. In each case there is an inevitable *time lag* between a change in one component and the resulting supply response. This lag may arise because of inadequate information on the market, excessive competition, inertia, or simply the time necessary to divert building resources (human and material) into housing construction.

Over time, the inventory of units under construction in turn acts to alter the current housing stock, just as demographic change alters the inventory of households. The net flow of new units is then the sum of housing completions, less removals (demolitions, abandonment, or withdrawal of units for other reasons), plus or minus changes in the vacancy rate. The rate of household formation, deriving from changes in life styles, demographic structure and rate of immigration (net migration at the regional or urban level), similarly adjusts the composition of demand. The resulting updated housing inventory in turn influences the perceptions of builders and redefines their incentives to initiate new starts in the subsequent period.

These perceptions will clearly differ depending on whether the builder is primarily involved in constructing single-family (owner-occupied) or rental housing. Not only do these two types differ in their demand schedule, but also in their financial requirements. Owner-occupied units are by definition sold on completion and therefore return equity to the developer and investor relatively quickly. Rental housing, on the other hand, is more of a long-term investment, which returns equity only slowly through monthly rent payments, depreciation allowances, and perhaps as an investment tax shelter. The latter attractions were major factors in stimulating rental housing construction in the U.S. and Canada during the 1960s and early 1970s.

A formal model: The above schematic framework can be made more concrete in terms of a statistical model which attempts to predict the aggregate number of new housing starts within a given time period. Similar models are available in the literature for several different countries.[1] Still other models have been adapted to fit a particular urban area in aggregate rather than the nation (Straszheim, 1975). The following equation, which may be taken as representative of a family of national housing models for the U.S., illustrates the specific factors which might be hypothesized as accounting for variations over time in the number of single-family starts:

$$\Delta H_{t_1} = a_1 + a_2 \Delta HH + a_3 D - a_4 V + a_5 P - a_6 I + a_7 \Delta H_{t_0} - a_8 \Delta H_{t_i}$$

where ΔH_{t_1} = number of new housing units added during time period t_1
ΔHH = net household formation during time period t_1
D = demolitions and other removals from the stock

$$V = \text{number of vacant units}$$
$$P = \text{index of average house prices (or rents)}$$
$$I = \text{average mortgage interest rate}$$
$$\Delta H_{t_o} = \text{number of units built in immediately previous time period } t_o$$
$$\Delta H_{t_i} = \text{number of units built in some earlier time period } t_i$$
$$a_1 \text{ to } 8 = \text{coefficients to be estimated}$$
$$t_i \, i = 1 \cdots = \text{monthly or quarterly lag}$$

The model asserts that the supply of new housing increases directly (positively) with the rate of net household formation, the rate of removals from the stock, average house price increases, and with the rate of housing starts in the immediately preceding period.[2] Supply decreases with higher vacancy rates, higher interest rates, and with unusually high levels of construction in still earlier periods. The latter variable attempts to pick up the short-term cyclical swings in housing construction noted above, with the length of the cycle as a variable to be estimated in any given study.

To adapt this kind of national model to individual regions or urban areas requires adding a number of additional variables: for example, net migration, income and wage differentials, and local land availability. The major difficulty in applying such models to single urban areas, aside from data limitations, is that local housing markets are much more volatile and more susceptible to local policy changes (e.g., development controls) and to fluctuations in the local economic base.

Housing from the Existing Stock

It should by now be obvious that the overwhelming majority of housing opportunities are supplied by the existing stock rather than by new housing construction, even over a period of several years. It is perhaps less widely recognized, however, that the supply of services flowing from that stock can shift relatively quickly, in terms of quality, tenure, or in the number of units provided. Our previous illustration of alternative forms of supply changes (Fig. 2.4) indicated that, excluding demolition and new construction, supply changes can take several forms:

> changes in the *number* (and size) of units through subdivision and merger (conversion);
>
> changes in *quality* and value (filtering) without physical alteration;
>
> changes in *occupancy* status (tenure), and density of occupancy;
>
> changes in quality with *physical modification*, including modernization, improvement, and rehabilitation;
>
> changes through various combinations of the above.

These changes may be, and usually are, interrelated. The most difficult to assess is that of quality change without physical alteration to the structure since, unlike the others, it is not commonly recorded in property registers or building permits, although it presumably is evident in price (or rent) and assessment (or tax rating) increases.

Table 5.1. Investment in New Housing Construction and in the
Existing Stock, U.S., 1965–75
(in billions $ 1973)

Year	Expenditures for new housing construction	Expenditures on housing maintenance & improvements	Total investment	Expenditures for maintenance and repairs as % of new construction
1965	33.8	17.8	51.6	52.7
1967	27.6	17.0	44.6	61.6
1969	33.2	17.3	50.5	52.1
1971	41.4	19.2	60.6	46.4
1973	47.9	18.5	66.4	38.6
1975	26.9	20.8	46.7	80.3

Source: U.S. Bureau of the Census.

Empirical data on all forms of physical modifications to the existing stock, however, are notoriously weak, and no doubt seriously underestimate the level of activity. As a proportion of total expenditures on housing, expenditures on conversion and rehabilitation have ranged from a low of 5% to a high of 30% during the great depression. If estimates of the costs of recurring repairs and maintenance are also included, total investment in the existing housing stock is now equal to at least 50 of new construction expenditures (or about 35% of total residential investment). In 1975, investment in the existing stock actually reached 80% of the expenditures on new housing (Table 5.1).

Subdivision, merger, and quality changes: There have been relatively few studies of residential conversions or quality changes in aggregate or within urban areas. Even those which have been undertaken provide conflicting evidence on the extent of these changes. The conversion process, as noted, generally provides only a small proportion of new units in any housing inventory, yet the type, tenure, cost, and size of the units so provided are often crucial for particular social groups (e.g., low-income and small households).

Of the two dimensions of the conversion process, the subdivision of larger into smaller units is most widespread. Subdivision is primarily related to the demand for rental housing by low-income earners and by small or transient households. Thus, conversions tend to increase when the housing market is tight, when prices (or rents) are high relative to income, and when in-migration is high. Merger, on the other hand, tends to reflect higher-income demand, often for homeownership, where suitable alternative housing is not available or when preferences turn back to the older stock. The latter may reflect in part the process of inner city revival in which the middle class occupies housing formerly belonging to the poor (see Chapter 8).

The flexibility of the existing stock to produce more and/or better quality units is impressive. In a study of the older (pre-1947) housing stock in the city of

Toronto, for example, Morrison (1978) estimated that of the 137,000 residential structures in that stock, some 24% provided at least one additional dwelling unit over two decades. Among those structures which were initially single-family properties, 35% subsequently produced one or more additional units. Similarly, nearly 17% of the structures received substantial improvements in quality through investment and over 7% underwent major renovation.

Measuring changes in the quality of housing from the existing stock is even more difficult. Most such measures rely on price increases to reflect quality changes—a subject we leave until Chapter 7. One example will suffice here. Ozanne and Struyk (1978) undertook to assess changes in the flow of housing services (those evident in price changes) through a controlled sample of single-family units in Boston which had not also been physically converted. They sought to measure the responsiveness of the existing stock to changes in neighborhood, social and locational variables between 1960 and 1970. Variations among the 10 neighborhoods studied were taken as reflecting the decisions of suppliers (both landlords and owner-occupiers) to alter the quantity of housing services provided.

Their results generally confirm those of other aggregate studies, that the immediate short-term supply response is limited; but note that this study ignores physical modifications and conversions. Based on their estimates, for example, a 10% increase in income for low-income households produced only a 3% increase in the flow of housing services, but a 7% increase in price. Even with a more generous allowance for the supply response, they still found a price inflation of 4%, all other things being equal.[3]

Rehabilitation vs. replacement: One of the specific choices facing suppliers and owners of older housing is whether to modernize, rehabilitate, or convert the structure or to demolish and replace it with a new one. The process of replacement, of course, has been a continuous one since cities began. Nevertheless, there has been a long-standing interest in the relative costs and benefits of replacement in both the policy and research literature. This issue has been brought into sharp focus in the recent debate on publicly-initiated urban renewal and slum clearance vs. conservation and rehabilitation (see U.S. Dept. of Housing and Urban Development, 1973b; Bagby, 1974; Kirby, 1979). The supply of housing which results from these two emphases is obviously very different.

In theory, replacement is justified (in economic terms at least) when the projected value of the future flow of revenue from a new residential structure (V_j) exceeds that of the existing structure (V_i) by more than the capital costs (c_{ij}) of demolishing structure i and building structure j. This is, when

$$V_j > (V_i + c_{ij})$$

when both values are suitably discounted. Needleman (1965) extended this analysis to include differences in interest rates, in the expected life span of the new vs. the old structure and in operating costs. He argued that rehabilitation is profitable if the costs of demolition and rebuilding exceed the costs of rehabilitation by an amount equal to the discounted current cost or rehabilitation and the present value of the differences in the operating costs of the two structures.

In reality, the balance of costs and benefits is much more difficult to determine. Reliable information on rehabilitation is scarce and inconsistent. The balance of costs varies widely between sites and areas, by the character of the structures and uses involved, and both are heavily dependent on the specific kinds of property tax and depreciation allowances which apply. Moreover, it is extremely difficult to assign relative benefits in rehabilitation and redevelopment. Generally, however, the effect of local and business tax systems, in North America at least, has been to encourage demolition over rehabilitation and to add a *double tax* to any improvement (the cost itself and the increased property taxes and rates due once the improvement has been completed). The negative effect is evident to anyone who has looked at older urban landscapes.

Only for specific projects has it been possible to obtain comparable data. Bagby (1974) estimated the costs of rehabilitation to be roughly 90% of those for new construction on small in-fill sites within the built-up urban area (excluding demolition costs), although the variability around the average was considerable. Listoken (1976), on the other hand, estimated the ratio in his Philadelphia study at around 60%. In most cases, however, the assumption is that rehabilitation is more costly. These figures also vary depending on whether one is considering the replacement of individual structures or the redevelopment of an entire area. The latter may involve extensive costs for replacing underground services.

Nor surprisingly, the tendency in most cities has been for the private sector to dominate in undertaking the replacement of single structures or small groups of buildings, where little or no renewal of existing utilities is required, while large-scale redevelopment—usually in the form of slum clearance—falls as a responsibility to the public sector. In general, however, the pendulum of support for either redevelopment or rehabilitation (conservation) swings back and forth depending on the market, public tastes, or on political whims rather than on the balance of real costs and benefits.

Relationship of new construction to investment in the existing stock: It is also important to ask whether the level of investment in the existing stock varies systematically over time with the aggregate rate of new construction. There is some evidence that the overall level of investment in the U.S. is inversely related to the rate of new construction. Certainly, during periods of extremely low rates of new construction, such as the great depression or WWII, investment in the existing stock did increase substantially in absolute as well as relative terms—primarily to obtain more dwelling units by subdividing (conversion) larger units (Firestone, 1951; Wheaton, 1966). In this way conversions acted as substitutes for newly-built units and in aggregate played a counter-cyclical role in the economy. Other evidence for Canada, however, suggests that the two indices often move together—particularly when the former includes all costs of home maintenance and repairs—following the ups and downs of the national economy (Morrison, 1978). Both views are correct, the difference is one of measurement and timing.

James (1977) offers some interesting evidence for two major cities (Atlanta and Washington) indicating that housing improvements (measured as building permits) are inversely related to rates of new house building. Intuitively, this relationship is perhaps obvious in that the demand for housing must be satisfied by both the new and existing stock. When the former declines, as our model of the urban housing market in Chapter 4 suggests, the latter must bear more of the load. This increased load might be reflected in several ways—increased prices overall, higher levels of conversion to meet low income needs, higher levels of rehabilitation to meet middle and upper income demand, and increased levels of maintenance and repairs. These indices do not necessarily move in the same directions, however. In fact, it seems that rates of subdivision and major renovations to the existing stock do vary inversely with the rate of new construction, but average levels of repairs and maintenance do not.

Resolution of this question is of considerable importance in predicting the fate of older housing stock and thus of older central cities. James (1977) goes on to argue that the collapse of the building industry in the U.S. in 1974–76 gave a remarkable boost to housing improvements in the inner cities. Conversely, very high rates of new construction, especially if that rate exceeds the level of aggregate demand, may undercut demand and thus levels of investment in older areas. The logical market outcomes of the latter relationship are disinvestment in the older stock and housing abandonment (see Chapters 7 and 8). If, on the other hand, the two do move together, then new construction can be encouraged without undue negative impacts on investment in older housing and areas. The implications are clearly very different depending on which view one adheres to.

Building and Development Costs

Housing prices and rents tend to reflect, at least over the longer term, the costs of producing that housing. During the 1970s, most countries have witnessed substantial increases in residential building and development costs as part of the general inflation trend and as the pressures on particular cost components have increased. These components, as defined in Chapter 2 and displayed in Chapter 3, include the normal costs of production (building materials, wages, land, and capital) and the costs of development. The latter represent the costs to the private builder or developer of managing the diverse activities which are involved in house-building and the cost of obtaining necessary planning permissions from local authorities, as well as the costs to those authorities of providing necessary services.

Obtaining precise figures on such costs is extremely difficult (Seidel, 1978). Many of the costs are buried in other aspects of the production process, while other costs are compensated by tax write-offs. Local building conditions and planning regulations also differ so widely that the costs of identical housing units will vary substantially from one area to another. Despite these difficulties, Figure 5.3 attempts a typical breakdown of the relative costs faced by builders in the construction of single- and multi-family housing, and the subsequent operating and maintenance costs faced by landlords (rental) and single-family owner-occupiers. The proportions are, of course, approximations, and will not necessarily apply to any particular area.

The largest production components, in order, are materials, land, and labor (with capital costs included in overhead).[4] Land costs are a particularly important variable. For single-family units, land costs may take from 15 to 30% of total

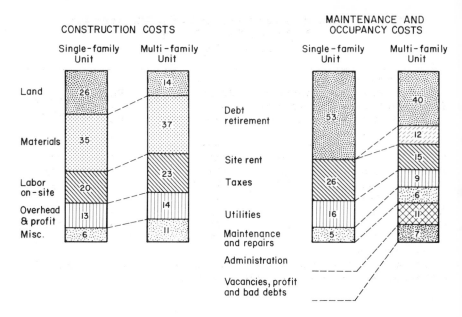

Fig. 5.3. Relative cost components for residential construction and maintenance, single-family and multi-family (in percentages).

costs depending on location and on whether the supply of developable land is tightly regulated or not. Since material and labor costs do not vary spatially as much as land costs within an urban region, a relative increase in the latter will alter both the type (and price) of housing produced and the location of that production. At the same time, however, variations in the degree and kind of building controls and land regulations among municipalities also influence the costs of development and thus the location decisions of land developers (Goldberg, 1978). There is substantial evidence that the increasing difficulty of obtaining permission to build has added directly to the cost of housing (see Chapter 8). On the other hand, time series statistics for England and Wales (Table 5.2) indicate that land has not increased as a component of the total costs of new housing over the longer term.

HOUSING SUPPLY AT THE LOCAL LEVEL:
THE ACTORS AND THEIR LOCATIONAL BEHAVIOR

It is obvious that housing does not just emerge, complete and in place, through the "invisible" hand of the market or by fiat of a public agency. It is instead produced by an army of individuals, firms, and government agencies—the "actors"

Table 5.2. Trends in the Components of Land and Housing Prices,
England and Wales, 1967–78
(1967 = 100)

Year	Site value as a percentage of the total cost of new houses (%)	Land prices for house-building	House prices (new)	Tender costs	Retail price index	Average earnings
1968	21.2	113	108	106	105	108
1970	21.6	155	120	119	117	132
1972	29.2	287	186	162	138	165
1974	24.3	449	262	258	174	220
1976	20.3	315	311	301	252	321
1978	18.7	na	429	367	308	409

na = not available.
Sources: Up-dated from U.K., *Housing Policy. A Consultative Document.* Cmnd. 6851, 1977; Hallett, 1977; and National Building Society Bulletins.

outlined in Chapter 4—participating in a complex, costly, and often time-consuming process which eventually delivers housing to the consumer. Each group of actors plays a relatively unique role and each makes decisions on the basis of differing objectives and perspectives and subject to differing constraints. To understand how the aggregate relationships defined above translate into housing on the ground, we must get inside the residential development process at the local level. This requires that we examine both the characteristics and operation of the building industry and the full range of actors who participate in that process.

Characteristics of the Building Industry

At the outset, in talking about residential construction one must first differentiate between builders and the construction industry on the one hand and the development industry on the other. The latter includes the full range of actors involved in producing housing. The following sections initially look at the house-building industry itself and then review the land development process in general, in which the builder is but one participant. The two sectors have rather different roles to play and very different characteristics.

The housing industry has as many unique characteristics as the product it produces (see Chapter 2). Briefly, those characteristics which impinge most directly on the themes of this volume are:

> *industrial fragmentation:* The heterogeneity of housing has (traditionally) tended to discourage vertical integration in the building industry. Instead, the industry is characterized by a proliferation of production services, specializing in particular aspects of building (Table 5.3).

Table 5.3. Size of Firms Involved in Residential Development,
U.S., 1976
(in percentages)

Type of firm (activity)	Number of housing units produced				
	0–15	16–100	101–500	Over 500	Total
Land developer	55.4	19.6	17.9	7.1	100
Builder	41.9	46.4	10.6	1.2	100
Developer and builder	19.5	46.5	26.9	7.1	100

Source: Center for Urban Policy Research, Rutgers University, quoted in Seidel, 1978, p. 26.

geographic fragmentation (localization): The diversity of local building regulations, combined with the importance of information on the local housing market and local politics, has meant that in North America much of the housing industry is restricted to relatively small geographic areas.

financial interdependence: The size of the investment necessary to produce housing is such that most house-building (and home purchase) is done on *credit*. This ties the housing industry to the "money" market more closely than most other consumer goods.

multiplicity of buyers and sellers: The housing industry faces a market consisting of an immensely large number of participants, each with different tastes, preferences, and motivations.

fluidity of membership: The erratic behavior of housing supply encourages (if not necessitates) a large transient component of firms and individuals who enter and leave the industry depending on the current level of activity.

These characteristics suggest that the residential building industry is disjointed, unstable, inefficient—if not chaotic at times—and prone to abuse by governments, institutions, and unions, and to misuse by some of its members. All of this is true to an extent. It is difficult to attempt to "rationalize" the industry, to achieve economies of scale in housing production, and to police its activities and performance. Few house-builders construct more than 100 homes a year in the U.S., unless they are part of a larger development firm (Table 5.3). Many small builders also suffer from low levels of capitalization, which restricts their ability to adapt to changing circumstances. Unions also tend to be fragmented and independently-minded. And financial sources for builders tend to be restricted, uncertain and unevenly distributed across regions.

These characteristics have numerous effects, but in general they have no doubt contributed to the relatively rapid increase in the costs of housing production, accelerated the growth of new building organizations—the large development firm—and fostered all sorts of special government inquiries into the structure of the industry. Of particular interest here is the emergence of an industry of "land development," or what Ambrose and Colenutt (1975) have called *the property machine*, as a component in urban real estate and housing markets. Before looking at this industry, however, we must first define what we mean by the development process generally.

Conceptualizing the Residential Land Development Process

It is only at the local level that we can link the actors—the land-owners, developers, financial intermediaries, and governments—through their position in and contribution to housing production. It is also at this scale of inquiry that housing becomes "fixed" to land: thus, housing supply becomes first and foremost an exercise in land development. The way that process actually works, as in the previous example of the housing market (Chapter 4), is so complex that it is immediately necessary to use generalized and selective examples.

Most research in this context has tended to focus on the mechanisms of converting raw (vacant or agricultural) land into urban residential use (Weiss, 1966), although the approach has been extended to include the redevelopment process within cities (Bourne, 1969). The conceptual framework employed here views land as passing through a series of *stages* from an initial undeveloped stage through different periods of negotiation, active site preparation, and building construction to a final stage in which the product (housing) is delivered to the consumer. Each stage involved the participation of different actors, each behaving according to their own norms, but with each dependent on what went before. One could visualize this sequence of stages, as Barrett, Stewart, and Underwood (1978) have done, as a "pipeline" in which there are barriers (such as planning approvals) and pumps (priming actions such as investment decisions) between each stage.

The stages of development: Figure 5.4 provides one generalized example of the sequence of land development for residential purposes, drawing largely on earlier work by Clawson (1971), Kaiser (1972), Drewett (1973), and Bourne (1976). Although the actual outline will vary depending on the area and time period under study, perhaps five major stages can be recognized in most areas:

> a parcel of land takes on an *urban interest*, based on an evaluation of emerging pressures and prospects for development;
>
> the parcel undergoes active *development consideration* and feasibility studies, including the initiation of negotiations for the sale or lease of the land;
>
> initiation of *planning for development* and for *implementation* of financing and government approvals;
>
> active physical site preparation and *construction*;
>
> *marketing* of the finished housing.

Of course, no real world example need fit exactly into this number or sequence of stages, but the above do represent the basic decisions which must be taken. Note that the term stages should not be understood to mean "discrete" changes; the process of land development is a continuous process but within which there are

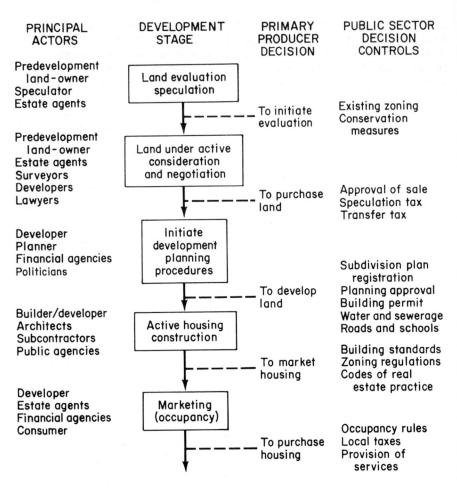

PRINCIPAL ACTORS	DEVELOPMENT STAGE	PRIMARY PRODUCER DECISION	PUBLIC SECTOR DECISION CONTROLS

Predevelopment
  land-owner
Speculator
Estate agents
    Land evaluation speculation
    To initiate evaluation
    Existing zoning
Conservation measures

Predevelopment
  land-owner
Estate agents
Surveyors
Developers
Lawyers
    Land under active consideration and negotiation
    To purchase land
    Approval of sale
Speculation tax
Transfer tax

Developer
Planner
Financial agencies
Politicians
    Initiate development planning procedures
    To develop land
    Subdivision plan registration
Planning approval
Building permit
Water and sewerage
Roads and schools

Builder/developer
Architects
Subcontractors
Public agencies
    Active housing construction
    To market housing
    Building standards
Zoning regulations
Codes of real estate practice

Developer
Estate agents
Financial agencies
Consumer
    Marketing (occupancy)
    To purchase housing
    Occupancy rules
Local taxes
Provision of services

Fig. 5.4. Actors and stages in the residential land development process (rural to urban conversion).

specific "discrete" decision points. Note also that we are concerned here with situations in which land is predominantly privately owned.

The key actors and decisions: Figure 5.4 also identifies who the key actors are in the development process, when the critical decisions are made, and generally what controls public agencies have (or should have) over the character and rate of development. Each actor makes decisions in reference to three major sets of characteristics: (1) those of the parcel of land (its size, location, value, current ownership, and zoning); (2) those of the actor or firm involved (size of firm, corporate structure, equity situation, and range of activities); and (3) external conditions. The latter include anticipated levels of demand for land and housing, available financing, the relative attractiveness of other types of investment, and the attitudes of local interest groups to new developments. Although it is not possible to say in general which actors have the most influence over the flow of land through each stage, since this varies by project and area, some actors clearly have *primary* roles (e.g., developers and planning agencies) while others have secondary roles (e.g., estate agents, speculators, etc.) in that their participation is often indirect and supportive of other actors.

Speculation is an important variable throughout the sequence of development, although it is not always clear exactly who the speculators are or what role they play.[5] To identify who is a speculator, for example, requires that we know the motivation behind each action, which we seldom do. Nonetheless, the issue of speculation in land has generated an avalanche of reports and public inquiries. Some argue that speculators, like estate agents, play a useful role in bringing available land and buyers and sellers together, thus facilitating the transaction process. This is obviously true—someone has to do it. But others see speculation as invariably increasing the costs of urban land and housing through the capture of excess and unearned profits.[6] The latter may result from overcharging zealous buyers, anticipating public improvements in an area (e.g., new roads or sewers), or by withholding land until prices rise further. There are numerous and obvious examples where these have happened, and land profits have been staggering; there are other examples where losses have been considerable.

It is the *pre-development land-owner*, however, who generally sets the stage, at least in a housing market where development rights are still in private hands. This owner may be the original occupant, a farmer for instance, or an investor (public or private) who has purchased the land for fun or profit. Whoever it is, their motivations, attributes, and actions contribute to defining the cost and availability of land for housing and the pace at which subsequent residential development takes place.

The key agent is most frequently the *developer*. Usually, but not always, the developer is a corporate entity who secures rights to the land—through various means—and then initiates the actual sequence of development. Their behavior differs depending on their corporate structure and financial backing and on the size of the developments undertaken. Their motives are usually a mixture of profit maximization and the need to maintain liquidity (a flow of developments) and thus survival. There are basically two types of developers: the *land developer*, who undertakes the initial site evaluation, assembles the necessary parcels, and perhaps prepares the site; and the property *developer* who facilitates, if not undertakes, physical construction on the site and may continue to manage the housing (if it is rental) or to market it for sale. Recently, however, the two kinds have become one as development firms expand through horizontal integration or merger.[7]

The critical decision here is the *land purchase decision*. That decision moves the parcel of land from one state (undeveloped) to another, when it effectively becomes part of the urbanized landscape. The financial commitment involved is also substantial in theory, although in practice it is possible, through such diverse means as "options to purchase" and "piggy-back" mortgages, (on other properties) for a developer to accumulate an impressive amount of land without putting out much cash.

The second critical decision point—*the decision to develop* the site—is usually the largest commitment. It generally follows extensive negotiations with all current participants, and after an extensive approval process for planning and building permits has begun (Seidel, 1978). The approval process itself can be both time consuming and costly; in some areas, a bureaucratic nightmare. It is, however, one of the few points in the development sequence when other actors and the community at large can express their views on the proposal. Increasingly they have done so, with considerable vigor and success (Lorimer and Ross, 1976). In any case, the actual timing of the decision to develop is clearly conditional on external conditions relating to demand, profitability, and community resistence.

Throughout the process, there are also a large number of *intermediaries* involved, of which real estate agents, and the speculators noted above, are perhaps the most numerous and obvious. These agents vary in size and resources from the part-time housewife or retired farmer to the large corporation. Although their principal role is as "peddlers of information" and facilitating agents—in bringing housing consumers together with the supply—they are also involved in seeking out potential sites for new developments (or redevelopments). In this case they often serve as "front-men" for developers in seeking to buy (or option) and assemble prime sites. Despite considerable interest in their activities, however, the empirical evidence on whether they act to significantly alter the outcomes of the development process remains unclear (Brown, 1972; Palm, 1976, 1979).

Local government agencies intersect with the residential development process at several points in time. Figure 5.4 lists examples of these specific points and the relevant policy instruments available to public agencies to influence decisions taken in the private sector. Although the list of instruments is long, and the powers are considerable, the crucial question is how consistently these controls are applied and for whose benefit. In many instances such controls are used in a negative fashion to slow or prohibit residential developments because they are considered to be undesirable, in social or economic terms, or because growth is seen to be too rapid. Some communities have used such controls to call a halt to further residential growth (the "lifeboat" principle) in order to preserve their present environment and to maintain or improve their existing tax base. Each agency or actor in the public sector, however, has its own objectives, and its own decision rules. Thus, to understand how the residential development process works in any area also requires that we examine each of these actors.

The number of agents involved in housing supply is obviously very large. A flow chart of the land development process constructed for an average size metropolitan area (an interesting exercise) would no doubt show far more stages than the above, with hundreds of different actors and decision variables at each stage. In an earlier study of Philadelphia, for example, Wheaton (1964) estimated that over 20,000 development decisions (i.e., decisions to build or to finance building) are made each year, although perhaps 3,000 of these are individually-ordered houses. Clawson (1971) and Drewett (1973) both noted a similar degree of complexity in their studies of the suburbanization process in the U.S. and U.K., respectively.

Emerging Corporate Structures: The Property Industry

For most urban areas, careful examination reveals a relatively small number of key agents and decisions in housing production, and the degree of concentration seems to be increasing. Perhaps even less than two dozen major landowners, developers, and financial agencies essentially determine what land gets developed, what housing is built, and where. Their decisions in turn set the ground rules for thousands of other decisions by smaller firms, building subcontractors, and public agencies as well as households. The degree of concentration in different cities appears to be related to historical conditions, the size and economy of the city, and the degree of previous public intervention. Tighter planning controls have often had the perverse effect of encouraging concentration in the land development industry (Bourne, 1977), but not to the same extent in the building industry itself.

The latter assertion raises the additional question of the degree of monopoly control in land and housing development. That is, to what extent can small groups of landowners or producers exert "market power" (i.e., act together to set overall prices)? Despite the large number of participants in the development process, the inherent properties of land (that it is finite) and housing (fixed in location) means that it is almost inevitable that a few producers will dominate the urban housing market—as oliogopolies—in small areas for certain periods of time. This does not necessarily mean that there is a monopoly in land and housing development in an entire urban area. That depends, at least in part, on whether distinct spatial submarkets exist and on the degree of public restrictions and physical barriers on land supply. In any case, the issue of a concentration of ownership in urban land has generated an intense debate among researchers which as yet remains unresolved.[8]

Clearly, we need to know more about the structure and behavior of the industry which produces housing in our society. Increasingly, studies are appearing on the role of particular agents: financial institutions (Harvey and Chatterjee, 1974; Duncan, 1977), developers and landlords (Goldberg, 1978; Morrison, 1978), real estate agents (Palm, 1978), the bureaucracy (Pahl, 1977) and the property industry in general (Ambrose and Colenutt, 1975; Lorimer and Ross, 1976). Additional research is needed on the complex linkages between firms and the often cosy relationship between those firms and local governments. Individual property firms frequently turn out to be "paper" organizations fronting for very large corporations outside the residential field. Such conglomerates, as noted earlier, are able to internalize (i.e., keep within the firm) the profits which accrue from the appreciation of residential land as it goes through each stage in the development process. They are also better able to overcome the usual ups and downs of the real estate market than small firms by shifting resources into those sectors or stages which remain bouyant. A second area of research, which we examine in the last section in this chapter, is the behavior of institutions providing consumer finance in the housing field. Equally interesting is the parallel process of residential land development undertaken within the public sector (see Chapter 10). How different is that process from that in the private sector described above?

Locational Considerations in Housing Supply

Although one might assume that each of the above decision agents in the private sector operated with a view to improving profit (and liquidity) levels, this does not tell us what locations are selected for residential developments. This section undertakes a brief outline of the considerations of private developers and owners in selecting locations for new construction, redevelopment, and conversions (or rehabilitation).

One approach might begin with a general hierarchical schema of locational evaluation involving three distinct steps (Bourne, 1976). The evaluation begins with a broad *area-wide* assessment by the developers of the attractiveness of an area or sector of the city for their proposed investment in terms of its general accessibility (within the urban area) and special accessibility to specific activities (shops, jobs, and utilities), and the nature of planning restrictions. Within that context, specific *subareas* are evaluated in terms of their relative potential, amenities, services, and the quality of adjacent housing developments (e.g., social status). Finally, the third level involves selecting particular *sites* in terms of their availability, taxes, zoning, ownership, physical properties, and, in the case of redevelopment, the demolition costs of existing buildings.

New construction: Out of this three-level evaluation process emerges a number of critical characteristics which influence the developer's choice of location. From numerous empirical studies with respect to new construction in suburban areas we know that developers do tend to choose sites which offer a combination of following attributes: (1) good accessibility to places of employment and transportation facilities; (2) proximity to public services, notably sewer and water utilities; (3) where land is available and reasonably priced; (4) where current zoning is appropriate or subject to change so that it conforms to the proposed development; and (5) the presence of environmental amenities. Which of these factors actually dominates in the choice of locations varies with the area and time involved, the condition of the housing market, and the nature of the planning process (see Kaiser, 1972; Drewett, 1973; Goldberg, 1978; Barrett et al., 1978).

Traditional site selection models, of course, emphasize accessibility, but this is a rather broad locational consideration. Clearly, not all areas of similar levels of accessibility are or can be developed at the same time. Within these accessibility constraints, then, developers emphasize more localized factors, including the price of land and whether or not it is available for development. Increasingly, however, with tighter planning controls and building codes, the two factors above which are direct policy instruments—the existence of public services and zoning—have become prominent in determining which locations are selected.

Site selection for redevelopment: The process of selecting sites for residential redevelopment (private apartments) responds to roughly the same locational criteria, but with several important exceptions. First, (re)developers are in most instances faced with a built-up landscape containing not only established structures (i.e., replacement costs), rigid property boundaries, obscure titles and absentee landlords, but a much more complex overlay of social and political constraints on changes to that landscape than is typical in new suburban areas. Second, they are more likely to encounter organized community resistence to their develop-ments, as indeed they did in the late 1960s. Third, the images which people hold of certain areas then become crucial since they tend to linger and thus to be trans-ferred to the new development. Hence, from the point of view of the residential redeveloper, one must alter the above list of location factors to include lot size (a measure of the ease of land assembly), established neighborhood images, replace-ment costs, and proximity to areas where apartments have been allowed previously.

In an earlier study of private apartment redevelopment in the city of Toronto, the author found that the above criteria were clearly important but were relatively weak (Bourne, 1969; Bourne and Berridge, 1973). Apartment construction was higher in areas of better accessibility, in above-average quality neighborhoods (but not in the highest), in areas of larger lot sizes, and in close proximity to areas which had witnessed rezonings for apartment development earlier. Developers also avoided areas of low environment quality, fragmented landownership and strong or tightly-knit ethnic communities. Municipal boundaries, where they represented substantial tax or zoning differentials, were also important, as was the developers' perception of the ease of obtaining planning permission.

Over time, however, the importance of these locational factors changed. By the early 1970s development controls and zoning restrictions on apartment con-struction and community resistence strengthened in most cities. Land values rose, replacement costs accelerated, and then rent controls were imposed. Several areas underwent extensive rehabilitation which meant that redevelopment was no longer economically feasible or desirable. As a result, the rate of redevelop-ment slowed, apartments were increasingly confined to specific areas, and the projects became smaller in size. The redevelopment "game" had changed. In any case, by the late 1970s few new apartments were being built for rent, as the pen-dulum of development swung to conversion and rehabilitation and the investment attractiveness of rental buildings disappeared.

The location of supply changes through conversion: The factors which influence the pattern of residential conversion are both more subtle and more localized than those for either new construction or redevelopment (Ingram, 1977). Unlike the latter, conversion can be undertaken by individual households or landlords as well as by developers. The actual process of location decision-making will therefore vary depending on who is doing the converting and for what purpose. Recall from our previous discussion that conversion for low-income households will have a different spatial pattern than that for high-income households. Moreover, as Morri-son (1978) argues, since the decision of whether to convert is generally made at the time of purchase, that decision reflects the relative prices of alternative sources of housing supply available to both low- and high-income groups.

Despite this complexity, the location of housing units undergoing conversion (in this case subdivision) within the older housing stock is far from random. The areas selected tend to be those which are most accessible to the CBD (or public transit), and those with particular environmental attributes. The individual housing units involved are, on average, larger, older, and less expensive than others in the area. Premissive zoning, on or near the site, and proximity to local neighborhood services also play a part in determining the resulting locations. Bradbury (1977) also observed that units selected for conversion tend to be those in rather poor condition, because the economic return from the existing structure which is lost through conversion is likely to be smallest, but not those whose age and structural material would make the costs of conversion prohibitive. The lack of comparative studies to date, however, makes it difficult to generalize very far about the location of conversion activity in the existing stock.

HOUSING FINANCE

The provision of capital to finance the construction and consumption of housing, as an immensely complex subject, is well beyond the scope of this volume.[9] Yet it is essential that the reader have a general sense of where housing finance comes from and who gets it. Earlier it was noted that the extreme dependence of both the housing industry and its consumers on *credit*—its costs, availability, and distribution—indicates that housing is particularly sensitive to changes in the financial system. Indeed, some would argue that housing is but an extension of the financial system in which it is produced. Similarly, it is possible to see the provision of credit as the cornerstone of most national housing policies (see Chapter 9). In this section we examine aggregate sources of finance for housing demand (not the supply side or building industry) and the spatial allocation of these sources to the consumers of housing.

The Origins and Scale of Housing Finance

Housing consumption is financed in general, like other forms of real estate, by a combination of two types of capital funds. One consists of *internal sources* of funding, which derive primarily from the savings of individuals or groups of investors, and are normally represented by down-payments on housing. The second source consists of *external* funding, primarily from institutions, which is obtained as credit through mortgages. As indicated in the previous discussion of the process of bidding in the housing market, these two sources represent distinct trade-off decisions for individual households, especially in the resale market. Unfortunately, we know very little about the former and only about the latter when they are registered or insured under government regulations.

Since the emphasis here is on external sources of funding, it is important to note just how recent is massive government involvement in housing finance. The U.S. federal government, for example, only became involved on any scale during the 1930s, as a result of continued chaos in the real estate industry generally, which was capped by a mortgage famine brought on by the great depression. Before that time, state governments acted as the principal regulatory units, but only in a very loose sense. Federal involvement has gradually taken the form of setting guidelines for housing finance, notably for mortgage lending, and the establishment of loan insurance and mortgage guarantee programs.[10]

One consequence of this intervention has been an explosion in rates of home-ownership financed primarily through the growth of mortgage lending by authorized institutions. Federal insurance made residential mortgages a more attractive investment for financial institutions, by making them safer, and fostered the emergence of numerous other institutions whose prime function was mortgage lending. As a result, in the U.S., the proportion of the national consumer housing debt held by credit institutions rose from under 50% before 1920 to 80% during the 1950s and to about 90% in the 1970s.

Mortgage provision is therefore important not only in social terms but because it is big business. Residential mortgage debts are the largest single source of personal indebtedness on a long-term basis.[11] For example, in the U.S., in 1976 over 63% of all single-family owner-occupiers reported having an outstanding mortgage— representing over 23 million houses.[12] Total indebtedness, which Grebler et al. (1956) estimated at $2.3 billion in 1890 and $69.1 billion in 1952, had risen to over $560 billion by 1977 (U.S. Congress, 1978). With these figures in mind, we turn to a consideration of specific sources of finance and their distribution.

Sources of Housing Finance

There are at least three distinct levels which must be differentiated in examining the sources of housing finance: first, the national level, involving the allocation of capital to the housing sector as part of aggregate capital markets; second, the firm level, at which capital is allocated to the producers and institutions which finance housing; and third, the provision of capital to consumers. The latter transfer takes place both indirectly, through such means as income growth, taxes, and other forms of household assistance, and directly, through the distribution of housing allowances, tax credits, and publicly-subsidized housing or mortgages.

The importance of various sources of mortgage funds differs between countries (and in some cases between cities), reflecting the institutional structures and historical conditions through which housing finance policies have evolved. Table 5.4 summarizes the origins of mortgage funds for owner-occupation in the U.S., Britain, Sweden, and Canada. Although some attempt has been made in the table to line up the columns for similar sources, it should be stressed that even simple terms such as "banks" do not necessarily have the same meaning in different countries, or for that matter within the same country.

Note first in Table 5.4 that the major sources of housing finance are limited in number.[13] In the U.S., savings and loan associations and private banks dominate the residential mortgage field, although an increasing role has been taken by secondary credit agencies, credit unions, and by some governments. In the U.K., building societies (of which there are now about 350) overwhelmingly dominate, but with local authorities also providing an increasing share.[14] In Sweden, the situation is again quite different. As expected, a large proportion of mortgages are provided through national agencies, such as the National Housing Board and the Mortgage Bank, as well as by other nonprofit organizations. In Canada, institutional sources of mortgage funds are relatively diverse, although dominated by private sources, with an expanding role played by specialized loan and trust companies, while government tends to act as a residual lender, or lender of "last resort."

Table 5.4. Sources of Residential Mortgage Finance:
U.S., U.K., Sweden and Canada, 1970–76
(in percent)

United Kingdom[a]	Building societies	Insurance companies	Banks	Local authorities	Other public institutions	
1970	87	3	3	6	1	
1975	75	2	2	16	5*	

United States[b]	Savings & Loan Associations	Insurance companies	Banks[c]	Pension funds[d]	Other institutions[e]	Private
1970	42	9	28	2	11	8
1975	46	4	26	1	16	8

Sweden[a]	Urban Mortgage Bank	Insurance companies	Banks[f]	National housing board	Credit companies
Average 1970–73	29	2	19	21	19

Canada[a]	Loan & Trust Companies[g]	Insurance companies	Banks	Government	Corporate, pensions, credit agencies
1970	23	26	3	23	22
1976	29	16	12	17	26

Notes:
[a]Institutional sources only.
[b]All sources.
[c]Includes commercial banks (15%) and mutual savings banks (10%).
[d]Includes private pension funds and those of state and local governments.
[e]Includes secondary credit agencies, state and local government, federal government, credit unions, etc.
[f]Includes non-profit (11%) and commercial banks (8%).
[g]Includes Quebec savings banks, fraternal societies.
*+10% cash, 10% inheritance.
Sources: U.K.–Financial Statistics, HMSO, 1977; U.S.–Board of Governors, Federal Reserve System, 1976; Sweden–Sveriges Riksbank, 1975; Canada Mortgage and Housing Corporation, 1978; Duncan, 1977; Colton, 1978; Stafford, 1978.

In all cases, however, the trend has been toward greater *concentration* in mortgage finance with an increasing share coming from a few large private, public, or nonprofit institutions. This trend has undoubtedly been accelerated by the extension of government mortgage insurance programs. Individual or noninstitutional mortgage sources represent only about 8% of the total in the U.S. and about 10 and 12% in the U.K. and Canada, respectively. While small, the latter are particularly crucial sources in some areas, such as the inner city, and in immigrant and ethnic communities.

Spatial Variations in Mortgage Lending: Who Gets What and Where?

Given the recent availability of disaggregate data on mortgage lending, there has been increasing interest in the spatial allocation of that lending.[15] Are there systematic differences in the provision of mortgages between regions and across an urban area? Is there a bias in lending in relation to the location of low-income or minority households and low-income or minority households and low-cost housing units? What is the impact of these variations on the operation of the housing market, on housing quality, and on neighborhood change?

Although there has been some concern for regional patterns of mortgage lending in the U.S. (Morris, 1978), most of the research in the geographical literature has focused on the allocation of mortgage funds to people living or wishing to live in different parts of an urban area (Harvey and Chatterjee, 1974; Stone, 1975; Harvey, 1977a; Boddy, 1976; Duncan, 1977; Morrison, 1979). The specific empirical results obtained will, of course, vary with the city and the institutional context under study (Listokin and Casey, 1979). Nevertheless, in most cities for which data are available, it has been observed that:

(1) the distribution of individual mortgage funds is spatially restricted, with the oldest and poorest residential areas receiving the least;

(2) both public and private institutions contribute to this form of discrimination;

(3) when lending is done in poorer areas the conditions are often harsh, in terms of down-payment, rate of interest, or length of term demanded;

(4) each institution has somewhat different criteria for allocating mortgages, but few are in the business of losing money;

(5) such discrimination in mortgage lending plays a major role in initiating or accelerating the process of housing and neighborhood deterioration.

In fact, the withdrawal of mortgage funds by institutions from an urban neighborhood can spell the death of that neighborhood as a viable living environment, especially if it was poor to begin with.

This bias is, in part, a reflection of the well-known procedure of *red-lining*. This term describes the practice whereby mortgage lenders remove neighborhoods from the map—with a red pencil—to which they will not then extend credit through mortgages. In effect, the red line is the "bottom line" on the institutional ledger below which insufficient returns or losses on mortgage lending are anticipated. Although developed in reference to American cities, the same practice is evident in the U.K. (Williams, 1977), Canada (Morrison, 1979), and in cities in most other capitalist countries. It also appears that such differentials persist even when discrimination in lending based on income, race, and age of housing, as well as variable interest rates, have been declared illegal.

There is now an impressive amount of solid empirical evidence to support the above assertions. Harvey and Chatterjee (1974), in a study of housing finance in Baltimore, were among the first to display the spatial patterns of mortgage finance. Their results show a clear bias in mortgage lending favoring higher-income neighborhoods (Table 5.5). In poorer areas of the city, a high proportion of housing transactions are strict cash sales, with the proportion declining systematically from the lowest to highest income areas. The proportion of privately-held mortgages declines in a similar fashion. Clearly, property transactions in lower-income, inner-city, and ethnic neighborhoods are far more dependent on the household's own limited financial resources than are transactions in higher-income neighborhoods.

Institutional lending, on the other hand, is heavily concentrated in middle- and upper-income areas. Federal savings and loan associations (SLAs) as well as commercial banks provide few loans in poorer areas, notably again in the inner city (see the redrawn map of Baltimore in Bourne, 1976). A few of the state-chartered SLAs extend their mortgage coverage into such areas. They do so, in part, because they tend to operate locally, given their charters, rather than as part of a regional or national chain. In addition, the proportion of housing transactions in which the lender is insured under FHA programs against default by the borrower is again highest in middle- and upper-income areas.[16] The absence of this insurance can add an important percentage point to the interest charged or simply result in prohibited lending where variable interest rates are not allowed. Parallel studies of the behavior of building societies in other cities have shown equally sharp differentials in mortgage lending patterns.

As one example, we reproduce here a map of the distribution of institutional mortgage-lending patterns in one city (metropolitan Toronto) at one point in time (Fig. 5.5). The obvious bias is toward the suburbs and to newer housing. In most respects these patterns are not surprising. Private lending institutions, such as trust companies and building societies, and quasi-public institutions such as state mortgage banks, often tend to behave according to the traditional objectives of other financial institutions: namely, financial security, an optimal (or at least satisfactory) rate of return relative to other possible investments, and the maintenance of liquidity. This means that mortgages are a scarce resource, whoever is giving them out, which must be rationed, and that lenders tend to avoid housing types, neighborhoods, and borrowers they consider to be "at risk."

Obviously, then, what you (as a potential or current homeowner) get in terms of institutional credit does depend not only on who you are but *where you live*. Unfortunately, it is often very difficult to differentiate the "who" from the "where" effect because of the very high coincidence between the location of poor households and poor housing conditions. Even so, it is one matter to identify differences in mortgage funding but quite a different matter to link these differences to specific consequences. In some areas, the absence of institutional lending may be more than made up by private sources (inheritances, local associations, family and friends, ethnic societies, etc.) at little or no additional cost to the borrower. In other cases, spatial differences are real inequalities, as appears to be the case in Baltimore. In other words, spatial discrimination in mortgage lending is but a symptom of other and deeper social inequalities.

Table 5.5. Sources of Housing Finance, By Spatial Sub-market, Baltimore

Examples of sub-markets	House sales per 100 properties	% transactions by source of funds:						% sales insured by FHA	Average sale price (in 000's $)
		Cash	Private	Fed. S & L	State S & L	Mtge and savings banks	Other		
1. Inner City	1.86	65.7	15.0	3.0	12.0	2.9	1.7	2.9	3.5
2. Ethnic	3.34	39.9	5.5	6.1	43.2	3.7	2.2	2.6	6.4
3. Hampden	2.40	40.4	8.1	18.2	26.3	7.0		14.1	7.1
4. West Baltimore	2.32	30.6	12.5	12.1	11.7	27.0	6.0	25.8	8.7
5. South Baltimore	3.16	28.3	7.4	22.7	13.4	19.3	9.0	22.7	8.8
6. High Turnover	5.28	19.1	6.1	13.6	14.9	39.7	6.2	38.2	9.9
7. Middle Income	3.15	20.8	4.4	29.8	17.0	19.2	9.0	17.7	12.8
8. Upper Income	3.84	19.4	6.9	23.5	10.5	36.9	2.8	11.9	27.4

Source: Harvey and Chatterjee, 1974.
Notes: S & L = Savings and Loan Associations.
FHA = Federal Housing Administration.

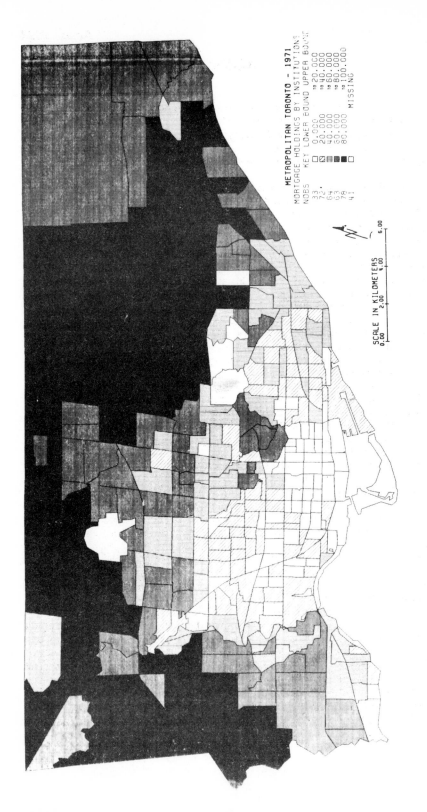

Fig. 5.5. Mortgage lending by financial institutions, metropolitan Toronto, 1971 (the percentage of first mortgages on single-detached owner-occupied dwelling units).
Source: Morrison, 1978.

NOTES

[1]For example, see Whitehead (1974) and Robinson (1979) on the U.K. housing market; L. B. Smith (1974) on Canada and Ingram et al. (1977) on the U.S.

[2]A slightly different model would be needed to account for multi-family starts since the latter tend to be more sensitive to current tax rates on investment and to the availability rather than cost (i.e., the interest rate) of credit than are single-family housing starts (see L. B. Smith, 1974).

[3]These estimates are based on a long-run price elasticity of supply of 0.3 and assumed income and price elasticities of demand for housing services of 1.0 and –1.0, respectively. The authors' suggested upper bound on the price elasticity of supply is 1.5, which produces the subsequent figure for price inflation of 4%.

[4]The engineering costs for land improvement before building roughly break down as follows: sanitary sewers, water mains, and storm drainage 35%; initial clearing, surveying, and grading 20%; curbs, gutters, and street paving 25%.

[5]Speculation, broadly defined, implies that someone has purchased a product (or taken an option to purchase) in anticipation that its value will rise in the future, presumably at a faster rate than could be obtained with other uses of that investment. In one sense, then, all homeowners are speculators since they are banking on an increase in house prices. At the other extreme is the professional speculator, the individual, group or firm who makes a living at buying and selling real estate as others do pork bellies or gold.

[6]The question of whether profits from land development are "surplus" profits or not is perhaps less important than the distributional question of who receives the profits. In particular, the question is whether the appreciating value of land resulting from public improvements should go to the private sector or be returned to the public sector and, if so, how?

[7]There were in 1976 some 25,000 members in the National Association of Home Builders (NAHB) in the U.S. The Center for Urban Policy Research estimated that of this membership some 3 percent were engaged in land development exclusively, 36 percent were in housing construction only and 61 percent were engaged in both.

[8]An interesting example of the diverse views and empirical evidence on landownership and concentration in urban areas is provided by a series of papers on Canadian cities (see Lorimer and Ross, 1976; Spurr, 1976; Markusen and Scheffman, 1977).

[9]Valuable historical accounts of housing finance in the U.S. are provided in Rapkin, Winnick, and Blank (1953), Grebler et al. (1956), and Wheaton et al. (1966).

[10]Such guidelines vary widely, but generally include limits on debt-income ratios, rates of interest allowed, and recall (default) provisions.

[11]The typical mortgage loan in 1976 amounted to 75% of the estimated value of the house at the time of purchase, with a median term to maturity (when the loan is due) of 27 years. The comparable medians for new homes only under Section 203(b) were 95% of the value of the house for a period of 30 years.

[12]The comparable figures for Canada and Britain are 61 and 57%, respectively.

[13]Note that not all sources differentiate between the lender of the initial mortgage and the current holder of that mortgage. A significant proportion of mortgages are subsequently sold to other institutions and investors as part of a secondary mortgage market.

[14]The figures in Table 5.2 tend to underestimate the expanding coverage of the building societies in the U.K. For example, in 1978 building societies provided mortgage loans on 89% of all new houses completed, compared to 78% in 1970 and 61% in 1958. At the same time, however, the proportion of all loans going to new houses declined, as the rate of new construction declined.

[15]Since different lending institutions vary in their participation in either the new or used housing sub-markets, some spatial bias is to be expected.

[16]Note that it is the lender not the borrower who is insured against default under such programs.

Chapter 6

The Demand for Housing
and Location

In its common, everyday sense, demand simply implies "what people want." Beyond that, however, it is not self-evident what is meant by the demand for housing nor how it should be measured. It becomes even more complex when we consider the demand for housing at specific locations and the determinants of choice in residential location.

In this chapter we examine the traditional side of the housing equation, but with an emphasis on the measurement and expression of demand in a spatial context. To do so, however, requires that we first step back and look at aggregate demand and its relationship to income, demographic change, and the question of housing needs. The second part of the chapter examines demand within urban areas: residential mobility, life cycle changes, and the process of selecting a house and a residential location.

AGGREGATE DEMAND RELATIONSHIPS

The Nature of Housing Demand and Needs

The demand for housing, in aggregate, represents the total of all household expenditures, government outlays, and institutional investment in what we have previously called the housing "sector." As in the case of other durable goods, the level of housing demand depends on the relative balance of changes in several different factors: (1) population growth, (2) demographic structure (e.g., age, household size), (3) disposable income, (4) housing preferences and tastes, and

(5) taxation and investment policies. Changes in any of these factors will alter both the level and direction of housing demand.

Yet as argued previously (Chapter 2), housing has a number of attributes which make the question of demand extremely complex. It is expensive to purchase (a "lumpy" investment decision for households), durable, and heterogeneous. It is also fixed in location and embedded in a particular real estate market and neighborhood context. This means that the demand for housing in any given area cannot be easily separated from the demand for land, location, and the services (e.g., schools) which that neighborhood delivers.

It is also clear that housing demand is a reflection of both its use value for *consumption* or occupancy purposes and its exchange value as an *investment* good for homeowners, investors, and landlords (as well as governments).[1] In addition, we must consider the difference between direct or *overt demand*, such as that actually expressed in patterns of residential location or the prices people are willing to pay for housing, and *latent demand* which is not directly expressed in the housing market.

When housing is defined as a social good or social necessity, on the other hand, one speaks of *housing need* rather than demand. Housing need, broadly defined, refers to the inadequacy of existing housing conditions when compared with some standard or norm of what is socially acceptable (Cullingworth, 1960). In theory estimates of housing need, unlike those of demand, take no notice of price or of market performance. In practice, however, the question is not as straightforward. Acceptable standards are relative measures based on the overall condition of the existing stock, which includes prices, as well as individual and collective perceptions of what future housing conditions might be. In practice, however, housing needs can be defined in several ways: such as in terms of (1) affordability (based on income), (2) suitability (based on dwelling size or design), or (3) adequacy (state of repair), or some combined definition which represents "core" need.

Types and Sources of Demand

The initial expression of demand is effectively *stock demand*, i.e., the demand for housing in the existing inventory at one point in time. Generally this is equal to the number of households (HH) plus a certain proportion of vacancies (V). Thus, the stock demand for housing (H) is equal to: $H = HH + V$.

More frequently, however, we are interested in changes in demand. First there is *direct growth demand* which arises because of a growth in aggregate population (in a country, region, or city) or through a change in the demographic structure of that population. The latter may be reflected in an increase in the rate of household formation because of bulges in the age pyramid (e.g., postwar baby boom), undoubling, household splitting or in-migration. As previously noted, this rate has increased dramatically in the last decade, even in those situations where aggregate population has not been increasing. Thus we can write growth demand as: $\Delta H = \Delta HH + \Delta V$.

In addition, we can differentiate a third source of demand, *replacement* demand (R). This refers to the demand for housing to replace existing units which have been lost through demolition, conversion, fire or other natural causes, and the demand for *improvements*. The latter, W. F. Smith (1970, p. 275) defines as consisting of those households with the desire and means to upgrade their existing housing standards. This demand may arise because of continued obsolesence of the existing stock, or through increases in real income and purchasing power, or more likely from both sources. We can thus write the component equation: $\Delta H = \Delta HH + \Delta V + R$. Here we do not refer to a change in replacement demand because that demand is new to each period.

Measuring Demand: The Concept of Elasticities

The most difficult type of demand to estimate is replacement or improvement demand, particularly that due to rising standards and expectations. It is, as noted in the previous introduction, even more difficult to make such estimates for different housing types, income groups, or for difficult regions of a country or areas of a city. A very useful and precise tool in this regard is the concept of elasticity of demand as used in traditional economics.

Since the most significant component in monitoring changes in improvement demand is income, the most common use of elasticities of demand is with reference to income. We can define the *income elasticity of demand for housing* as the proportional change in the demand for housing which results from a unit change in the level of real income.[2] In a similar way, the *price elasticity* of demand is defined as follows: if a 1% increase in the relative price of housing—relative, say, to the CPI—produces a decline in the demand for housing of 3/4 of 1% below what it might otherwise have been, then the price elasticity of demand is 0.75. These measures, subject to all of the usual assumptions, will be most useful in our following discussions of the location of housing demand and subsequently of housing patterns and policies.

Empirical Evidence

There has been little agreement on what the real income elasticities of demand are for housing, either in aggregate or for groups or individuals by age, race, or tenure. Historically, the major debate has focused on Engel's Law,[3] which asserted that the proportion of income spent on housing remained constant with rising income, and Schwabe's Law which asserted that the proportion decreased with rising income. As defined above, the income elasticity of demand in the former case would be 1.0 and in the latter case less than 1.0. More recently, the debate was reactivated by Reid (1962) who demonstrated that the elasticity was considerably higher than 1.0.

There is now an ample literature in this area,[4] so we need go no further than to draw out very general conclusions relevant to the following sections. Generally, estimates of the elasticities of demand vary widely between countries and over time. For the U.S., such estimates have ranged from 0.55 to 1.63 (Grebler et al., 1956; Muth, 1969; Quigley, 1978), which is presumably why a figure of 1.0 is so frequently taken as an average.

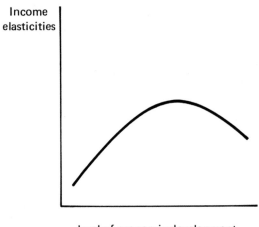

Fig. 6.1. Relationship of housing demand to economic development.

It is also evident that the demand for housing varies directly with the current level of economic development in a country and with that country's level of urbanization. The general hypothesis is that income elasticities of demand are low in the early stages of development, when a nation's resources are directed to other basic or productive sectors, then increase rapidly in the middle stages of development as the housing sector catches up. Finally, at high levels of development, housing demand again declines in relative terms as resources shift elsewhere. The result is a reverse U-shaped curve (Fig. 6.1). In a recent study of 31 developed and developing countries, Lakshmanan, Chatterjee, and Kroll (1978) find considerable empirical support for this hypothesis.

In addition, the proportion of household income spent on housing in different countries appears to have a U-shaped relationship with the rate of urbanization. According to Burns and Grebler (1977), that proportion tends to be lowest for countries with modest rates of urban growth and highest in areas of very slow or very rapid urban growth (Fig. 6.2). The latter reflects the relatively high housing consumption expenditures in very large and rapidly growing cities.

Most studies of the demand for housing in urban areas have tended to focus on aggregate populations and to assume uniform preferences or housing elasticities (Quigley, 1978). This is now clearly inappropriate. There is mounting evidence that such relationships differ substantially between groups of different income, age, and ethnic background.[5] Moore and Clatworthy (1978), for example, have shown in their studies of Wichita, Kansas that income elasticities of demand do vary widely within and between income and racial groups and over stages in the

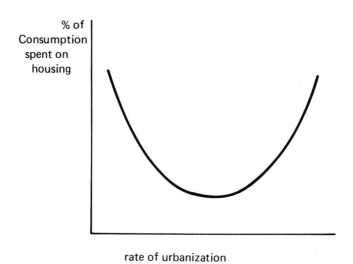

Fig. 6.2. Relationship between housing consumption and population shifts to urban areas.

life cycle. A given increase in income, for instance, produces a far smaller increase in housing consumption among low-income households than among those of medium income where they also found elasticities to be higher among families without children. And both groups exhibit marked difference in the types and attributes of housing consumed as income increases. These assertions are particularly relevant to those interested in housing policies targeted at lower-income groups, rather than at the population as a whole.

Other Components of Demand

We know very little, however, of the relationship between aggregate housing demand and other variables such as migration, labor turnover, and immigration. Migration, for example, has two different effects. One, it obviously adds to (or subtracts from) the total population in a city and therefore alters total housing demand. Second, it also becomes part of the explanation of differences in demand. While it seems unlikely that differences in housing conditions between cities would in themselves generate inter-urban migration let alone immigration, there are specific circumstances in which such relationships would hold. For example, in many new town development schemes housing has been used as a policy instrument in attracting labor, and in turn the availability of housing could be an additional inducement for labor to migrate. Johnson, Salt and Wood (1974) found some evidence of the importance attached to housing in the interregional migration of labor within the U.K., particularly housing conditions at the destination.

Finally, it is generally agreed that changes in tax rates and taxation policies can sharply alter the level of housing demand (Peterson et al., 1973; L. B. Smith, 1977; Stafford, 1978). For example, if interest on mortgages is tax deductable, changes in the allowable deduction or in tax rates will shift the demand for housing, relative to other consumer expenditures, upward or downward. Similarly, the exclusion of the personal home from capital gains tax will produce a transfer of household investment into housing (rather than, say, stocks and bonds) and thereby increase the demand for housing. On the other hand, proportionally large increases in local property taxes or rates can render housing—at least larger houses—less attractive and thus reduce the level of replacement demand. Again, these aggregate relationships will vary widely among local taxing authorities.

DEMAND IN SMALL AREAS: RESIDENTIAL LOCATION, MOBILITY, AND HOUSING CHOICE

Our concern must now turn to translating these aggregate demand perspectives into the demand for housing at particular locations or within small areas of a city. How do people select housing and a residential location? What is the role of mobility and occupancy change in meeting changing demands for housing within cities? What factors influence locationally-specific housing demand?

In attempting to respond to these questions, we could take one of several approaches. These include micro-economic models of land use (Alonso, 1964) and residential location (Evans, 1973); large-scale simulation models of the housing market, such as that of the Urban Institute (de Leeuw and Struyk, 1975) or the National Bureau of Economic Research (Ingram, 1977); residential development simulation models (Kaiser, 1972); or more micro-level behavioral studies of household mobility and of the location decision-making process in selecting a house and a neighborhood. Here we select but two: the micro-economic models and the behavioral or decision-making approach.

Micro-economic Models: Or Housing in Legoland

Certainly the most formal approach mathematically and perhaps the best developed theories of residential location are those from micro-economics. Chapter 4 briefly outlined the basic concepts involved in reference to the competitive operation of an urban housing market in aggregate. In these theories, housing is but one good consumed by households located at a specific distance from the center of the city or place of employment. In fact, rather than models of housing they are more appropriately labelled as models of residential land use.

These models have been extensively developed since the early pioneering work of Muth (1961, 1969), Alonso (1964), and Mills (1967). In general, these models are similar in design and output to the von Thünen model of agricultural zonation around a central market place. They attempt to replicate the pattern of residential land use in urban areas based on the assumption that households trade off housing against other goods and both against accessibility to the city center. These models incorporate classical economic concepts on the behavior of consumers—that they are rational animals who know their preferences and attempt to optimize their net benefits in selecting a residential location—into a framework of a long-run general equilibrium (that is where supply equals demands in the long term).

Such models are subject to a number of limiting assumptions. Housing is considered to be a unidimensional product, competition is perfect, household tastes are invariant, information on market prices is widely available, and legal restrictions on the land are nonexistent. The existing housing stock itself is either ignored or assumed to adapt immediately to new needs, almost in the fashion that children build with lego sets. Space has only one dimension, distance from the city center, as measured by accessibility or commuting costs; and since, traditionally, all employment (and shopping) is assumed to be concentrated in the city center, these costs are known. The outer boundary of the housing market under these assumptions is that distance from the city center at which all leisure time is consumed in commuting to work.

The principal measure of housing demand is income and the preferences expressed by households through their respective indifference curves. In this context, housing essentially becomes a derived demand, i.e., the household consumes land (the size of the residential parcel) and a location (or distance—in time and money costs), according to its relative preferences for space, accessibility, and all other nonhousing goods, including leisure time. Overall consumption of all three is subject to a total budget limit, i.e., an income constraint.

In its simplest form we can summarize these concepts as follows: households will choose a location such that the marginal savings in their payments for housing obtained by moving an additional unit of distance from their centrally-located workplace will be exactly offset by the increased charges for transportation to that workplace. If the latter costs are assumed to be of lesser importance relative to housing as household income increases (i.e., lower income elasticities), then the wealthy will tend to live on the periphery; if the reverse is the case, they will tend to live nearer to the city center with the poor on the periphery.

To reiterate, if one assumes that higher-income households in general have an income elasticity of land (and housing) consumption which exceeds that of the income elasticity of the cost (and time) involved in commuting to work, then they will select residential locations more distant from the city center. If the reverse is the case, then they will select locations nearer to the city center. The assumption in most of this literature is that the former relationship holds. More likely, however, if one were to look at subgroups within the higher-income strata, one would find that the relationships (the housing elasticities) differ considerably. People of similar socioeconomic status do not necessarily have the same housing preferences. The result is what we observe in reality: higher-income groups living both on the periphery and near to the city center.

What other outputs from such models are directly relevant to the housing theme of this book? The models provide, simultaneously, a market-based optimal distribution of location rents (which are, in effect, housing prices), and an equilibrium residential pattern for all households based on the maximization of their individual preference or utility functions. In spatial terms, the outcomes may be summarized as follows: (1) population densities decrease regularly with distance from the city center; (2) residential lots increase in average size with distance; (3) household income increases with distance; and (4) lot size increases with income.

Criticisms of and Extensions to Micro-economic Models

Among the many criticisms of micro-economic models, most of which relate to their restrictive assumptions, perhaps the following are of the greatest interest here:

> They are, for the most part, exercises in comparative 'statics.'
>
> They emphasize a single workplace (the CBD) and assume uniform transport costs.
>
> Competition among urban land uses is limited.
>
> Household tastes are assumed to be invariant, and the prices of all goods other than housing are assumed to be uniform.
>
> Many of the interesting factors which influence housing location, such as changes in income, public expenditures and policies, are external to such models.
>
> Interdependence between actors (collusion) is ignored.
>
> Environmental quality issues, and the role of spatial externalities in housing, are sidestepped.
>
> The housing stock is treated as relatively homogeneous.
>
> The role of government, in setting zoning standards or taxes, is generally ignored.
>
> The costs (to a household) of adjusting to a new set of housing conditions, including the obvious costs of moving, are not considered.

This long list of criticisms derives in part from the obvious need to simplify reality for purposes of theory construction and in part from the fact that the models are basically economic, not social models. They are important here precisely because they set the stage for much of the discussion to follow.

It would be unfair however, if we did not acknowledge the extensive modifications which have been made in these models over the last decade, many of which are directed to the above criticisms (see Richardson, 1977; Quigley, 1978). Attempts have been made, for example, to incorporate varying tastes and utility functions (Beckmann, 1974); to incorporate a fuller range of housing services (Evans, 1973); to relax the assumption of a single employment center (de Leeuw and Struyk, 1975); to incorporate racial discrimination (Kain and Quigley, 1975); to incorporate heterogeneity in the housing stock (Straszheim, 1975); to measure environmental amenities (Berry and Bednarz, 1975); and even to incorporate the costs of moving (Muth, 1974).

Of particular concern here, however, is their treatment of the existing housing stock. Earlier models, such as Alonso's, were criticized in that they ignored the built environment of existing structures. Subsequent attempts to incorporate into such models a heterogeneous, historically durable and complex housing stock have only met with partial success (Muth, 1978). Evans (1975) refers to the mechanistic way the stock is treated as similar to that of playing with lego; thus our heading for this section "housing in legoland."

These models have also been criticized not for what they tend to leave out, but for what they include. Harvey (1973), for example, has brought into question the fundamental logic on which such models are based and the purpose for which they are developed. He sees the latter role as perpetuating the status quo by developing theory which rationalizes the inherent inequalities in our society in the consumption of land and housing. On the former, he criticizes the logical structure of neoclassical economics, as reflected in assumptions such as homogeneous "utility" functions, because it reduces household behavior to a set of unidimensional laws which mirror the preferences of the dominant social class. Such models are then at best descriptions of a distorted reality, rather than explanations of behavior, and at worst they act to obscure underlying social conflict and diversity and real housing needs.

Other more specific criticisms have been directed at the assumptions regarding the relative size of income elasticities for land and location. Wheaton (1977) has argued that the elasticities for land and commuting *are roughly the same*. If this is the case, then the explanations behind the spatial models of Alonso and Muth are open to serious question. Wheaton suggests that other factors—such as neighborhood externatlities, fiscal incentives (e.g., lower taxes), and the political fragmentation of urban areas—are more useful in explaining why the rich tend to live on the periphery of American cities. Others, such as Downs (1975), would augment this list by including the relative cost of new houses, the ease of financing, the lower cost of developing vacant land, differing life-style needs and the social status of suburban living. The first three sets of these factors were examined in Chapter 5; the latter are explored in the remainder of this chapter.

Still other writers have criticized the assumption that people actually know what they are buying. Many people lack information, or are unaware of what they are getting into when moving into a dwelling unit and neighborhood (Whitbread and Bird, 1973). We can only evaluate these kinds of criticisms by actually looking at the residential decision process.

Household Mobility: Reasons for Moving House

The principal means through which changes in the demand for housing are satisfied, especially in the short term, is by residential mobility. The factors involved in moving house and in selecting a new residential location are of course considerably more complex than the above models allow. The specific reasons vary with each household and their current housing and income circumstances; since both are sufficiently well-documented, the reasons do not need to be repeated here in detail.[6]

In general, people move houses because of a dissatisfaction with their current housing status, relative to their income or needs, or a desire to improve their

Table 6.1. Reasons for Changing Residence

I. Life Cycle Changes		*III. Housing Attributes*	
Marriage	33.1%	More modern house	8.5%
Increase in family size	1.9	Obtain garage	0.6
Decrease in family size	0.8	Better garden	0.7
Retirement	0.6	Accommodation too small	16.1
	36.4%	Accommodation too large	1.6
			27.5%
II. Income and Employment		*IV. Neighborhood and Accessibility*	
Changes		*Needs*	
Change in job	12.0%	Nearer to schools	0.5%
Change in income	1.9	Nearer to social facilities	0.1
	13.9%	Nearer to work	5.3
		Nearer to shops	0.1
		Nearer to relatives	11.1
		Better neighborhood	3.9
			21.0%

Source: U.K. National Building Society.

housing and neighborhood amenities, or both. Or, they may be compelled to move by changes in jobs, life-style or life cycle, or because they be physically forced to move (Table 6.1). Most moves are also over a relatively short distance, especially those related to social and housing factors. Longer distance moves tend to be much less frequent and are primarily related to job changes. Further, long moves are more common among members of skilled and professional occupations than among unskilled and manual workers.

The reasons for moving house, however, may well be unrelated to the actual factors considered in selecting a new house and location. Moreover, both sets of factors will vary depending on aggregate conditions in an housing market at any given time. These conditions include (1) the growth rate of the urban area and the strength of its economic base, (2) demographic changes and the rate of in-migration, (3) income growth, (4) changes in overall accessibility levels and costs, and (5) shifts in financial policies with respect to housing. To the extent that these changes are spatially differentiated within a city, they will in turn affect the demand for housing in particular neighborhoods.

Within this context, we do know that residential mobility in North American cities averages between 15 and 20% per year.[7] Excluding multiple moves, approximately 70% of all urban households will have moved within 10 years and perhaps 90% in 20 years (see Fig. 6.3a). We also know that the frequency of moves declines with the age of the household and with the length of time in one location (the "duration-of-stay" effect). Similarly, it has been shown that residential movements are considerably higher for rental housing than for owner-occupied housing at all ages and income groups, since buying and selling a house (the transaction

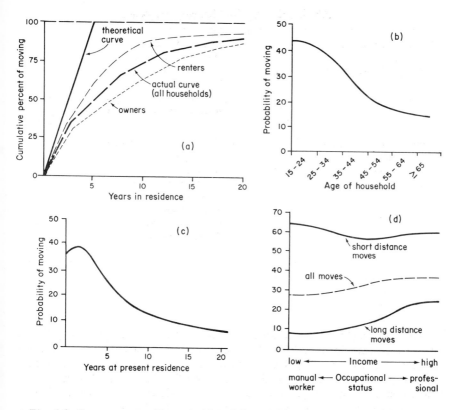

Fig. 6.3. Components of household mobility and housing turnover: (a) aggregate mobility rates, by tenure; (b) the age effect; (c) the duration-of-stay effect; (d) income and occupational effects.

cost) is more cumbersome and expensive than rental transfers. Finally, mobility tends to increase with income, but at a decreasing rate.

Demographic and Life Cycle Changes

It has been widely documented that the principal reasons people change houses are associated with their housing needs at different stages in the life cycle (Rossi, 1955; Simmons, 1968; Moore, 1972). In part, these needs are demographic; young singles and elderly households usually require different housing attributes than do families with young children. In part, the needs are related to life-style. It must be acknowledged, however, that in a modern, affluent, and relatively open society there is now a proliferation of different life-styles and thus wide variations in the changes which follow from the life cycle. Aging is one of the few common demoninators.

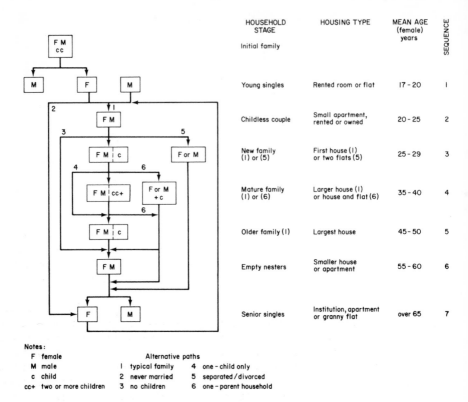

<table>
<thead>
<tr><th>HOUSEHOLD STAGE</th><th>HOUSING TYPE</th><th>MEAN AGE (female) years</th><th>SEQUENCE</th></tr>
</thead>
<tbody>
<tr><td>Initial family</td><td></td><td></td><td></td></tr>
<tr><td>Young singles</td><td>Rented room or flat</td><td>17 - 20</td><td>I</td></tr>
<tr><td>Childless couple</td><td>Small apartment, rented or owned</td><td>20 - 25</td><td>2</td></tr>
<tr><td>New family (I) or (5)</td><td>First house (I) or two flats (5)</td><td>25 - 29</td><td>3</td></tr>
<tr><td>Mature family (I) or (6)</td><td>Larger house (I) or house and flat (6)</td><td>35 - 40</td><td>4</td></tr>
<tr><td>Older family (I)</td><td>Largest house</td><td>45 - 50</td><td>5</td></tr>
<tr><td>Empty nesters</td><td>Smaller house or apartment</td><td>55 - 60</td><td>6</td></tr>
<tr><td>Senior singles</td><td>Institution, apartment or granny flat</td><td>over 65</td><td>7</td></tr>
</tbody>
</table>

Notes:

		Alternative paths	
F	female	I typical family	4 one - child only
M	male	2 never married	5 separated / divorced
c	child	3 no children	6 one - parent household
cc+	two or more children		

Fig. 6.4. Idealized household life cycles.

Nevertheless, there is some merit in looking at a typical set of alternative household life cycles as one basis for anticipating the changing demands placed on the housing stock. The unit of analysis here is the household, although with emphasis on the traditional family unit. This emphasis is not inappropriate in that such units still count for a majority of long-term, intra-urban moves and since, in the final analysis, most societies—as Michelson (1977) points out—are at least serious about the welfare of children.

Figure 6.4 outlines a typical life-cycle progression beginning with a stereotype family unit consisting of two adults (F, M) and 2 children (c). It follows one of the children through as many as seven stages until their children have left home and they have retired. The number of stages is, of course, arbitrary. In this illustration, we follow the young woman (F) through the sequence, at each stage recognizing that alternative life-cycle paths are possible and increasingly frequent. For example, some of the alternative paths include being married (F, M; path 1) or never married (path 2); divorced or separated, with or without children (paths 5 or 6); remaining childless (path 3); having one child (path 4), or two or more children (path 1).

In each stage, the housing requirements are usually different as is the household's ability to satisfy those requirements. A typical individual household might move many times during this sequence, but normally only three to five moves involve substantial shifts in the type of housing involved. The typical sequence perhaps is from a rented room, flat or apartment for newly-formed households through a sequence of larger apartments into the owner-occupied market, likely occupying their largest unit between the ages of 45 and 55 when real income tends to reach its peak and space requirements (in terms of the number of bedrooms or outside play space) are highest. In later stages, when space needs (and possibly income) decline, the household—now smaller through the departure of children, death of a spouse, divorce or separation—will likely move into a smaller house or return to the rental sector.

This highly simplified illustration at least allows us to order our expectations on how demographic changes will alter housing needs and demand. Recent shifts in demographic structure, notably the trend toward declining fertility, smaller household size, and an overall aging of the population, combined with an increasing diversity of life-styles, confirm that society's housing needs in the next decade or two are likely to be very different from those in the past.[8]

This hypothetical life cycle progression through the housing stock also has a spatial imprint. Typically the new household would seek rental accommodation in the inner city or suburbs, then move into the newer suburbs when children arrive, and subsequently into more mature suburbs or exurbs as the family matures. Older families or seniors might then retire into a city flat or leave the urban area altogether. To the extent that these spatial patterns are manifest in a real city, the impacts of demographic change on the distribution of housing demand can be considerable. The aging of the population during the 1970s in what were predominantly young, single-family suburbs in the 1950s and 1960s is but one example.

Household Decision Making and the Search for Housing

The actual process of decision making which people go through in deciding to "adjust" their housing situation is generally not part of micro-economic models of residential location. The process clearly has two components: the initial decision to move, and the decision on where and into what kind of housing to move. In practice these two major decisions are taken as part of series of linked decisions in which people continually evaluate their housing needs and alternatives.

One of the most succinct conceptual frameworks for examining this process in a spatial context was developed by Brown and Moore (1970), and has subsequently been widely extended (Clark and Cadwallader, 1973). In their initial model, Brown and Moore drew on Wolpert's (1965) integration of the concepts of *intendedly rational behavior* and *place utility* as a basis for explaining differences in intra-urban migration behavior. Place utility, simple defined, measures an individual household's level of satisfaction or dissatisfaction with respect to a given location (house and environment).[9] When the place utility of the present residential location diverges—usually, but not inevitably, downward—from the immediate needs of the household, "stress" builds up and the search for alternative housing locations begins.

At some unspecified "threshold reference point" a psychological process is triggered which converts that stress into "strain," the latter involving a motivation for action (in this case residential mobility). The position of this threshold point is largely a function of previous residential experience, which produces a set of expectations or "housing needs set" of real (or perceived) aspirations.

Figure 6.5 provides a somewhat extended version of the initial model, with the two decisions on whether or not to move and where to move ordered for simplicity. On the basis of an initial set of attributes, and a stimulus for change, the household undertakes an assessment of the feasibility of a move. The stimulus can arise either through changes internal to the household and its housing needs, or through changes in the immediate environment. The latter provide examples of what forces can lead to a change in the demand for housing at a given location: physical improvement or decay of the built environment, nonresidential land use succession, social or racial transition as well as accessibility changes. As a result of its own assessment of these changes, the household can decide to move or to stay in place (in "situ") and to adjust, as far as is possible, to the changes. Most of the literature has, for obvious reasons, looked only at those who decided to move.

Given the decision to actively consider alternative housing and locations, a number of additional factors must be considered by the household. They must, for example, have a particular strategy, explicitly or implicitly, for identifying and evaluating housing alternatives, subject to a number of constraints (of which income is but one). We can summarize these considerations in terms of the following concepts:

> the action or *awareness space*—the cognitive map—or subset of all locations (i.e., of housing units) in an urban area for which the household has sufficient knowledge to assign place utilities to different alternatives.
>
> *aspiration region*—the upper and lower limits of the set of housing attributes specified by the household as including their preferred set (this corresponds to the distribution of bid prices described in Chapter 4).
>
> *search space*—is that part of the awareness space, defined by the boundaries of the aspiration region, within which the household actively searches for a new dwelling.
>
> *behavior path*—the term "path" is used here to convey the importance of ordering the sources of information utilized, and of recognizing that households attach implicit probabilities to the likely success of each source of information and to each sequence of searching.

The constraints on the processes of search and evaluation derive from both limited household resources (income, information, and the time available for search) and the housing inventory (prices, and the number and location of available vacancies). The combined result of these constraints is the feasible *decision space*, within which the evaluation takes place. If available vacancies fall within

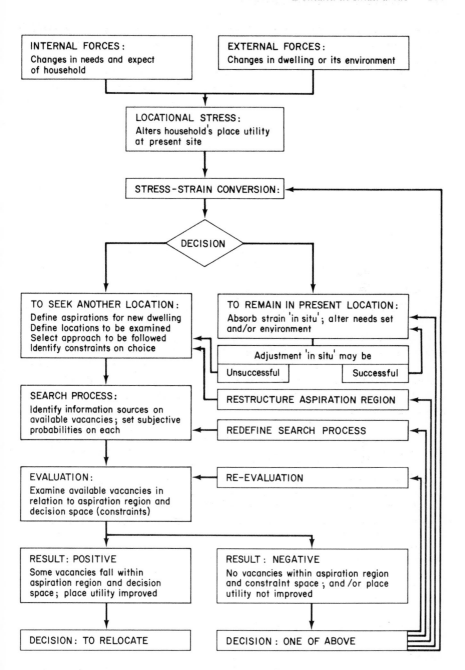

Fig. 6.5. The household relocation and search process.

that decision space, and within the household's aspiration region—and thereby increase that household's place utility—then, in theory, a decision to move will be made. All of this process also occurs within a *time constraint*, either one imposed from outside (by pressures to move or rising prices) or from inside (the ability and willingness to invest one's time). Households must, as a result, adjust the length and strategy of their search accordingly, which also means altering the criteria involved in evaluating alternatives and the sources of information used.

The role of information on housing opportunities is obviously critical. The sources of information available and used by households, as Palm (1978) and numerous others have shown, act to shape the pattern of housing demand and the workings of the housing market (Chapter 4). Those sources include the mass media (newspapers, radio, TV), specialized agencies (estate agents, citizen bureaus, and housing authorities), informal networks of direct and indirect social contacts (friends, relatives, work associates), and simply "looking around."

Although the specific balance of information sources used varies with the area studied, a surprisingly large proportion of households rely on a limited number of informal sources (Barrett, 1973). Johnson et al. (1974), for example, estimate that nearly 33% of their sample found their new accommodation through friends, relatives, business contacts, or work-mates (Table 6.2). They noted that newcomers tend to rely on more formal channels of information, as do higher income and professional households. Lower-income households tend to rely more on informal channels.[10] This perhaps is not surprising given the relatively high costs of engaging real estate agents. Reliance on personal contacts also tends to restrict

Table 6.2. Sources of Information in the Search for Housing
(in percent)

Source	Initial information sources		Source for final choice	
Real estate agencies	13.3		39.6	
Local government agencies	2.9		2.5	
Citizens' bureau	1.1		–	
		17.3		42.1
Friends and relatives	19.8		21.6	
At work	4.4		2.5	
Business contacts	6.2		9.1	
		30.4		33.2
Looking around	18.7		4.7	
Accidental observation	1.8		2.5	
		20.5		7.2
Other		2.0		3.6
No response		9.0		0.5

Source: Johnson et al., 1974, p. 236.

the geographic area of search, often to the household's current residential area or to other neighborhoods which are familiar and of roughly similar social status. Some researchers have found empirical evidence that these restrictions lead to a *sectoral bias* in housing search (following established sectors of socioeconomic status) and a *distance-decay effect*, in which the alternatives examined fall off sharply with increased distance from the home. But these are perhaps less significant than the simple fact that the search is restricted to a limited range of housing and neighborhood types.[11]

Despite the rather formal and mechanistic nature of the preceding model formulation, it does at least provide an idealized context within which to identify the basic components in a process of decision making which is far from simple or straightforward. In fact, the difficulty of applying this formulation to any real-world situation—and there have been few detailed empirical studies—is precisely that the information required to test each concept is excessively large. This should not, however, deflate the usefulness of the rich array of ideas contained in the model as a framework for studies of specific areas or groups of households.

Tenure Choice

As well as choosing between housing and all other goods, making the trade-off between accessibility and housing, as in the micro-economic approach, and undertaking the search procedure as in the second model, a household has to select a type of tenure. The principal choice is between owning and renting (with cooperative ownership somewhere in between). The preceding behavioral model was principally concerned with home purchase. Generally, however, these decisions are all made simultaneously, or at least as part of deciding on the appropriate housing "package."

Tenure choice is extremely complicated and not well understood. There are, of course, strong economic and social motivations for home purchase (Struyk, 1976). Homeownership is an asset, a tax-free benefit and a status symbol. Under some conditions it is clearly economically rational to buy. Others choose to rent because of life-style preferences, the need for flexibility because of frequent job-related moves, or because of limited equity (for down payment) or simply because of low income.

Generally homeownership increases with household income, but at a declining rate. Doling (1976) provides a strong argument that the probability of homeownership increases sharply as incomes increase and then levels off and stabilizes at between 65 and 75% of all households, depending on local conditions. These proportions, it should be noted, relate primarily to the English-speaking world (Kemeny, 1978). Homeownership rates (see Chapter 3) are substantially lower in most continental European countries where renting, public ownership, and cooperatives are traditionally more common.

In any case, tenure choice is part of the fabric of housing demand at specific locations within an urban area. If, as is typical, an urban housing stock is spatially differentiated by tenure, a shift in tenure preference or choice will alter the spatial pattern of demand. Similarly, a changing pattern of housing tenure in new construction will alter the movements of households accordingly. The suburbanization of the high-rise rental apartment in North America during the 1960s also irreversibly remade the image of the suburbs, and the geography of housing demand and opportunities by tenure.

Life Cycle Plans, Anticipations, and Housing Ideals

Among the many extensions and criticisms of the preceding models of residential mobility and choice, two are worthy of elaboration here. One criticism is that while such models are cumulative, in the sense that households are continually faced with pressures to relocate, they are not dynamic. That is, they do not recognize the relative position of households in terms of their anticipated sequence, or *life plan*, regarding housing. Not everyone, or necessarily even a majority, move because of stress created by the inadequacy of their current housing or its surroundings as outlined in the preceding model. A second concern is the emphasis placed in such models on *freedom of choice* in housing. Clearly, not all households have a choice in whether to move or not, or where to move if forced to.

Michelson (1977) provides a good example of one elaboration of the housing relocation model. He introduces the concept of a progressive, evolving life cycle in which the criteria people use to evaluate their housing needs and preferences change over time. While the search process might follow that outlined above, the inference regarding their behavior would be one of a premeditated course of "action" rather than a "reaction" to stress.

The basic argument in this approach is that people have anticipations about their future residential moves, perhaps not the number and frequency of moves but certainly what they expect to get out of the moves. Their current location may be viewed as temporary, as a step into other types of housing or other locations and living environments.[12] Michelson (1977) found that nearly 66% of the (male) residents moving into downtown apartments viewed the likelihood of moving again in the next 5 years as "very great," while only 5% of those moving into a suburban house thought that a subsequent move was very likely. Thus, even while this group of movers was carrying out one cycle of mobility, based on decision criteria relevant to the housing unit and environment into which they were moving, they were also anticipating their move into still another unit with different characteristics and intended to satisfy differing needs and preferences.[13]

The empirical results suggest a "family-mobility" cycle with respect to housing use and demand comprised of three distinct stages: (1) the initial or *baseline* stage; (2) a stage of short-term *incremental* changes or adjustments toward some longer-term ideal; and (3) the attainment or *approximation of the ideal*. Stages 2 and 3 are by definition dynamic, with the ideal housing environment evolving through personal experience and changing household conditions. The opportunity to attain one's ideal in the future allows a household to appear quite satisfied with housing conditions in stages 1 and 2, even where those conditions do not meet current needs or preferences.

This approach helps to explain two dilemmas: the presence of widespread housing satisfaction, despite a gap between preferences and current housing conditions, and the apparent contradiction between high levels of satisfaction and the intention to move. It might also help to pinpoint some sources of dissatisfaction in housing, i.e., with the perceived infeasibility of attaining an ideal rather than with current living conditions, even when the latter appear inadequate to the observer.

Restricted Choice

The latter point raises a particularly critical question regarding who exactly has a choice in housing or location. The above approaches, as well as most other studies in housing mobility, admittedly assume that choice is relatively free or unconstrained (except by tastes and budget). For many households, however, there is, as Gray (1975) argues, very little choice of where to live or what to live in. Although this is a question we take up in more detail in a subsequent chapter (Chapter 8), at this junction we must at least acknowledge the kinds of constraints that exist and their respective sources.

The most obvious constraint on choice in a private market is *low-income*. In the housing policy literature, the usual rule of thumb is that at least one-third of all households in a competitive housing market have little or no choice and need some form of public sector assistance. These people may be the real working poor, the elderly, the very young, the unemployed, or the transient. In any case, their numbers are large.

Other constraints on residential choice affect different groups of the population. These include households who:

> because of *discrimination* due to their race, ethnic origin, language or religion are precluded from relocating to specific neighborhoods or types of housing;
>
> because of the *psychological stress* of moving from familiar environments, are unwilling to move;
>
> are *physically incapable* of relocating, because of personal handicaps, family situations, or medical needs;
>
> *lack the necessary information* to be aware of what choices are open to them;
>
> are residents in *public sector* housing, where freedom of mobility within that sector is traditionally limited;
>
> live in *isolated locations*, even within cities, for whom a residential relocation involves a lengthy move and a dramatic change in living environments;
>
> have *special needs*, such very different groups as the large family, one-parent households, non-married couples, former in-mates of institutions, and problem families.

Although the existence of a restricted choice for groups such as these is well known, it is still a sobering exercise for any student of housing to undertake an inventory of the proportion of the population which is affected. What it means is that residential and housing location models, such as the micro-economic or behavioral models outlined above, must be seen for what they are: idealized constructs of reality which primarily apply to specific segments of the population with the freedom of choice, and even then under severely restrictive assumptions. This does not mean that they are wrong. Rather, they are only partial explanations.

NOTES

[1]In practice it is not easy to separate the two, particularly for homeowners (see Harvey, 1973).

[2]If, for example, a 10% increase in real income leads to a 5% increase in the quality of housing (services) demanded, then, all other things being equal (ceterius paribus), the income elasticity is 0.50.

[3]Ernst Engel, a German statistician, not F. Engels, the associate of Karl Marx.

[4]Excellent reviews of housing demand studies are provided in Muth (1969), Kain and Quigley (1975), Ball and Kirwin (1975), Burns and Grebler (1977), and Quigley (1978).

[5]See, for example, Grigsby's criticism of aggregate elasticity measures in Bourne and Hitchcock (1978).

[6]Detailed reviews and empirical studies of mobility are provided in Simmons (1968), Lansing et al. (1969), Moore (1972, 1973), Yeates and Garner (1976), Clark and Moore (1978), and Jones and Eyles (1977).

[7]The corresponding figure in Britain for the number of families who change residence each year is 8.6% (U.K. Central Statistical Office, *Social Trends*, Vol. 9, 1979). For owner-occupied housing in the U.S., the mobility rate is between 9 and 10%.

[8]The fact that the divorce rate has tripled since the mid-1960s is one example of how the demand for housing can change (in this case, primarily for more and smaller units) without a change in total population size.

[9]More formally defined, place utility is ". . . the net composite of utilities which are derived from the individual's integration at some point in space" (Brown and Moore, 1970). The concept of place utility has a parallel in welfare economics in the idea of a consumer "surplus" for households, as well as in the difference between use (occupancy) and exchange (market) value—although not strictly in the sense in which Marx used these terms.

[10]Rossi (1955), in his study of housing mobility, estimated the effectiveness of different sources of information on housing opportunities as follows: personal contacts (.76), driving and walking around (.33), newspapers (.29), and real estate agents (.28).

[11]These restrictions on choice are considerably more severe in public sector housing (see Murie, Ninar, and Watson, 1976; and Chapter 10), particularly in restricting moves between local housing authorities.

[12]For example, Duncan and Newman (1975) also found this tendency in their report on a massive survey of the residential history of 5,000 American families aptly titled "People as Planners."

[13]It is not uncommon in housing surveys to find that very high proportions of households indicate that they are satisfied with their current house and environment. The U.K. National Dwelling Survey, 1977, for example, found 82% satisfied with their houses and 80% with their residential environment. This is not the same thing, however, as asking whether there are undesirable features of the house or neighborhood.

Chapter 7

Outcomes and Processes of Change

The principal outcome of the interaction of supply and demand, as these are outlined in the two previous chapters, is to place people of different characteristics and needs in housing of different types situated within particular kinds of residential environments, at any given point in time. The reader might then have anticipated in this chapter a detailed description of spatial patterns of housing conditions and household attributes within cities. Instead this description has been introduced throughout the volume, wherever such patterns are relevant to the discussion.

This chapter examines those basic processes operating within the urban housing market and their spatial outcomes, i.e., the results of the allocation process. To allow for a detailed discussion, however, requires that we be selective. Here we look at six major processes of change: (1) occupancy turnover and the movements of households within the housing stock; (2) the filtering process and changes in housing quality; (3) housing and neighborhood change viewed as an "arbitrage" process; (4) the progression of housing vacancies through the stock (vacancy chains); (5) spatial variations in house price changes; and (6) revitalization and the return-to-the-city movement. Chapter 8, then, looks at particular kinds of processes and outcomes which are considered to be either market failures or social problems, or both.

HOUSING OCCUPANCY AND TURNOVER

The Matching of Households and Housing Stock

One would assume from the preceding discussions of constraints on housing supply on the one hand and of life cycle needs and income on the other, that the

Table 7.1. The Match Between Households and Housing Stock: The Toronto C.M.A., 1971[a]

No. of households		Household income				Age of household		
		Under $5K	$5–8K	$8–12K	Over $12K	Under 30	30–50	Over 50
Tenure								
Own		438	535	1089	2188	335	2194	1721
	b	(34.8)	(41.4)	(52.7)	(70.2)	(21.1)	(63.8)	(63.6)
	c	(10.3)	(12.6)	(25.6)	(51.5)	(7.9)	(51.6)	(40.5)
Rent		820	757	976	928	1254	1243	984
	b	(65.2)	(58.6)	(47.3)	(29.8)	(78.9)	(36.2)	(36.4)
	c	(23.6)	(21.7)	(28.0)	(26.7)	(36.0)	(35.7)	(28.3)

		Household income				Age of household		
Owned dwelling unit value:								
<$22.5K	c	85	57	76	77	11	89	195
		(28.8)	(19.3)	(25.8)	(26.1)	(3.7)	(30.2)	(66.1)
22.5–32.5K		119	181	405	598	93	634	576
		(9.1)	(13.9)	(31.1)	(45.9)	(7.1)	(48.7)	(44.2)
32.5–42.5K		52	93	233	597	69	568	338
		(5.3)	(9.5)	(23.9)	(61.2)	(7.1)	(58.3)	(34.7)
Over 42.5K		29	20	68	464	25	326	230
		(5.0)	(3.4)	(11.7)	(79.9)	(4.3)	(56.1)	(39.6)

Notes: [a]From the 1:100 public use sample; [b] = column percentages; [c] = row percentages; [d]Expected selling price; owner-occupied single-detached units only.

matching of people to houses would be relatively straightforward. We might, for example, expect to find that wealthy households would consistently tend to live in larger, expensive housing on the edge of the city or in older better quality housing, with the poor occupying smaller and lower quality units, often rental, located nearer to the CBD.

In reality, however, the matching of households to housing units is considerably more complicated. Moreover, these simple occupancy relationships become more diverse when we look at conditions in different cities and countries. Table 7.1 provides one example of who lives in what kind of housing based on a sample of individual census records for households in the Toronto metropolitan area. Note that households of different income and age distribute themselves over a rather wide spectrum of the housing stock, in terms of the tenure and value of housing occupied. Some young and many older households do own their housing, the wealthy often rent, and those of the lower (current) income do live in some of the more expensive housing. There are problems here with measuring both income and housing value at any point in time.[1] Yet, these data do suggest that the attributes of both the stock and households act primarily as broad "constraints" on the likely behavior of those households and thus on the occupancy of the stock, rather than strict determinants of that behavior.

Household Movements Between Tenure Classes

Any summary of the matching of households to housing, by tenure, price or size of unit, is then a snapshot of ongoing processes of change. We can convey this dynamic property by referring the reader back to the discussions of market transactions in Chapter 4 and of the changing interdependence between supply and demand in Chapters 5 and 6, respectively. Here we demonstrate the frequency of household movements between housing tenures, for samples drawn from both the U.S. (Table 7.2) and the U.K. (Table 7.3). Although an attempt has been made to put the two tables in roughly similar form, the numbers are not strictly compatible. Note that both tables include not just the movement of existing households but the entry of newly-formed households and in-migrants into the market as well as out-migrations and household dissolutions.[2] Note also that these do not say how many or what proportion of households actually moved (see Chapter 6), but what tenure transitions took place among those that did move.

Despite definitional difficulties, the tables do suggest that although most moves are within the same tenure class, there is a considerable movement between classes, and that rates at which households are dissolved or leave the market are high.[3] The highest level of containment, as expected, is in the owner-occupied sector, while the lowest is in private rental (unfurnished) housing. In-migrants tend to occupy the same tenure as they did in their previous location, while newly-formed households distribute themselves across all tenure classes.

These rates of movement will vary with local conditions, as reflected in a complex array of factors. These include: (1) rates of in-migration and household formation, less out-migration and dissolutions; (2) the rate and tenure of additons to and deletions from the housing stock; (3) the rate of growth in personal disposable

Table 7.2. Movements Between Tenure Types, U.S.
(in percentages)

Tenure	Newly-formed households	In-migrants			Movers	
		Former owners	Former renters	Total	Former owners	Former renters
Owner-occupied	67	88	20	24	[54	41]
Rental[a]	33	12	80	76	[23	52]
Out-migrants or dissolved	–	–	–	–	23	7
	100	100	100	100	100	100

Source: Grigsby, 1963.
Note: [a]Excludes public rental.

income and employment opportunities; and (4) changes within the existing stock itself. The latter, for example, may involve the conversion of existing units from rental to owner-occupied (or the reverse), with or without the occupant household actually moving house. Tenure changes do not always involve household moves, and of course most moves do not involve a change in tenure since households tend to stay in the same housing sector.

Table 7.3. Household Movements Between Tenure Types, England and Wales, 1971
(in thousands of households and percentages)

Present tenure	New households entering[a]	Previous tenure			Total
		Owner-occupied	Public rental	Private rental	
Owner-occupied	176	385	66	174	801
	(35)	(66)	(18)	(23)	(37)
Public rental	57	28	197	172	454
	(12)	(5)	(57)	(23)	(21)
Private rental	265	36	25	276	600
	(53)	(6)	(7)	(36)	(27)
Dissolved, moved out, etc.[b]	–	134	66	139	339
		(23)	(18)	(18)	(15)
Totals	496	583	354	761	2194
	(100)	(100)	(100)	(100)	

Sources: Calculated from U.K. Government, *Housing Policy*, 1977, Technical Vol.; and C.S.O., *Social Trends*, Vol. 9, 1979.
Notes: [a]Includes newly-formed households and in-migrants.
[b]Estimated.

We can illustrate the complexity of flows which follow from household movements and stock changes by referring the reader to studies of a single metropolitan area. On example is Murie, Ninar, and Watson's (1976) detailed study of the West Yorkshire conurbation in England. Here we can see the full diversity of movements by tenure group within a single housing market area; in this case, a market sharply differentiated by public sector and private rental housing. The interested student might wish to construct a table of household movements from such studies and to compare the results with the figures given in Tables 7.2 and 7.3. It is also revealing to compare these figures with those obtained for other metropolitan areas with quite different housing stocks.[4]

It would also be instructive to examine movements within and between structure types and through different quality levels, in each case cross-classified by income, age, and perhaps race. But space does not allow us to consider all of these permutations. Instead, we turn over attention to consider examples of those basic processes which are commonly used to measure and explain household movements, housing and neighborhood quality changes, and housing prices over space.

THE FILTERING PROCESS

Perhaps the most common interpretation of changes in the quality of housing is that of the *filtering process*. In its broadest form, filtering refers to any change in the relative position of a housing unit *or* household in the inventory, or matrix, of housing units in an area. Dwellings or households are said to "filter-up" if their position improves over time or to "filter-down" if their position deteriorates. As this concept, and the process itself, underlies much of our previous discussion and the policy reviews to follow, it is imperative that we understand what it is and how it has been applied.

History of the Concept

The general idea of a filtering process in housing has been known since the 19th century but has its primary roots in the classical ecological studies of the 1920s. As described in Chapter 2, these saw the growth of cities as reflected in a series of concentric rings expanding outward from the city center (Park et al., 1925). As the urban population grew and incomes rose, and as the housing stock in each ring aged, the innermost rings were occupied by a succession of social groups of decreasing income. In effect, each zone, and its housing stock, filtered down over time.

This result is based on a number of specific assumptions in the ecological literature, mostly implicit, regarding housing. Among these are that the demand for housing is positively related to income and that households of higher income prefer newer over older housing and suburban space over accessibility (as in the micro-economic models above). Moreover, it is assumed that housing inevitably depreciates with age, thereby reducing the flow of services from the existing stock and encouraging those of sufficient income to relocate, and that new housing construction is both a necessary component in quality changes and a direct stimulant to filtering.

Applying this concept to individual housing units rather than rings or entire neighborhoods was a logical step. Hoyt (1939) developed the concept of filtering in his study of the growth of high-status residential areas, but left it as an empirical measure of change. Subsequently, others (notably Ratcliff, 1949) added a welfare component: that new construction would release existing housing units which could then filter down to lower-income groups, improving their housing quality and thus their welfare. The latter definition has, in turn, set off a long debate on what filtering means and on what it implies for social welfare.

More recent contributors have sought to define the term more explicitly. Grigsby (1963), who argued that filtering was "... the principal dynamic feature of the housing market ... ," defined the conditions under which filtering occurred as follows:

> ... filtering occurs only when values (of housing) decline more rapidly than quality, so that families can obtain either higher quality or more space at the same price, or the same quality and space at a lower price than formerly (p. 17).

In other words, filtering only occurs when price declines more rapidly than housing quality. Note that in this context the focus is on the housing unit, i.e., on the supply side, and on changes in the physical quality of housing consumed.

An alternative approach is to focus on the households rather than the housing units. Leven et al. (1976) in their study of neighborhood change redefine filtering as taking place when:

> ... a household, without a change in its income or tastes, experiences a change in its housing bundle to a different place on its scale of preferences (p. 46).

Thus, filtering-up only occurs when the change is to a more preferred bundle of housing services.

Three important implications emerge from the latter definition. One is that households can undergo filtering in situ, i.e., without moving house. This the authors call *passive filtering; active filtering* involves a relocation. This distinction ties back directly to our previous behavioral model of household decision making in Chapter 6 and to that of market and nonmarket changes in Chapter 4.[5] Both concepts can be applied to individual households as well as groups (neighborhoods). In addition, this definition recognizes the importance of external factors in determining housing conditions and, equally important, it incorporates consumer preferences and their expectations regarding the flow of housing services available to them in the future.

Measuring Types of Filtering

It may be seen from the above that filtering can be measured in numerous ways, for quite different purposes. Four measures stand out: (1) changes in housing supply, usually quality or price; (2) changes in the position of households, by income, preferences, or needs; (3) changes in the matching of households to units;

and (4) changes in household welfare. All four are relevant and useful, but each measures a slightly different component of the nature of housing supply and occupancy. Here we examine all but the last through a simple hypothetical example.

Figure 7.1 illustrates the dimensions of the filtering process, incorporating the differentiation between passive and active filtering as defined above. Assume, for simplicity, that at one point in time we have three similar dwelling units S_1, S_2, and S_3, ranked by value or price, and occupied by three households H_1, H_2, and H_3, respectively. In theory, the households would be ranked by income, but this unnecessarily complicates the analysis at this point. Over time (from time t_1 to t_2), no households move, but we can visualize three different types of outcomes: downward filtering (S_3 and H_3), upward filtering (S_2 and H_2), and no change (S_1 and H_1) in relative value.

Active filtering is considerably more complicated. In the second part of Figure 7.1, we examine what is perhaps the conventional view of the filtering process. Again the example begins with three housing units, S_4, S_5, and S_6, which are initially occupied by households H_4, H_5, and H_6, respectively, and ranked by relative value. At time t_2, new housing unit S_7 is added to the stock at the highest value category. Household H_6 moves into that unit from its previous location in S_6. Since S_7 is of slightly higher value than S_6, household H_6 in the process has

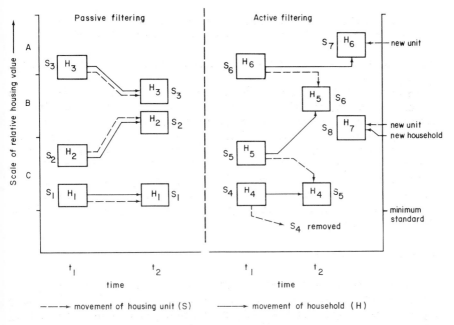

Fig. 7.1. Simplified examples of the *filtering process.*

improved its housing position and, in theory, its "welfare" through upward filtering. In the meantime, unit S_6 filters downward in value to the point where it can be occupied by a household of lower income, such as H_5. In this illustration, H_5 has also improved its housing position since even though S_6 has filtered downward, it is still at a higher value level than H_5's previous residence (S_5). A second new unit, S_8, added at a lower quality level and immediately occupied by a newly-formed household, would not involve filtering of any form, according to this definition.

A third variant of the filtering process is illustrated by the movement of housing unit S_5. This unit has filtered downward and is now occupied by household H_4, but since S_5 is now in roughly the same value position as the previously-occupied unit S_4, the household's relative position has not changed, i.e., no filtering. To complete the traditional picture, unit S_4 becomes surplus to this simplified housing market and is therefore removed from the stock (vacant, converted, abandoned, or demolished).

These quality changes can be succinctly represented in the form of a tally or *transaction matrix*. For convenience here, we assume only three broad value categories (A, B, and C) for the seven housing units cited above. The absolute frequencies of movements of units between these value categories are displayed in Table 7.4. Two units initially in category A have filtered down to category B; while of the four beginning in category C, one filtered up to category B, two remained in C, and one was removed from the stock. In addition, one new housing unit was added in category A. The initial distribution of housing units ordered by value, 2-0-4, has become 1-4-2 by the second time period, but note that these are not the same units nor do they necessarily have the same occupants.

The purpose of this highly simplified illustration—and one can easily visualize how the numbers in such transition matrices could explode in any real situation—is twofold: to demonstrate the complex nature of housing quality changes, and to

Table 7.4. A Matrix Representation of Filtering: (a) Housing Units and (b) Households

		Final value category t_2							**Final value category t_2**			
		A	B	C	Units removed	Initial total			A	B	C	Households removed	Initial total
Initial value category t_1	A	0	2	0	0	2	Initial value category t_1	A	1	1	0	0	2
	B	0	0	0	0	0		B	0	0	0	0	0
	C	0	1	2	−1	4		C	0	2	2	0	4
units added		1	1	0			households added		0	1	0		
new total		1	4	2			new total		1	4	2		
(a)							(b)						

stress the need for concepts and methodologies which capture this dynamic characteristic. If the actual movements recorded in matrices similar to Table 7.4 are converted to proportions, the latter can be interpreted as "probabilities" of transitions in housing quality. Grigsby (1963), Watson (1974), and Jones (1978), for example, used such matrices to illustrate the interrelationships between different housing sub-markets in urban areas. Others (Clark, 1964; Gilbert, 1972; Sharpe, 1978) have used similar transition matrices to project the movements of specific types of housing using the methodology of Markov-chains.

Does Filtering Work?

The debate on filtering in urban housing markets has been continuous for at least three decades. The principal difference of opinion is that between filtering seen as either: (1) an elementary descriptive concept, or (2) a normative concept in which filtering is said to work *if and only if* households improve their housing condition, their "welfare," through the filtering process.

The latter concept is particularly crucial since it is the implicit (if not explicit) concept lying behind housing policies in most western countries. That is, simply, that new housing tends to be added to the stock at the higher value levels, for middle- and upper-income groups (as in Table 7.4). The housing left behind by these groups is then available for lower-income groups—just like used cars. If the rate of new construction is faster than the rate at which the existing stock is filtering downward (i.e., deteriorating), then most lower-income households will be able to improve their housing condition.

Here we can see the origins of policy thinking which emphasize new construction (starts or completions), but with little or no regard to their distribution by price and quality. This emphasis is by no means recent; it is, in fact, explicit (although the term is not used) in many housing documents in the 19th century (Alden and Hayward, 1907). If filtering works, the argument goes, people will get improved housing regardless of the value level at which new construction takes place. In part, this can be seen as a justification for policies which emphasize the construction of middle- and upper-income housing. What is also implicit in such policies is that new housing will exceed household formation and that real incomes will rise.

But used housing is not like second-hand cars; in fact, even used cars do not filter-down neatly either. The principal criticism of filtering in housing, from a normative point of view, is precisely that housing, at least housing of reasonable quality, does not filter-down to those of lower income. Either it is not available, because it is still occupied by middle- and upper-income households, or it may be converted to other uses (such as offices) or some other forms of tenure (multi-family rental) for investment purposes. In some cases it is demolished for roads, commercial redevelopment or parking. Or, even if it becomes available, restrictions on access to that housing, in terms of the lack of mortgage availability, high rents or discrimination, may prevent the household from occupying such units. Data from Lansing et al. (1969) indicate that less than 10% of the households which benefit from the construction of expensive units would be classed as poor.

Even when older housing does filter-down, it is often low-quality housing, suffering from a lack of maintenance and a protracted decline in neighborhood or environmental quality. At best, it may provide a residence temporarily not much better than the previous one (in quality/price or space per person), and at worst it may help push low-income groups further down the ladder of housing quality. To some observers, this is precisely the implicit purpose—to maintain and legitimize inequalities—of those policies based on the filtering concept (Boddy and Gray, 1979). More specifically, and as Lowry (1960) argued in his earlier critique of filtering, the decline in housing quality through filtering—even if it worked—would so burden the low-income occupant with long-overdue maintenance costs, which they cannot afford, that any benefit from filtering would be both small and temporary.[6]

The filtering process might then be thought of as analogous to a person walking up a down escalator. People walk up at a speed related to increases in their income and their mobility (ability to change houses), while the down escalator represents the downward movement of housing units over time. Those who can move faster may advance up the escalator, but for those who cannot or who do not have the means, even staying in the same place is difficult. A disruption in income, such as unemployment, death of a spouse, or restrictions in the freedom to move, can send a person downward fast. Some inevitably end up at the bottom. Seen in this light, filtering is *neither an efficient nor humane* way of providing housing for those of modest or low income.

In part, the debate on filtering reflects a confusion between filtering as both a process and as an outcome. The *process* is a structural change in the market, in either or both of supply and demand. One *outcome* of that process is a change in the welfare of particular households or groups. The fact that the latter change does or does not conform to one's objectives, that the poor benefit most, does not negate the fact that relative changes in housing value (i.e., filtering) do occur.

The critical question is the reliance of housing policies in many western countries on the process of filtering-down as the best means of improving the quality of housing available to those of lower income. This reliance directly affects the level in the price hierarchy at which governments introduce—or influence the private industry to introduce—new units into the stock. Cullingworth (1966) expressed the view that the maximum benefit to the poor occurs through construction aimed directly at that income level. Even though the multiplier effect of such housing, as defined in the following section, is likely to be lower than that of more expensive housing, the difference is not that great (Downs, 1975). Accordingly, most governments have in the past accepted the objective of building housing for those households in greatest need (Chapter 10).

THE ARBITRAGE MODEL OF NEIGHBORHOOD CHANGE

One recent variant on the filtering theme and on the dynamics of urban housing markets is the "arbitrage" model of neighborhood change (Leven et al., 1976; Little, 1976). This model focuses on the conditions and the mechanism involved in the movement of the boundaries between neighborhoods of different socioeconomic status or racial composition in an unstable housing market. It helps to bring together diverse elements from the literature on neighborhood change, sub-market interrelationships, filtering and housing preferences. Unlike filtering, however, the arbitrage process is a direct response to changes in preferences.

Outline of the Model

The model, as outlined in Leven's study of St. Louis (Leven et al., 1976) begins with an aggregate mismatch between housing supply and demand which triggers a shift in the boundaries between neighborhoods. The dynamic aspect of the process is a change in the expectations of households regarding the future flow of housing services in that neighborhood. What might otherwise be an orderly process of change, say from higher-income to lower-income occupants, can become chaotic if, as in many American cities, residents' anticipations of neighborhood change also involve racial transition and the deterioration of neighborhood quality. This uncertainty creates a self-generating process in which expectations become self-fulfilling and the rate of transition accelerates.

To illustrate how the process works, we can draw on Leven's simplified model of two adjoining neighborhoods—one of high-income households and one of low income. Further, the authors assume that households in the high-status area have access to new housing located outside these two neighborhoods, while low-income households do not. In addition, they assume that most households prefer to live in neighborhoods of similar status (and presumably similar race). These preferences are then expressed in four different sets of prices within the two-neighborhood system: the price for (1) high-income households in the center of the high-status area, (2) for high-income households near the boundary of the low-status area, (3) for low-income households near the boundary of the high-status area, (4) for low-income households in the center of the low-status area.

The boundaries and prices in these subareas may in theory remain stable. More likely, however, given some exogenous change, such as an increase in the demand for housing by one or other group (through in-migration, demographic change, or income growth), the boundary between the neighborhoods will move. Which way it moves depends on which group is expanding (or contracting). Conventionally, and as most studies show, it has been the expansion of low-income migrant groups which puts pressure on the high-income area—creating what Harvey (1973) called a "blow-out" effect. Increased demand and continued deterioration of the poorest housing stock within the low-income area, combined with the filtering-down of housing in the high-income area, set the stage for the operation of an "arbitrage" process.

The explanation for the four sets of house prices is that higher-income households will demand a *locational discount* for living near the low-income area. Similarily, lower-income households living near the high-income area will pay a *premium* for that location. This premium might arise either because the latter simply want to improve their housing conditions, or they may actually prefer living near those of higher status. More likely, however, they are forced to pay these premiums

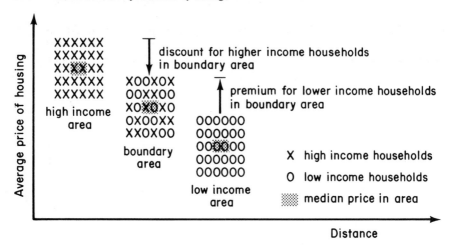

Fig. 7.2. The dynamics of residential transition: the arbitrage model (adapted from Leven et al., 1976).

in order to out-bid higher income households, even when the latters' bids include the discount. As a result, median prices decline from a high in the center of the high-status area through the boundary zone, to a low in the center of the poorest area. An outline of these conditions is given in Figure 7.2.

How the Process Works

The arbitrage process follows from these assumptions on household preferences and expectations set within an overall context of disequilibrium in the housing market. The story is a familiar one. Higher-income households perceive a future decline in their housing bundle through neighborhood transition and seek to move out. They also have the choice, and attraction, of newer housing. Those who stay as the boundary moves will find their property discounted. High-income migrants into the boundary area will lower their respective bids. Lower-income households, without the same degree of choice in housing and faced with a shrinking supply of housing in their area (through deterioration, demolition, or abandonment), are forced into the initially high-income neighborhood. The only "profitable" market alternative is to convert—or "arbitrage"—housing for the wealthy into housing for the poor. If, as noted, the low-income households are also racially different, the transition is accelerated and price changes become accentuated, but the sequence is much the same.

The outcome of this process, as in the traditional filtering process, is that the discount attached to housing formerly occupied by high-income households results in a lack of maintenance and physical deterioration. This may occur because of an oversupply of such housing, if higher-income groups move out rapidly, as well as the expectation of lower incomes among those moving in. In fact, because of these expectations, house values start to drop even before the transition begins, as existing owners undertake to devalue their property simply to "get out." The end of this cycle of changing expectations and continued deterioration is the abandonment of housing (see Leven et al., 1976, p. 39 and the following chapter).

In conclusion, the dynamic of arbitrage, when set in motion, continues precisely because of disequilibrium in the housing market. Falling prices, physical neglect, and declining incomes produce a "syndrome" of declining household and landlord expectations. These expectations are reinforced by the behavior of institutional lenders, such as banks and SLAs, who then withdraw their investments or demand higher down-payments. Other actors, such as speculators, may intercede by purchasing housing, but only to extract a quick return, further accelerating the process of underinvestment and deterioration. The process, of course, is not inevitable, but when it begins it is difficult, if not almost impossible, to reverse.

HOUSING LINKAGES, MULTIPLIERS, AND VACANCY CHAINS

Another relative of the filtering model, and a technique for directly linking the housing units involved in household relocations, is that of vacancy chains. More a method than a theory, vacancy chains provide a useful index of linkages within the housing stock. A vacancy chain may be defined as:

> . . . the sequence of moves made by a vacancy subsequent to its arrival in the system . . . where each vacancy is created by the construction of a new unit or by the "death" of a family (White, 1971).

The logic of the vacancy chain model is that a new vacancy opens up a unit to be occupied by a given household. The unit previously occupied by that household, in turn, then becomes available to a second household, and so on. These relocations can be seen as forming a linked sequence or chain in response to the creation of the initial vacancy. Note that it is the vacancy which moves, a difficult concept to grasp, and that the vacancy is said to be displaced when a household moves in.

The principal measure of interest is the number of moves (or chain links) generated by a new vacancy and the reasons for termination of the chain. When the household moving into that unit is new (newly-formed or an in-migrant), the chain ends (chain length = 1). Figure 7.3 provides a simple illustration of chains of 2 and 3 links in length. In addition, one can measure the spatial pattern of the chains and the characteristics of households and the housing units involved at each link.

Applications and Empirical Evidence

Aside from some early applications in the real estate literature (see Firestone, 1951), the vacancy chain approach has been applied with one or more of the

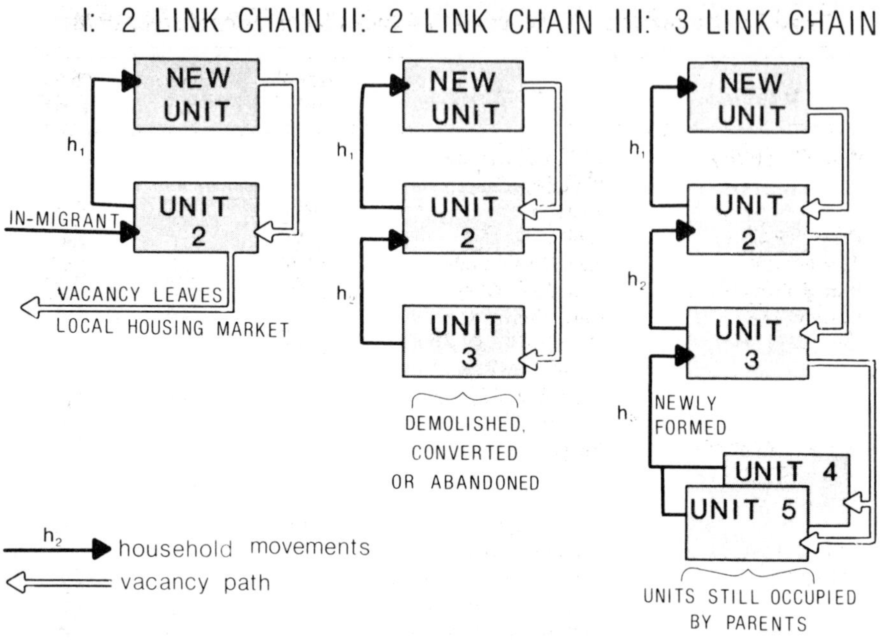

I: 2 LINK CHAIN II: 2 LINK CHAIN III: 3 LINK CHAIN

Fig. 7.3. Examples of the vacancy chain model.

following objectives in mind: (1) as a descriptive measure of the *multiplier* effect of the construction of new housing units, i.e., the number of moves made possible by constructing a new unit (the chain length); (2) as a means of measuring the *benefits* to households resulting from relocations generated through new construction, in terms of whether their housing conditions are improved (i.e., filtering); (3) as a means of evaluating *linkages* between housing sub-markets.

The technique has been used most extensively to measure the first two dimensions of housing turnover. Kristof (1965) used it to evaluate the filtering process and the distribution of housing benefits in New York City. Lansing et al. (1969) applied it in order to trace household relocations across the United States, while White (1971) formally introduced the concept of "chains of opportunity" to housing research.[7] More recently, there have been numerous applications of vacancy chains to the distribution of moves between tenure types and locations in specific cities, including Minneapolis-St. Paul (Adams, 1973), Detroit (Sands, 1976), Glasgow (Watson, 1974), Manchester (Jones, 1978), and Toronto (Sharpe, 1978). Table 7.5 summarizes the results of these and other studies with reference to the average length of the chains.

The empirical evidence is very mixed. Chain lengths tend to be short and variable—from 1.0 to about 2.4 in the cities in Table 7.5. This variability is attributable

Table 7.5. Estimates of the Length of Vacancy Chains (after Sharpe, 1978)*

Author	Study area	Year of survey	Sample size	Chain length
Firestone (1951)	Montreal, Ottawa, Winnipeg, Calgary, Victoria	1949	500	1.3
Kristof (1965)	New York, N.Y.	1963	65	2.4
Pack (1970)	New Haven, Conn.	1969	151	1.9[a]
Brueggeman (1971)	Columbus, Ohio	1969	658	2.3[b]
Duffy (1972)	Christchurch, N.Z.	1971	584	1.9
Adams (1973)	Minneapolis–St. Paul Public housing	1972		
	(senior citizens)		116	2.0
	Private ownership		93	2.2
Department of the Environment (n.d.)	England	1971	363	1.5
Watson (1974)	Central Clydeside Conurbation	1970	896	1.7
Sands and Bower (1974)	Rochester, N.Y.	1973		
	Inner city (subsidized)		75	2.2
	Inner city (private)		77	1.7
	Suburban (subsidized)		85	1.8
	Suburban (private)		58	1.8
Sharpe (1976)	Toronto, Ontario	1971	263	1.5
Romsa (1977)	Windsor, Ontario	1972	157	2.1[c]
	Single detached		90	2.2
	Condominium		67	1.8

Notes:
*The size and composition of the samples, and the method of calculation of chain length, vary considerably in each of these studies. As a result, the chain lengths are shown in this format for illustrative purposes only. See Sharpe (1978) for references.

[a]Mean chain length calculated by the author from data provided in Pack (1970), Table 2.

[b]Weighted mean chain length calculated by the author from data provided in Brueggeman et al. (1972), Table 2.

[c]Weighted mean chain length calculated by the author from data provided in Romsa (1977).

both to the diversity of the housing stocks in each city and the weakness of the method itself. Chain lengths tend to be shorter in rapidly growing cities where more housing is occupied by new households, and in others such as Glasgow where demolitions for slum clearance have removed many of the existing units vacated for newly-built units. Chains also tend to be shorter for public sector housing construction.

The routes taken by housing vacancies and the reasons for termination of the chain are highly diverse. In a study of chains created by newly constructed units in Toronto, Sharpe (1978) showed that most vacancies are quickly dislodged at link one through their occupancy by new households (21%) or in-migrants (26%) or by their removal from the stock. Only 33% moved into link two and 17% to link three. Very few vacancies pass into link four. The average chain length—the multiplier—was only 1.5.

Evaluation

Vacancy chains have come in for substantial criticism, largely because of their weak theoretical base. One obvious criticism is that the actual links in the chain may be but accidents of chance and that it is misleading to put them together in a sequence which by its nature implies a causal linkage. The households involved usually do not know each other, except perhaps in marginal pairs, nor is there any other actor in the transaction process which knows all the units or households linked in the chain. While this is true at an individual level, the aggregate rates of movement of vacancies through different spatial or hierarchical sub-markets does provide, in a more restricted sense, a descriptive index of interactions between such sub-markets, and of the turnovers generated by new construction.

In terms of measuring whether or not filtering improves the quality of housing available to the poor, however, the vacancy chain is clearly an unsuitable technique. The poor seldom appear in the vacancy chains recorded in most empirical studies, except for those beginning with public sector construction (Watson, 1974), and when they do appear the evidence that their housing conditions are improved as a result is inconsistent. Of those studies which have included average price (or rent) of housing units at each link, most have not found a consistent decline in such prices through descending links in the chain.

This suggests that the main beneficiaries of new construction (the multiplier) are households in roughly similar levels of the housing market to those entering the new home market. This, in turn, suggests that the level of new construction may be the critical variable. Indeed, some studies have shown chain lengths to be greater for lower-priced housing units. Thus, the vacancy chain may still have a useful descriptive role in monitoring the links between levels of new construction and the existing stock.

SPATIAL VARIATIONS IN HOUSING PRICES

It has already been documented in previous sections that housing prices vary systematically across an urban area. Since price is in fact the most common index of housing market performance, despite its many measurement difficulties (Wilkinson and Archer, 1973; Quigley, 1978), it warrants special attention here.

Determinants of Spatial Price Variations

Attempts to account for the actual variations of house prices (and rents) over an urban area at one point in time have tended to focus on four sets of factors:

> the *structural characteristics* of the house (size, age, style, quality) and its improvements (number of baths, garage, modern kitchen, etc.);
>
> *external neighborhood characteristics:* the character and quality of the local physical and social environment, including physical amenities, racial composition and local tax rates;
>
> *location*, particularly accessibility to places of work, shopping and recreation;
>
> *institutional* behavior; financial and real estate agents.

These four sets of explanatory variables mirror our earlier definition of the flow of housing services. Table 7.6 summarizes the variables used in several of the better known studies of house prices.

Clearly there is now a sufficient inventory of empirical studies to allow us to generalize about the sources of house price variations, at least in cross section (at one point in time). Again, the results vary with the urban area studied, its local topography, building history, transportation system, social composition and its rate of growth. They also vary depending on the methods used (primarily various forms of regression), the level of aggregation (individual units or areal groupings), and, of course, the variables selected. Table 7.6 amply demonstrates the diversity of hypothesized predictor variables.

Most studies, however, have reconfirmed that measures of the attributes of the housing stock are overwhelmingly dominant. In particular, as one might expect, these include the size of the housing unit (in floor area or lot size), the number of bedrooms, and the level of improvements. Among the latter, the presence of a garage or air conditioning are often highly significant in differentiating relative house values. Ball and Kirwin (1977) found the number of rooms to be the only consistent variable in accounting for price differences across all areas of Bristol, except for the inner city (where the presence of central heating was critical).

Neighborhood and environmental variables do influence house prices but with little apparent consistency from one area to another. Some relationships are perhaps obvious: housing values do tend to be higher in areas with more attractive physical environments, scenic views, less air pollution, and of course more homogeneous higher-income neighbors. In part this diversity is a simple measurement problem, given the difficulty of finding suitable measures of either the neighborhood or the environment. In part it also reflects the fact that environment differences, unlike the number of bedrooms, are not valued the same way from one neighborhood to another. This is not to suggest that the role of "neighborhood" factors can be avoided; far from it. Instead they require a careful assessment based on individual case studies.

Variables denoting ethnicity, race, and recent immigration do emerge as more consistent correlates of housing price differences, at least in those urban areas which have a heterogeneous population and a segmented housing market (McKay,

Table 7.6. Determinants of Housing Value: A Sample of Recent Studies

Author and date	City	Dependent variable	Location variables	Race/ethnic/class	Neighborhood variables		Housing variables	
					Neighborhood characteristics	Environmental quality	Housing characteristics	Housing improvements
Kain and Quigley (1970)	St. Louis	House price	Distance to CBD	% white	Median schooling, crime index	—	5 factors (from 39 variables), Age, no. of rooms, lot area	No. of baths
Wilkinson and Archer (1973)	Leeds	Factor analysis results	Distance to CBD	Socioeconomic index	Residential dens., No. of schools/pop.	—	House type, age, no. of rooms, area	Attics, bedrooms, garage, bath, inside toilet
Berry and Bednarz (1975)	Chicago	House price	Distance to CBD	% Blacks % Cubans/Mexicans % Irish	Med. family income, % Apts., migration rate	SO_2 levels, particulates	Sq. ft., age, lot area	Air cond., garage, improved basement, No. of baths
Ball and Kirwin (1977)	Bristol	Purchase price + improvements	Distance to CBD	Fitted to social areas	Nonresidential street	—	Bungalows, No. rooms, age, floor & plot areas	Central heating, garage, amenities, condition
Sumka (1977)	North Carolina (small cities)	Annual contract rent	Distance to CBD	% Blacks	Population density, Average rent, Lot value	—	Dwelling size, lot area, tenure: length of tenure, a lease, resident landlord	Plumbing, furnished, heating, quality
Palm (1978)	San Francisco	House price trends	Distance to city (for suburbs)	Chicano . . . all other variable are principal components . . .	Occupation, demographic uniformity, taxes, crime rates	Scenic views, air pollution	New housing, single-family owner-occupied	F.H.A. mortgages

1977; Berry, 1979). The difficulty however is separating out the effects of ethnicity or race per se from those with which they are commonly associated, such as low-income, poor-quality housing and neighborhood disamenities. The specific question, "do minority groups pay more for housing" is taken up in detail in the next chapter.

Finally, accessibility to the CBD now appears to be relatively less significant in accounting for house price variations. This is also not surprising, as Hoyt (1939) demonstrated long ago, since in the multi-centered modern metropolis with several major work locations one would not expect the distance-to-CBD relationship to exert its previous dominance. It is still there, in that the per unit price of housing services generally declines outwards from the city center, but it is swamped by structural attributes of the housing stock, by neighborhood differences and by the growth and expansion of local suburban labor markets. In some cities, we now find that residential land prices increase slightly as one goes outward from the center.

Variations in House Price Changes

Even less research is available on factors accounting for spatial variations in the rate of house price changes. Here researchers are confronted with severe data as well as analytical problems (Richardson, Vipond, and Furby, 1975). Data on house price trends, suitability disaggregated, are scarce and of uncertain quality. If, for example, prices are based on market transactions, then there is the problem that price differences will in part reflect the different units on the market at each time (the "composition" effect–Chapter 2). In addition, an examination of house price changes draws us back full circle to reconsider processes of neighborhood change as well as the overall level of inflation in prices.

In general, studies have shown that variables which are significant in accounting for different levels of house prices in cross section do not perform nearly as well for changes in those levels over time (Berry, 1976; Palm, 1977; Morrison, 1978). For example, Palm (1977) found that a small but nonetheless significant proportion of price trends among municipalities in the San Francisco area were related to differences in socioeconomic status (income), the level of municipal services, and the presence of racial minorities. But these differences are in part also related to the existence of distinct sub-markets, which as Straszheim (1975) notes, can lead to substantial price differences at least over short periods of time.

These relationships, as Palm (1977) concludes, are due as much to institutional behavior as to correlations between the variables themselves. In other words, they are the result of non-market forces as well as market forces. Chapter 4 also included an example of the price effects of these forces from Harvey's research on housing sub-markets in Baltimore. One of the key variables in the Baltimore study was the spatial pattern of mortgage-lending behavior. Palm (1977), in fact, identified a negative correlation between the presence of FHA-insured mortgages and price changes, presumably reflecting the absence of conventional sources of mortgage financing in those areas.

Other more traditional variables are also important. Changes in accessibility and in the location of employment do influence house price trends. These effects, however, are often long-term or highly localized, such as those which result from subway construction or from redevelopment pressures (Maher, 1974). Moreover, over the longer term, these trend differences tend to even out in line with overall levels of price inflation in that urban area. One useful index of spatial differences in price changes is the relative increase in the price of older houses compared to new houses in most North American cities (James, 1977). This trend, part of the revitalization movement we discuss subsequently, has reduced the price differences between central city and suburb.

Any review of this literature suggests just how difficult it is to rank the determinants of relative house prices, at one point in time or over time. As Stafford (1978) notes, there is no unique theory of residential location and house prices which can accommodate such a diverse range of characteristics as is evident in the variables listed above. These variables interact in such complex ways as to defy simple generalization, except perhaps by some real estate agents.

Hedonic Price Estimates

Studies of housing prices are complicated by the fact that housing is not a homogeneous good (or social service). As argued earlier, housing consists of a bundle of attributes, which we might expect individual households to value somewhat differently and perhaps independently. Consequently, we might also expect that different prices would be attached to these attributes, although largely as *implicit* prices. The price of housing units we observe in the aggregate, then, is a "composite" price of all of these attributes.

The technique commonly used to measure such implicit "attribute" prices is *hedonic price estimation*. Typically, such prices are estimated through standard multiple regression techniques in which each regression coefficient is a measure of the price effect of adding an incremental unit of an attribute (a bathroom, a new kitchen, air conditioning, etc.).[8] The actual forms of the analysis differ in detail but are similar in design (see Sumka, 1977).

Analyses of this form have been widely used to estimate aggregate prices for the bundle of housing services and in particular to determine how prices change when one or other measure of housing quality is controlled (see for example, Ball, 1973; Kain and Quigley, 1975; Carvalho, Hum, Sahay, and Falconer, 1976; Quigley, 1978; Rosen, 1978). In fact, several of the studies cited above would qualify as hedonic price analyses. Berry and Bednarz (1975) used similar techniques to examine the relationship between market values and assessment ratings. Others have used such techniques to test for systematic differences in the prices of housing between cities (Rosen, 1978), between subareas of a city (Goodman, 1978), as well as changes in price levels over time (Palm, 1978).

The results of these studies are widely available and need not be repeated here (see Quigley, 1978). They do, however, show the existence of wide differences in the "implicit" attached to specific housing attributes, both between sub-markets and over time. The detailed results of such analyses are, of course, specific to the area, data base, and methodology used. Nevertheless, they do reiterate the importance of viewing housing as a composite good (or bundle of services), of spatially disaggregating price into distinctive sub-markets, where they exist, and of linking specific housing attributes to changes in local demand and policy initiatives.

REVITALIZATION, GENTRIFICATION, AND THE RETURN-TO-THE-CITY MOVEMENT

One of the most interesting and visible trends of the 1970s has been the reversal of declining housing quality and social status in some inner city neighborhoods. This process—known by such labels as revitalization, gentrification, resettlement or white-painting—in turn raises the issue of whether there has been a "return-to-the-city" movement on the part of suburban middle- and higher-income households. It also links our previous discussions of supply changes within the existing stock to that of recent shifts in housing demand and prices, and it raises fundamental questions for both research and policy.

Definitions and Empirical Evidence

Perhaps the broadest term is revitalization. Generally it refers to an improvement in housing and neighborhood quality, usually combined with an increase in the average incomes of those who live in the area. Gentrification has a more explicit class connotation in which "traditional working-class neighborhoods are invaded and occupied by middle and upper income groups" (Hamnett, 1973). The return-to-the-city question then becomes a matter of determining who exactly is involved in this transition, where they come from, and their status relative to that of the previous residents.

Revitalization not only takes several forms but derives from different sources. It may be done privately, by individuals or corporations, involving either streets or single housing units. It might also occur through the efforts of quasi-public housing associations and self-help groups or through direct public grants action. The following summary is concerned primarily with the first form—private, spontaneous revitalization—which has been the topic of most interest and, at least in North America, is the most substantial. The emphasis here is on housing as both cause and effect of the revitalization process.

Despite overt public awareness, and considerable policy interest, there is surprisingly little comprehensive data on revitalization and gentrification and few detailed studies of how the process takes place, in part because of measurement difficulties.[9] A recent study by the Urban Land Institute (1977) estimated that some private revitalization is taking place in about 75% of all U.S. cities with populations over 500,000. The bulk of the activity, however, is concentrated in relatively few cities. Lipton (1977) has provided some evidence of the extent of inner city revitalization in U.S. cities, through an examination of change over time in the number of neighborhoods of above-average income and occupational status located within a fixed distance (2 miles) of the CBD. The resulting picture is very mixed. Some cities showed an increase in the number of such areas (Philadelphia, Houston), others showed a decrease (Atlanta), while still others (Newark) have no such areas, period. Cybriwsky (1978) and Gale (1979) provide fascinating case studies of the revitalization process in Philadelphia and Washington, respectively. We draw on these studies to demonstrate the conditions which act to encourage revitalization in some cities and not others and what social and neighborhood changes accompany revitalization.

The cities most likley to witness inner city revival are those with a combination of the following attributes: (1) a historic and attractive central area, (2) a high proportion of professional occupations and office jobs, (3) a tight housing market, (4) older housing which has some architectural merit, (5) some inner city amenities (e.g., parks), (6) an absence of racial strife, and (7) relative difficulties in commuting to new suburban locations. It should be stressed, however, that there has always been some shifting back and forth between low- and high-income areas, as Hoyt (1939) demonstrated, and that there have always been upper-income areas within easy access to the central area.

Why the trend? Although the conditions which generate revitalization vary with the city in question, a number of common denominators can be identified. Demographic and employment shifts have resulted in smaller families and more two-income households, making a choice of housing in the inner city both more attractive and more feasible. Young, smaller households mean fewer children and thus less need for outside play space and less concern for school quality. The increase in two-income households has also substantially increased the disposable income available to purchase older housing (which normally requires a higher down-payment), while their need to consider two journeys-to-work often renders a central city location more attractive (Kern, 1977). In addition, the general slowdown in new residential construction in the mid-1970s increased the costs of new suburban housing relative to the older stock. At the same time, the difficulties and costs of commuting from increasingly more distant suburban estates has placed a greater premium on accessibility to central area jobs and amenities.

Finally, there may also have been a shift in tastes and housing preferences. Older housing does seem to be in vogue, at least housing of specific architectural styles, and different life-styles appear to value a central city location as both "trendy" and amenable. The difficulty here is one separating changes in life-style and housing tastes from the demographic transition which has resulted in proportionately more households in home-buying age cohorts during the 1970s.

Why are certain locations selected? In nearly all studies, such areas tend to be conveniently located near the city center and to contain housing which is of good quality but (initially) relatively inexpensive. Cybriwsky (1978) also noted that in the case of Fairmount in Philadelphia the process of racial transition was not well-advanced and appeared to have been halted. In fact, the success of that neighborhood in resisting racial turnover seemed to pave the way for the subsequent invasion of higher-income groups. In addition, there is little doubt that areas of unusual housing design (e.g., Victorian townhouses in the U.K.), in which the stock is old, but not too old, and which contain or are near to environmental amenities, cultural institutions, or attractive shopping, are those selected for revitalization first (Gale, 1979).

Private developers can also do much to create an image for a neighborhood favorable to revitalization, presumably because they own the housing involved, and financial institutions can act to expedite the transition by extending mortgage lending to what may become "in-areas." In Britain, parallel research on the role of financial institutions in mortgage lending, and specifically the impact of government housing improvement grants, has shown that such financing has accelerated the rate at which lower-income areas have been invaded and occupied by higher-income groups (Williams, 1976, 1978; Duncan, 1977; Boddy and Gray, 1979).

Social, Neighborhood, and Policy Impacts

The most obvious impact of revitalization is the extensive physical improvement of the housing stock in such areas, and of course much higher prices and rents. The density of occupancy also normally declines with smaller households (and perhaps with fewer dwelling units). At the same time, and this is the policy dilemma (Chapter 9), it reduces the inventory of low-cost, lower quality housing available at that location. In the private market, the dislodged original residents are simply ignored, especially low-income tenants, although some homeowners do escape with sufficient payment to purchase improved housing elsewhere.

In terms of external effects, the quality of the local residential environment also improves considerably, but in the process the entire social fabric of the neighborhood changes. Social relations within the community are dramatically altered, as are the relations between that community and the city at large. Similarly, the demand for local services shifts, sometimes "up-market" services, in other cases toward fewer services (e.g., schools). Equally marked changes take place in overall land use densities and patterns, in the local retail structure, and in the political orientation of that community. In the case of Fairmount, revitalization also reduced racial tension, but apparently replaced it with class tension.

Many of these changes are not by definition bad or good. That depends on one's perspective. Neither is the process entirely new in historical terms, nor is it restricted to the inner city.

Nor is there sufficient evidence to conclude that revitalization represents a movement of certain groups back to the city, although some have no doubt done so (James, 1977). Many of the households involved are young, newly-formed households who are buying their first home. Many of these already lived in the city rather than the suburbs or were newcomers (Gale, 1979). Thus revitalization does not (as yet?) appear to have altered the inner city-suburban migration balance significantly. Yet it has altered the housing conditions of selected parts of the older city and challenged our views of what the future holds for those areas. Strategic changes in public policy could dramatically alter the rate of private market revitalization, either upward or downward. It is, however, unlikely to be the solution to all or even a majority of the problems of deteriorated and unwanted housing in our inner cities.

NOTES

[1]The first such problem is whether to use current income or some measure of permanent (long-term) income or accumulated wealth (see Bossons, 1978). The second problem relates to determining the value of housing when that housing has not been on the market for some time.

[2]Household dissolutions occur through either a death of one or both spouses, divorce, undoubling, remarriage, or with first-time marriages by two individuals previously living as separate households.

[3]Household formation and dissolution rates are also related to income. In Reid's (1962) classic study of income and housing, she demonstrated that a 1% rise in income led to a 2.3% reduction in the number of other persons attached to the household.

[4]For comparison purposes, see Grigsby's (1963, p. 63) diagram of household movements in the Philadelphia housing market.

[5]The distinction here is between market (active) filtering, when in the process of moving the household "enters" the market, and nonmarket (passive) filtering when the household's housing status may change, but without going through a market transaction.

[6]Ratcliff (1949) made the same point over 30 years earlier when he concluded: "The end product of filtering is substandard housing; thus filtering produces the very blight which we seek to remedy" (p. 333).

[7]The concept derives from studies of the sequence of job changes within large organizations which follow from the creation of a vacancy at different levels in the organization.

[8]To consider these coefficients as "prices" one has to assume that the urban housing market is in some kind of long-run equilibrium. This is analytically convient but highly unlikely in reality.

[9]One dimension of this problem is the difficulty of differentiating between an area undergoing substantial maintenance and repairs and one undergoing revitalization. What is implied, but seldom verified, in this literature is that the housing stock in the latter area has significantly changed its position in the hierarchy of all housing units in the city such that it is now in a different sub-market. As shown in Chapter 4, however, sub-markets are not easy to measure.

Chapter 8

Market Failures and Housing Problems

Despite the vast improvements in housing supply and quality noted in Chapter 3, housing remains a persistent and divisive social issue in all western countries. Why this apparent paradox? Perhaps the basic reason, as previously emphasized, is that housing problems are to a considerable extent subjectively defined, depending on the particular social, economic, and political conditions prevailing at any given time, and on our attitudes regarding living standards. It seems that our expectations have grown even faster than our record of housing improvements.[1] In addition, housing remains a divisive issue precisely because the inequalities in the distribution of housing have become even more prominent as overall prosperity increased.

This chapter can do little more than illustrate the range of current and emerging housing problems in western industrial cities. Rather than simply inventory all such problems here, we undertake to explore the processes underlying a selection of these problems in more depth. Those selected are ones which relate to the themes developed in earlier chapters, notably Chapters 2, 3, and 4, and those which have an important spatial dimension.

The Range of Housing Problems

A majority of countries agree they share most, if not all, of the following types of housing problems:

> *substandardness:* far too many households still live in housing which is physically substandard or located in substandard neighborhoods.
>
> *inequitable distribution of supply:* although aggregate housing supply now equals or exceeds the number of households in almost all countries, this supply is

inequitably distributed by income group, by race and ethnic status, family size, and by location.

needs of special groups: groups such as the elderly, the handicapped, single-parent families, "problem" families, the young, and the transient are often faced with severe difficulties in finding housing suited to their needs and budgets.

the very poor: these people, although numerically small, are the all but forgotten members of the housing problem even in the public sector. In almost all countries, the amount of public housing available is inadequate, and in some cases they are excluded from the public sector because their incomes are too low.

segregation and discrimination: all too often the process of allocating housing—in both the private as well as the public sectors—produces a pervasive spatial separation of social groups by income and ethnicity.

obsolesence, underinvestment and deterioration: in many urban areas the older housing stock suffers from an acute and long-standing condition of inadequate investment in maintenance and repairs.

price escalation and affordability: for many households, the recent inflation in housing prices and in the costs of owning (mortgage, taxes) or renting is assuming an uncomfortably large proportion of their income.

financing, subsidies, and the distribution of benefits: this massively complex area incorporates such problems as the proportion of a nation's national wealth and productive resources which should be directed to housing, the extent to which certain sectors of society and of the housing industry should be subsidized, and the unequal distribution of benefits which result from housing policies (see Chapter 9).

supply problems, instability, and concentration: the private housing industry, as described in Chapter 5, remains beset by wide fluctuations in rates of new construction, instability in financing and in labor force requirements, maintenance of liquidity, corporate concentration, property speculation, and corruption.

local market imperfections: most local housing markets display a variety of illogical, or illegal, and certainly unfair practices—e.g., under-the-table land deals, collusion among estate agents, excessive transaction fees, price fixing and price jumping (called gazumping in the U.K.), bribery and corruption—which benefit those in positions of power.

In the following section, aspects of these problems are regrouped under four broad headings, within which selected examples of each problem are presented. The four headings are: housing quality and substandardness, segregation and racial discrimination, obsolesence and abandonment, and prices and affordability.

The Sources of Housing Problems: Market or Policy Failures?

It is necessary at the outset to see these problems in their political (and ideological) as well as historical context. In some instances, perhaps most commonly, students of housing interpret these problems as "failures" of the market and thus the rationale for government intervention (Downs, 1975). Others, who place more faith in the functioning of the market, see such problems as precisely the result of extensive government intervention in the housing market and of misdirected and mismanaged public policies (L. B. Smith, 1977). Still others view such problems not as failures of the market process but as the inevitable outcomes of a "laissez-faire" market system in which housing is produced for profit rather than to meet needs and in which inequalities are an essential part of the system (Harvey, 1977b; Boddy and Gray, 1979).

All three views are partly correct. The crux of the debate is the ability or inability of the private market to provide adequate housing for all. Few would now subscribe to the view that it can do so. In each of these views, the policy response is also rather different, varying from reduced government involvement to "corrective" policy measures and to outright nationalization of the housing sector. This text cannot be expected to sort out the relative merits of each interpretation, but it can at least alert the reader to the diversity of perspectives which is necessary in understanding housing problems.

HOUSING QUALITY, SUBSTANDARDNESS, AND INEQUALITIES

Previous sections have demonstrated the dramatic improvement in the quality of urban housing in western societies and the corresponding reduction in the incidence of inadequate or substandard housing. They have also demonstrated that quality is an elusive concept, and that it is not, as Goodman (1978) argues, reducible to a single composite index. In fact, for most census agencies, housing quality has presented a statistical nightmare, as reflected in the wide margins of error and frequent changes in definitional criteria.

Traditionally, public concern has focused on physical measures of quality, such as structural defects, the absence of plumbing facilities, or standards of occupancy such as overcrowding which submit to easier measurement. As these problems have diminished in importance over the last two decades, attention has shifted to the use of other indices of quality, including household furnishings, excessive costs, social satisfaction, environmental quality and neighborhood services—measures which define the quality of "living" as much as the quality of housing.

Quality Improvements and Inequitable Supply

Chapter 3 provided aggregate statistics on housing quality changes. Between 1940 and 1976, for example, the proportion of all housing in the U.S. lacking some or all plumbing facilities declined from 45% to less than 3%. During the same period, the frequency of dilapidated housing declined from about 18% to less than 4%. Even a more comprehensive attempt to measure quality, based on 15 variables relating to physical quality, still identified only 8% of all occupied units as in need of some rehabilitation (Table 8.1). In the same survey, only 2.8% of households interviewed considered their housing as "poor" (Weicher, 1978). In almost all surveys, well over 80% of households describe their housing as adequate.

Space standards have also improved. The proportion of married couples sharing their accommodation with another household (i.e., doubling up) decreased from 7% in 1940 to just over 1.2% in 1976. Similarly, overcrowding declined from over 20% to less than 5% in the same period. The principal reasons for these increases

Table 8.1. Percentage of Households Occupying Housing In Need of
Rehabilitation in U.S., By Income and Race, 1976[a]

Race of head of household	Average annual income			Total all households[b]
	Less than $10,000	$10,000– $19,000	$20,000 or more	
Black	24.9	11.5	7.1	19.6
White	10.6	4.7	2.4	6.4

Note: [a]Defined as a unit with incomplete or inconsistent facilities (sewer, water, heating, light) or one with structural faults such as a leaking roof, wall cracks, falling plaster or inadequate wiring.
[b]Total = 8.1%.
Source: U.S. Congressional Budget Office, *Annual Housing Survey*, 1976.

have been the growth in supply and in personal income and social wealth, and current conditions tend to vary geographically in relation to the strength of an area's economic base and its rate of growth.

In many instances, the rate of improvement has been greatest among low-income and minority populations. Among non-whites, for example, the proportion lacking complete plumbing facilities declined between 1940 and 1976 from nearly 80% to less than 4%. Of the lowest 40% of the profile of household income, roughly those eligible for federal housing assistance, some 57%, were living in housing which was dilapidated or had inadequate facilities in 1950. By 1976, that proportion had declined to 12% (U.S. Congress, 1978).

Nevertheless, inequalities in the distribution of housing quality remain severe. Low-income households are still three times (12%) more likely to live in substandard housing than middle- or upper-income households (4%). As shown in Table 8.1, black households are also more than three times as likely to live in housing needing rehabilitation, or in housing which is without plumbing or is overcrowded (Headey, 1978). Moreover, non-whites are more likely to live in such conditions compared to whites, *at all income levels*. Similarly, in the U.K., colored households are also (in 1977) more than three times as likely as white households (23 to 7%) to live without adequate plumbing facilities (Central Statistical Office, 1979).

These inequalities are perhaps more obvious when set in their appropriate locational and neighborhood setting. Many of the low-income and racial minorities are trapped in older inner city areas, systematically cut off from access to the expanding employment opportunities in the suburbs and an adequate level of public services. Even when their own housing is structurally sound, as is often the case, the quality of housing and neighborhood services, in the sense defined in Chapter 2, are often unacceptably low (U.S., HUD, 1973; Downs, 1975). For those at the very bottom, the effects of poor housing and inadequate services are cumulative and socially destructive.

What we cannot easily or adequately convey here, however, is the truly appalling housing conditions in which many of these people live. It does not take much imagination to construct an image of deteriorating structures, garbage smells, leaking pipes, and of rat-infested halls, wall cavities, cellars, and alleys. Equally disturbing are the urban neighborhoods in which these households often live—dirty, vandalized, dangerous, and demoralizing. Numerous articulate authors, such as Herbert Gans, Jane Jacobs, and Lee Rainwater, have painted vivid pictures of life and living in such neighborhoods and the attitudes and behavior it encourages.

Although inadequate housing as such is not the cause of these conditions, it is one vehicle through which they are expressed. It can become a prison for the poor and the disadvantaged. We clearly have come a long way in achieving a decent home for all, and equally clearly inadequate housing will never be completely eliminated.[2] But there is obviously still a long way to go and an urgent need to reduce inequalities in housing quality, particularly those which include neighborhood services.[3]

Overcrowding: Of People or Houses?

Traditionally one of the most frequently used and important indices of housing quality, overcrowding has diminished rapidly in recent years as both a problem and a policy priority. As noted in Chapter 3, the level of overcrowding—using the current criteria of 1.00 or more persons per room—has decreased to the point where less than 5% of households are now classified as living in overcrowded conditions in the U.S. and 9% in the U.K. Yet one must remember that the number of people involved (over 10 million in the U.S.) is still numerically large, and that it will be a long time, if ever, before overcrowding is effectively eliminated.

It is somewhat ironic that as the problem itself has diminished, our understanding of the process has increased. Overcrowding is a state, a condition, of occupancy and thus it can refer to either housing units or households. It is also a highly fluid state (Grigsby and Rosenburg, 1975). For example, Moore and Clatworthy (1978) have demonstrated how variable the process is through their analyses of the changing conditions of individual housing units and households based on the annual enumerations conducted by the city of Wichita, Kansas. They show substantial shifts from year to year in the specific houses and households which are overcrowded, particularly in the rental sector (Table 8.2). Houses which were overcrowded last year frequently are not the same ones as those overcrowded this year. The previous household may have moved, to be replaced by a smaller household (<2.00 persons per bedroom) or one or more members of that household may leave, rendering it no longer overcrowded. Other houses remain consistently overcrowded, even if the households have changed, while some households remain overcrowded even when they move from one dwelling to another.

Overcrowding, then, is for many people a transitional state from which they may escape for only short periods of time. Although the tendency is to classify units as overcrowded, it is obviously preferable to follow households which are overcrowded wherever they move. It is only through disaggregate level data, for

Table 8.2. Transitions Among Overcrowded States, Wichita, Kansas, 1971–72[a]

	% shifting from overcrowding			Remaining overcrowded %	% of total overcrowded
	Unit demolished	Household moved	Unit no longer overcrowded		
Owned	2	17	14	67	7.9
Rental	4	55	7	34	9.9

Note: [a]2 bedrooms with more than 4 persons.
Source: Moore and Clatworthy, 1978.

individual housing units and households, that the dynamics of this condition can be understood and specific problem areas or households identified.

SEGREGATION, RACIAL DISCRIMINATION, AND CLOSED HOUSING MARKETS

One of the most pervasive characteristics of urban housing markets in western and pluralistic societies is their intense spatial segregation. One need only think of the Falls Road area in Belfast, Harlem in New York, or Watts in Los Angeles to solicit the appropriate images. This segregation varies widely among cities, regions, and countries in degree, extent, and in who is being segregated. It also differs in origin: the first is *voluntary* segregation, due to residential self-selection; the second is *involuntary*. The latter may result from differences in income or tastes among groups, or in the information available in the search for housing, or it may be caused by discrimination on the basis of ethnic origin, religion, lifestyle, or race. Although it is not possible to separate the effects of these processes precisely, our concern here is primarily with the latter.

Segregation and Access to Housing

Although the context and processes of discrimination differ, the results are often the same: one group is systematically denied access to its *fair share* of a nation's housing resources through the attitudes and behavior of others. These "others" might include real estate agents, bankers and financial institutions, government agencies, or any of the actors outlined in our earlier conceptualization of the housing market (Chapters 2 and 4). Generally, however, they are the social group which holds political power.

A recent and extensive assessment of racial discrimination and segregation in American urban markets, undertaken by the Office of Policy Development and Research in the Department of Housing and Urban Development, stressed the

Table 8.3. Aggregate Measures of Discrimination By Real Estate Agents
In the Search for Housing
(percent)

Search for:	Blacks and whites treated equally (1)	Whites favored (2)	Blacks favored (3)	Difference (2)–(3)
Rental housing	30.3	49.4	20.3	29.1
Housing for sale	10.5	55.5	34.0	21.5

Source: Yinger et al., 1978.

complexity of measuring discrimination as such, but concluded that the evidence of the existence and importance of discrimination was now overwhelming (Yinger et al., 1978). In a survey of the actual practices of real estate sales and rental agents, authors concluded that blacks faced discrimination in over 29% of their attempts to find rental housing and in nearly 22% of their attempts to find housing for sale (Table 8.3).[4] The difference between the two sectors is due, in part, to the simple fact that rental agents are much more likely to discriminate on the basis of a wide variety of criteria against people they do not expect will be good tenants. If one considers the more limited housing options open to them, as well as restricted sources of information, blacks are likely to encounter discrimination 75% of the time in the rental submarket and 64% of the time in terms of housing for sale. This also ignores the presence of *racial steering* by agents, i.e., directing black or minority households into particular areas or away from others.

The direct and indirect effects of this discrimination are clearly substantial. The disadvantaged group usually has less choice in housing than the majority population, consumes less housing at greater per unit cost and housing which is of lower quality. Since housing is inevitably married to a local environment, and since such groups tend to be restricted to poorer areas of the city, they also receive fewer and lower quality public services and are subject to higher costs (such as crime). Further, given that most segregated ghettoes are centrally located within urban areas, while jobs are increasingly decentralized, the same groups have lower accessibility to employment. The result is *cumulative*—a *vicious circle*—in which discrimination, low incomes, and residential location interact to perpetuate poverty, segregation, and housing inequalities.

The accumulated evidence on the spatial extent and configuration of segregation by race—the classic urban ghettoes—is now staggering and widely available (Rose, 1972; von Furstenburg, Harrison, and Horowitz, 1974; Kain and Quigley, 1975; Jones and Eyles, 1977; Lee, 1977; McKay, 1977; Schnare, 1978). We need not repeat this evidence. Instead, the following section focuses on one dimension of the process of discrimination: racial discrimination and price "mark-ups" or premiums for housing in American cities.

Racial Discrimination and Housing Premiums

The question "do blacks pay more for housing?" has been a long-standing issue in housing research (Muth, 1969; Lapham, 1971; Bonham, 1973; Olsen, 1974; Sumka, 1977; Yinger et al., 1978). The almost universal assertion is that they, along with other minority and racial groups, do pay more. In the majority of studies, housing located in predominantly black neighborhoods was shown to be more expensive than similar housing in neighborhoods which were exclusively white.

It is one thing, however, to assert the existence of a "racial" premium or mark-up for black households because of discrimination and "collusive-like" practices on the part of landlords, real estate agents, and financial intermediaries, and yet another to demonstrate it systematically by empirical observation and analysis. To do so requires that the researcher identify similar types of housing for comparison—i.e., essentially identical housing "bundles." This is extremely difficult to do given wide differences in housing style and quality within cities, coinciding with marked differences in neighborhood quality (e.g., in terms of schools and public services as well as levels of vandalism and crime). It is also difficult to separate, as Olsen (1974) notes, price discrimination due to households being poor or black, or likely both.

In assessing what are commonly called discriminatory "mark-ups" or premiums for housing, one then has to differentiate between two distinct types of discrimination, even when both are interrelated with race.

> *neighborhood or location "mark-ups"*—these are premiums paid for housing by all households in a given neighborhood because of the perceived disadvantages or costs of transitional and racially-mixed neighborhoods. These may arise because of the aversion of one racial group to living next to another group, or the view that racial change means more violence, increased crime and therefore higher costs to the owner or greater risk to the lender. These differentials are reflected in the prices (or rents) paid by *all* households in that area for similar housing units regardless of race.

> *racially discriminatory "mark-ups"*—these are premiums paid by members of one racial group, usually the minority, for similar housing within the same area, because of "overt" discrimination against households in that group.

Obviously, as the proportion of a neighborhood's population becomes increasingly black, however, the two forms of "mark-ups" become essentially the same.

Why might blacks pay more? Several different but complementary explanations are possible for why might blacks, or other racial minorities, might pay more for housing with identical attributes.

> *limited housing supply*—rapid growth of the minority population, combined with racial segregation which restricts housing choices, have acted to put upward pressures on prices and rents.

> *racial change and risk aversion*—landlords and real estate agents may be averse to renting (or selling) to black households because they perceive that racial change will lead to increased social problems and higher maintenance costs. They will

seek higher rents to compensate for these expected costs. Mortgage lenders may charge similar premiums on interest rates, or more likely restrict funds.

limited spatial mobility – blacks have more limited spatial mobility because of the newness of many to the urban area, their more restricted choice of job locations, and because of segregation.

limited equity – since blacks and other racial minority groups tend to have lower homeownership rates, they bring to the owner-occupied market fewer capital assets for down payments.

restricted information – as previously noted, blacks are likely to have less access to information sources on the housing market because of discriminatory practices by real estate agents and associations, and because of a reluctance to use services dominated by whites.

racial prejudice and preferences – if blacks are color blind, and whites prefer to live in neighborhoods dominated by those of similar race, then house prices or rents will be greater for blacks than whites in racially-mixed areas.

Empirical evidence. Despite this complexity, most empirical studies based on data for the 1950s and 1960s have demonstrated the existence of a significant relationship between racial composition and average house prices or rents. For example, King and Mieszkowski (1973) and Kain and Quigley (1970) found "mark-ups" for rental housing in all-black neighborhoods of New Haven and St. Louis, respectively, of roughly 8%. Sumka (1977) identified a similar mark-up in smaller urban areas in North Carolina. Schnare and Struyk (1976) found even greater mark-ups of 20 and 12% in Pittsburgh and Boston, respectively.

Yet the evidence is not consistent. Numerous studies, including those by Muth (1969), Lapham (1971), and Olsen (1974), found no significant differences. In their study of Chicago, Berry and Bednarz (1975) found a small discount for owner-occupied housing in all-black areas. Part of the difficulty here is in obtaining a "controlled" sample on which to base comparisons, and part is that such premiums or discounts do vary widely between cities, depending on prevailing conditions in the local housing market, as well as between rental and ownership sectors.

It is also clear that the premium differs with the racial composition of the neighborhood and with the degree of stability in that composition. In a study of five SMSAs, Gillingham (1973) found that mark-ups for black households varied from 9 to nearly 23% (Table 8.4). In three of the five cases, the premium increased in neighborhoods which were over 80% black, but the relationships, again, were complex and inconsistent.

There is additional evidence, however, which suggests that the relationship between race and housing prices may have changed significantly in recent years. Again referring to Schnare and Struyk's (1966) analysis, using 1960 data they found that rent levels were at a minimum (i.e., discounted) in mixed neighborhoods with 25% black populations, rising from there to a rent premium of 12% in all-black neighborhoods. But with 1970 data, they discovered that the premium had disappeared. Rents in all-black areas of Boston were at least 5% lower than those in all-white areas (Fig. 8.1). In Pittsburgh, the rent premium still existed for housing in all-black areas but it had been reduced from 20% to 7%.

Table 8.4. Rent Premiums Paid By Black Households in Five SMSAs

SMSA	Proportion of black household rents in mixed residential areas over rents for white households in all white areas		
	Blocks less than 20% black	Blocks 20–80% black	Blocks over 80% black
Chicago	12.8[a]	17.6[a]	22.9[a]
Detroit	6.4	9.3	10.3[a]
Washington	16.1[a]	2.2	2.1
Baltimore	13.1	18.8[a]	17.2[a]
St. Louis	5.8	4.7	11.4[a]

Note: [a]Regression significant at .05 level or higher.
Source: Gillingham, 1973, Table V-2.

Why might such a decline be taking place? Schnare and Struyk (1976) hypothesize that the traditional racial mark-up for housing derives not simply from discrimination, but, as argued above, from a shortage of reasonable quality housing in predominantly black neighborhoods. The 1950s and early 1960s were indeed periods of massive growth in the black population of the central cities of most

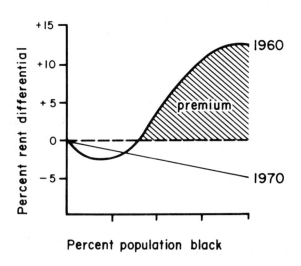

Fig. 8.1. Changing rent differentials in selected Boston neighborhoods, by race, 1960 and 1970 (after Schnare and Struyk, 1976).

major northern U.S. metropolitan areas, leading to a very high level demand for housing. The relatively inelastic supply of the housing stock in such areas, making it difficult to adjust supply to meet the new demands, combined with the limited locational alternatives available to blacks, meant that landlords and owners could charge a rent premium to the new migrants.

With the recent decline in the rate of black in-migration and of population growth generally, demand has subsequently declined. At the same time, housing supply has expanded through neighborhood racial transition and vacancies have increased. As a consequence, the permissible "mark-ups" on housing have declined or disappeared. It may also be true that recent federal legislation against discrimination in the selling and financing of housing, and policies for more *open housing* generally, have contributed to this trend. The evidence, however, is not yet sufficient to draw firm conclusions. We must await publication of the 1980 Census to obtain a more comprehensive picture.

OBSOLESENCE, PHYSICAL DECAY, AND ABANDONMENT

One of the universal problems of urban housing is that of maintaining the physical quality of the existing stock. We have all seen pictures of urban slums, deteriorating houses, and in many American and British cities the abandonment of housing. Given the pervasiveness of the filtering and arbitrage processes described in previous chapters, the racial discrimination-poverty cycle described earlier, and the obvious fact that buildings, like other capital goods, require substantial reinvestment in maintenance and repairs, some degree of obsolesence or deterioration is almost inevitable. The problem, then, arises when deterioration becomes widespread or when certain groups of households suffer as a result.

Concepts of Housing Obsolesence

The concept of obsolesence, as with housing quality generally, is in part a subjective concept. It is defined, most broadly, as a process leading to a decline in the ability of a structure to meet the demands placed on it, relative to other structures (Nutt et al., 1976). This decline results from three principal sources: (1) poor quality of initial construction, (2) wear and tear due to aging (as in Chapter 5), and (3) inadequate maintenance through misuse, abuse (overcrowding), or neglect. It is the latter—the question of a lack of investment—which to an extent incorporates aspects of the first two sources and which concerns us here.

Obsolesence, as it relates to the inability of a housing unit (or any building) to meet current needs, may reflect several different sources of change. A typology of obsolesence might include the following:

> *physical:* the deterioration of the physical structure through aging or the lack of maintenance;
>
> *style* (or social): due to changing tastes or rising standards of living;

functional: when the structure is inadequately designed or equipped for current uses;

economic: when it is no longer viable to maintain the structure due to high costs and low returns;

environmental: when the decline of a neighborhood renders it uneconomic, undesirable, or impossible to continue to maintain (or even occupy) a structure;

financial: when external constraints on credit (mortgages), maintenance and repair, and the property tax system discourage investment;

planning: or planning "blight," when a planning authority or other public agency through such actions as designating an area of clearance or renewal invites uncertainty and undermines the incentive for improvement.

These various forms of obsolesence are neither mutually exclusive nor independent. They overlap in numerous and complex ways, although most are reflected in the same outcomes: physical and economic decline. Each acts to produce a continuous downward "spiral" of disinvestment in the housing stock of many cities, culminating, in some instances, in a state of physical obsolesence which is not reversible.

Disincentives to Housing Improvements: The Prisoner's Dilemma

The spatial interrelationships—or externalities—linking housing units with a given geographic area play an important role in determining which areas of the city undergo improvement and which see this continued lack of investment. This process must be seen in the context of a market in which housing is individually owned (the "atomistic" market) and each owner is uncertain what his neighbor will do. In fact, it is in the interest of each owner not to tell. Under these conditions, and given certain external changes, it can be easily shown that the most common result will be that both owners do nothing—that neither invest in their property.

To illustrate the process, and the rationale for government intervention in land and housing markets, we draw on a simple example of decision making under uncertainty and adapt it to the housing situation (Davis and Whinston, 1966). In an urban area undergoing gradual deterioration, the presence of uncertainty about the future often produces a situation known as a *prisoner's dilemma*. Assume, as in Table 8.5, that we begin with a neighborhood consisting of only two resident homeowners (I and II), each of which has savings that could be invested either in the house or in safe bonds. Say the latter would each each a 5% return. Let's further assume that if both invest their savings in housing (option A) the cumulative result, through the spill-over effect noted earlier, would be not 5 but a 10% return. If, however, only owner I invests (option B), his return will not be 5 but, say, 3%, because the neighbor's house has not been improved and thus his investment is somewhat depreciated. Meanwhile, the neighbor might gain a modest return (say, 1%) by doing nothing; at least he would not lose, and would still have the 5% return from the bonds.

The end result of this process is that even though it may be in the interest of both owners (and society as a whole) to invest in their housing, the optimal

Table 8.5. Why Owners are Reluctant to Invest In Housing Improvements: A Prisoner's Dilemma Interpretation

Options:	Pay-off matrix = % return (gain or loss)		
	Owner I	Owner II	Total housing investment gain
A If both invest	10 (+5)	10 (+5)	+10
B If only I invests	3 (−2)	1 (+1) + 5[a]	+4
C If only II invests	1 (+1) + 5[a]	3 (−2)	+4
D If neither invests	5[a] (+5)	5[a] (+5)	0

Note: [a]From leaving savings in bonds at 5%.
Source: Adapted from Stafford, 1978, p. 62.

strategy (unless there is collusion) for any single owner under such conditions is not to invest. Neither owner is guaranteed a 10% return, but each is guaranteed a 2% loss if one invests and the other does not.

It is not surprising then that neighborhood decline continues in a self-reinforcing fashion once uncertainty and self-interest become paramount. Although the figures in Table 8.5 are artificial, and in any real world situation the number of actors and variables involved is very much greater, the example nonetheless is indicative of the strength of spatial externalities in urban housing and the importance of owners' expectations about future changes in their environment. When we add in the negative effects of absentee landlords on housing investment, the importance of "block-busting" by speculators in neighborhoods undergoing racial transition or redevelopment, the pressures for housing disinvestment become even stronger. One obvious outcome of this process is not only deterioration but the abandonment of housing. Both outcomes warrant a brief elaboration here.

Block-busting and Speculation

The unethical but often very profitable practice of block-busting is a means of securing rights to a block of properties at the lowest possible cost to the developer or speculator. This process takes several forms, but commonly begins with the purchase of one or more existing houses on a street which is considered "ripe" for redevelopment. These houses may then be let out to tenants who have no stake in the neighborhood and often those who are culturally different and of lower income or status. These tenants, either intentionally or unintentionally, tend to lower the quality of the neighborhood, or at least are seen to do so by longer-term residents.

As a result, uncertainty—if not outright panic—begins to set in among those owners who refused to sell out earlier or who were holding out for a higher price. Rumors spread rapidly about others on the street selling out at reduced, but still adequate, prices. Some of the rumors are true. Inevitably, without organized community action or policy intervention, the process culminates in a flight from the neighborhood and deteriorated housing (the arbitrage process), but speculative gains for some owners and, for the developer or his agents, a very successful land assembly. Ironically, designation of housing units or entire areas for rezoning or renewal by public authorities can have roughly similar effects. The implications for housing quality are of course even more serious since many residential areas destroyed in this way are not rebuilt, at least not for housing purposes. Even when such areas are redeveloped for residential purposes, housing is seldom provided for those persons initially *displaced* in the process.

Housing Abandonment

The scale of housing abandonment in the inner areas of some U.S. cities in the 1970s has become staggering. The U.S. Department of Housing and Urban Development (1973) estimated that in the city of St. Louis over 10,000 units (4%) of the housing stock were vacant and derelict.[5] In specific problem neighborhoods, the percentage rose to over 20%. In Baltimore, it was estimated that nearly 5% of all inner city housing units were boarded up, and the rate of withdrawal was estimated at about 4,000 units annually. In New York, perhaps 100,000 units are lost each year in this way. In most instances, the rate of abandonment is highest in older neighborhoods near the CBD, as in Philadelphia (Fig. 8.2), but not necessarily so.

Why has this abandonment taken place? The specific reasons for abandonment, of course, vary from city to city as well as between neighborhoods, but in general they mirror a *decline in the demand for housing* in particular areas. This phenomenon continues to be rare in countries other than the U.S., particularly those which still have an overall housing shortage. In the U.K., aside from losses due to vandalism, almost all of the vacant dwellings are the result of government action, either in clearing substandard 19th century housing or through restrictions on private rental. In the U.S., it has been argued (Grigsby and Rosenburg, 1975) that about half of the boarded up units are due to the abandonment process itself, and about half to government actions in renewal, highway building, or what we called earlier planners' blight.

The factors leading to the abandonment process are many. Grigsby lists six major factors: (1) the rising cost of maintenance; (2) absentee landlords who are indifferent, unwilling or unable to maintain their properties (Sternlieb and Burchell, 1975); (3) poor management of rental properties; (4) high rates of occupancy turnover, creating uncertainty and reducing the incentive for regular maintenance; (5) racial change in the neighborhood; and (6) the threat of government action. The low income of some households, in itself, is not considered by Grigsby to be the single major factor, although it is still important. Others would disagree.

Some researchers have attempted to develop a theory of the abandonment process in its spatial context and to link that process to broader changes in the housing stock. Dear (1976), for example, proposes a direct link between

Arbitrage process of
neighborhood change p155

p139 - model on decision
to move a stag

Prisoner's Dilemma- p.180

Housing abandonment
p.183

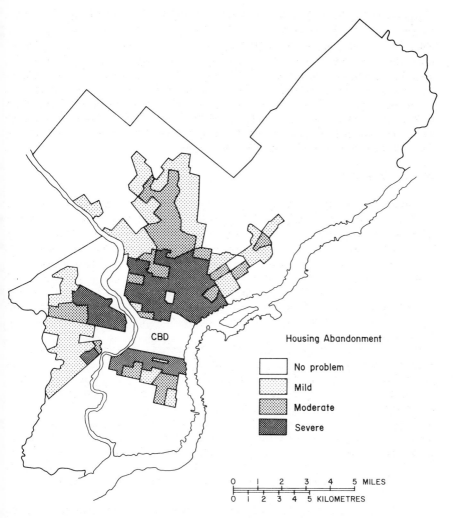

CBD

Housing Abandonment

☐ No problem

▨ Mild

▨ Moderate

■ Severe

0   1   2   3   4   5 MILES

0   1   2   3   4   5 KILOMETRES

Fig. 8.2. Patterns of abandonment housing in Philadelphia, 1972 (after Dear, 1976).

suburbanization, specifically the massive construction of postwar housing in suburban areas, and the decay and subsequent abandonment of older housing in the inner city. Briefly, suburbanization and low in-migration lead to a reduction in the city's economic base (the decline in demand) which results in a spatial concentration of low-income households, lower levels of housing investment, and a loss of confidence in the market. These become "initiating" conditions within which specific adverse conditions in certain neighborhoods lead to specific cases of abandonment.

Once set in motion, like the arbitrage process described in the last chapter, abandonment can develop its own internal dynamic. It spreads (the "contagion" effect) through the externalities noted above. Other owners become restless as abandonment spreads in their neighborhoods. Hazards such as vandalism and fire combine with a rapid deterioration in neighborhood quality to lower property values. Investment declines still further as the possibility of selling or renting the property decreases. In some cases, vacant houses are put to the torch, to rid the neighborhood of undesirables, or are vandalized for fun and spare parts. Eventually entire streets are abandoned and the process is complete.

Public Sector Abandonment, Vandalism, and the High-Rise Block

Such outcomes are not limited to private sector housing. Almost all readers will know of such spectacular public housing disasters as Pruitt-Igoe in St. Louis and the "piggeries" in Liverpool. Most cities have some similar but smaller examples. In these cases, an excessive large concentration of "problem" families, in badly-designed and poorly-maintained, high-rise buildings lead to discontent, vandalism, and eventual abandonment. Pruitt-Igoe was blown up; the piggeries were sold to a developer for next to nothing.

This process, as yet numerically small despite the publicity, is perhaps one of the most worrying trends in public sector housing policy. In the U.K., where public sector housing is considerably more important, the problem takes two forms: one is the rapid deterioration of many recently-built council housing estates, notably high-rise towers, and the other is the overzealous acquisition of private sector housing by local authorities for eventual modernization. Many of the latter units remain empty, because of a lack of money or tenants, and are subsequently vandalized, boarded-up and, in some cases, demolished.

This situation in turn emphasizes two recent and major housing problems which warrant elaboration: vandalism and the misfortunes of high-rise housing projects. The two do not necessarily go together, but frequently they appear to do so. Vandalism may be a short-term behavioral problem, or it may reflect a deep-seated reaction to inadequate housing and social injustice. In both cases, it is an expression of social alienation, of ghettoization and of a feeling of being trapped in bad housing. These social causes are capped by a private real estate market which all too frequently encourages depreciation of the housing stock and its environment, and often by the indifference of public authorities. Pruitt-Igoe may be but the tip of the proverbial iceberg.

The second problem, expressed in the question "what is wrong with high rises," is (as noted in Chapter 5) a subject of widespread debate, primarily in reference to public housing construction.[6] While there is little evidence of a consistent relationship between high-rise living and social pathologies (Schafer, 1974; Sutcliffe, 1974; Michelson, 1977), there is little doubt of their inadequacy for some people—notably for families with small children (Gittus, 1976), and for those with no choice as to where they live (Taylor, 1978). Vandalism also increases under such conditions, particularly when the apartment blocks are ill-equipped, poorly designed, and badly maintained. All of the problems of a downward spiral of deterioration evident along a street are accentuated in the enclosed space of the high-rise tower.

PRICES, RENTS, AND AFFORDABILITY

Perhaps the crucial dimension of housing supply and quality, and certainly the most common concern expressed in the popular press, is that of increasing housing prices and rents. This in turn raises the difficult question of the distribution or incidence of such increases: who suffers and who now has a problem in "affording" housing?

The difficulty every student of housing has in investigating questions of housing cost and affordability is that of separating rhetoric from reality. One must differentiate between cost increases due to our greater consumption of housing and those for a "standard" housing unit, as well as between perceived costs and real costs where the latter are deflated by increases in income and inflation. In addition, one must ask the thorny question, when is housing too expensive, by what, and whose standards? The fact that most of us have income constraints on the maximum amount of housing we consume should not obscure the fact that some people are paying more than they should for housing they receive.

Price Escalation and Affordability

Previous chapters have demonstrated that the 1970s has been a decade of escalating house prices and rents. Whether they have increased relative to income is a debatable point: it varies with the measure used, the time period, and location under study. In the U.S., for example, between 1970 and 1976 homeownership costs rose 49% (measured by the CPI index) while median family income grew by 52%. In Britain and Canada house prices exploded in the early 1970s, at a much faster rate than average earnings, but then declined in real terms during the mid-1970s. In 1978 house prices in Britain were still some 20% above the retail price index (for 1970) and they were again increasing. The interested student must look at specific indices of price (and cost) and incomes for each community before drawing firm conclusions (Bourne, 1977).

Nevertheless, it was also shown that the proportion of household income spent on housing decreases steadily with increasing income, and that the costs borne by low-income groups, especially renters, was often excessively high (see Chapter 3). The latter inequality may differ if, as in the U.K. and Sweden, the provision of public sector housing for many low-income households shields them from some of the very high costs in the private sector (Headey, 1978). Moreover, in those countries which subsidize homeownership through tax relief on mortgage interest, price escalation in housing can result in a *massive redistribution* of wealth from renters (and future generations) to current homeowners.

Table 8.6. The Degree of Inequality: The Percent of Households Paying
25 Percent of Family Income for Housing, 1976

Ratio of housing costs[a] to income	Annual family income			Total all households
	Less than $10,000	$10,000– $19,999	$20,000 or more	
Renters spending:				
more than 50%	18.5	0.3	0.1	10.8
more than 35%	37.8	2.0	0.2	22.6
more than 25%	61.1	10.9	1.3	39.0
Homeowners spending:				
more than 50%	9.7	0.4	0.0	3.0
more than 35%	23.1	3.2	0.3	8.0
more than 25%	39.0	15.4	3.9	19.3

Note: [a]Housing costs for renters include rent payments plus heating and utility costs
if not included in the rent; and for homeowners include mortgage payments, property
taxes, heating, utilities and public services such as garbage collection if not otherwise
included.
Source: U.S. Congressional Budget Office, *Annual Housing Survey*, 1976.

Perhaps the single most common indicator of affordability is the proportion of
households who pay more than 25% of their income for housing. Table 8.6 suggests
again that in the U.S. renters are, on average, worse off than homeowners. Fully
39% of all renters pay more than 25% of their income for housing, compared to
19% for homeowners. For low-income households, these figures rise to 61% and
39%, respectively.

These proportions also tend to be highest for those living in the inner cities
and for minority populations. A recent survey by the Department of Housing
and Urban Development (U.S., HUD, 1978) found that some 30% of all households living in the central city paid more than 25% of their income on housing,
and that proportion was increasing. The corresponding figure for low-income
minority households who were also renters rose to nearly 80%. Although there
is no single or unique value (such as the 25% rule) of what is or is not affordable
housing, the latter percentages are clearly excessive and socially unacceptable
by any standard.

These trends have not, however, discouraged homeownership, at least up to
1976. The U.S. 1976 Annual Housing Survey reported that the proportion of
homeowners among young and formerly-rental households (head <30 years old)
increased from 30 to 48% between 1970 and 1976. The proportion of their income spent on housing did increase, but only marginally. For low-income, first-
time buyers the proportion was much higher (34%) and clearly constituted a
short-term (if not long-term) burden. The situation appears to have deteriorated
since 1976.

The conclusion from this brief review is that the "affordability" of housing, however complex and difficult to measure, is primarily a problem for specific groups—notably the poor, racial minorities, those on fixed incomes, and inner city residents. Many of these people are already homeowners but are subjected to the increasing costs of household operation and maintenance. There are few policies designed to help them in either the U.S. or Canada.

Why is Housing so Expensive?: Alternative Perspectives[7]

While the debate on the extent to which housing prices have increased in real terms continues, it is worthwhile here to attempt to synthesize the arguments put forward to account for such increases. This approach allows us to represent a large volume of contemporary literature which would not otherwise be represented, and it should help to bring together various ideas scattered through previous chapters on demand, supply, and the urban housing market. In particular, it might assist in understanding why real house prices vary so widely over time and space.[8]

At the risk of extreme generalization, at least five different sets of arguments, or explanations, have been advanced for an overall housing price escalation. These five argue that housing price increases are primarily a function of:

> increases in *demand*, due to the growth of income, a desire and willingness to consume more housing and tax changes which have made housing a relatively more attractive investment (the "demand-pull" argument);
>
> land speculation and *monopoly* concentration in land ownership, financing, and housing development which have allowed a small group of companies and institutions to extract excess profits (the "manipulated-city" argument);
>
> escalating *development costs*, including increases in the basic costs of production—materials, land, labor, and capital—as well as increases in the costs of servicing residential land and the property taxes on that land (the "cost-push" argument);
>
> the *bottlenecks or red-tape* created by an increasing number and complexity of development and planning approval procedures which have combined to slow the rate of residential development and thereby increased housing costs and prices (the "multiple-bottleneck" argument);
>
> the *behavior of financial institutions*, and more generally of the capitalist system through which housing is provided, combine to ensure that housing is in scarce supply, expensive, and unevenly distributed, particularly with respect to low-income groups (the "radical" argument, dominated by Marxist or neo-Marxist groups).

Each of these five sets of arguments, and there are obviously many different permutations and combinations of each, offer, at best, partial explanations of what has happened to housing prices. They are not, however, mutually exclusive explanations; nor can they be simply added together to form a more comprehensive interpretation.

Which set of arguments provides the most powerful explanation depends on the market conditions prevailing in different housing markets, on the time period under study, and of course, on one's political views. The first (demand-push) explanation is perhaps the most widely accepted, at least among academic researchers (Scheffman, 1978). Average incomes have indeed risen rapidly in the last decade, and that rate of increase is highly correlated with increases in house prices. When combined with changes in household size, and with the increasing proportions in different age cohorts (early 20s), the effects of income growth are multiplied. There is no reason to assume that housing demand would not increase with income, and that prices—given the lag in adjusting supply—would rise accordingly. The effect on prices of an increasing proportion of households with two or more income earners is difficult to assess, but it too must be substantial.

National and local governments and institutions have also come in for considerable criticism. In the U.S., for example, it has been estimated that the average length of time required to complete a residential development increased from just 5 months in 1970 to nearly 14 months in 1975 (Seidel, 1978). The additional cost of each month of delay was, in turn, estimated at 1% at then current rates of interest.[9] Some financial institutions have also played a major role in house prices. For example, in the U.K. a massive injection of mortgage funds into the housing market by building societies was clearly instrumental in creating the explosion of house prices in the early 1970s (Mayers, 1979).

At the same time, changes in tax policies in several countries—such as the exemption of the private residence from capital gains—have also shifted household investment into housing and away from taxable investments (L. B. Smith, 1977). Similarly, government programs to stimulate demand, such as housing allowances, grants for homeownership, etc., without corresponding incentives for the supply side, have also contributed to price increases. Whether there has been an upward shift in the demand curve for housing—i.e., a change in the income elasticity of housing—is difficult to say, but it too could be a contributing factor.

Once an *inflation psychology* begins to prevail, still other factors come into play. Rapidly rising prices encourage speculation and the exercise of monopoly power in land and housing markets in local areas. This tends to draw additional investment into the housing market, thereby expanding the credit base for both house purchase and rental. If consumers believe that prices will go up still further, they increase their own bids and prices begin to explode. Eventually, higher prices begin to eat into available credit, because mortgages have increased in size in line with the inflated price of housing. Mortgage funds then become scarce, they are rationed, and eventually prices stabilize (or decline). It is this combination of circumstances which produces the boom-and-bust cycle of house price increases.

Whatever view one subscribes to, the critical question relates to the distributional effects of house price increases. Clearly, certain groups have suffered more than others in recent years, notably first-time house buyers (a cash-flow problem), those on fixed incomes (an inflation problem), and obviously the poor.   Others, including existing homeowners, have benefitted. Equally clearly, the former groups are concentrated in particular locations—in poorer cities and regions and the inner city—which tends to exacerbate the pressures of price escalation. The following chapters provide an overview of some of the policy responses to these issues.

NOTES

[1] For example, at the turn of the century overcrowding was defined as those situations in which the number of persons per room was more than 2.0 (Alden and Hayward, 1907).

[2] To illustrate the point, and the potential for error in quality statistics, Weicher (1978) reports that the 1976 survey of housing in the U.S. showed some 22,000 households with incomes over $25,000 living in housing without complete plumbing facilities.

[3] In the 1976 survey, over 34% of central city low-income households declared a dissatisfaction with their environmental conditions in reference to litter or abandonment, vandalized or run-down buildings, and local services.

[4] It should be noted that differential treatment of consumers by the real estate industry regarding whether housing is available or not is a potential violation of Title VIII of the 1968 U.S. Civil Rights Act.

[5] There is an obvious difficulty here in differentiating between housing units which are vacant but available for reoccupancy, those which are vacant and abandoned, and those which are abandoned by their owners but are not vacant (e.g., squatters). The most common definition of abandonment is when there is nonpayment of taxes and when owners cannot be traced.

[6] We should, of course, be careful of assigning any deterministic connotation to the effects of living in high-rise buildings. The vast majority of such buildings, even in the public sector, serve their purpose adequately. The problem is when tenants unsuited to such living conditions are concentrated in such buildings and when they see no prospect of getting out should they wish to do so.

[7] Much of this discussion is taken from a paper by the author (Bourne, 1977).

[8] By real terms is meant the rate of price increase discounted for inflation generally.

[9] For an average $40,000 house, a delay of say 8.3 months at this rate would add $3,320 to the value of the house, with no benefit to compensate for that increase (Seidel, 1978, p. 35).

Chapter 9

The Role of Government: Housing Policies and Programs

Throughout previous chapters, it has been stressed that governments play a large and increasing role in almost all aspects of housing production and consumption. They act as financiers, insurers, regulators, speculators, administrators, builders, landlords, and frequently destroyers. Even in the most market-oriented of economies, the role of the state in housing is pervasive. There is no pure market for housing.

In this and the next two chapters we examine three distinct dimensions of government involvement: first, housing policies (primarily national policies), examples of specific policy issues, and the impact on housing of other policies whose objectives are not explicitly related to housing; second, the role of the state as house builder and landlord (Chapter 10); and third, the variety of alternative systems of housing policy (Chapter 11). There is no need here, however, to provide a detailed chronology or inventory of housing policies and programs in the U.S., U.K., Canada, or any other country. There is now an extensive literature, much of it recent, which provides such reviews.[1]

Why Does the State Intervene?

The simplest response to this question is that government intervenes in the housing market precisely because, unlike the market for T-shirts, but like that for food, it is far too important—socially, financially, economically, and politically—to be left exclusively to an unfettered, unregulated, private market. This should not be surprising since what is primarily a competitive economic market could not be expected (even in theory) to produce outcomes which are entirely in accord with social needs or political objectives.

The rationale for government intervention in housing has generated a lengthy debate on the relationships between political structures and the established housing system (see Donnison, 1967; Downs, 1975; Stafford, 1978). Essentially the arguments boil down to one's view of the structure of society in general and of housing's role in that society in particular, as well as the prevailing concept of "equity" and the means available for achieving that equity. Here our concern is primarily with means rather than ideologies, but we must not lose sight of the context provided by the dominant ideology of the society we live in and of the government in power.

Most governments recognize at least three major purposes for public intervention in the private market, even if that intervention is approached reluctantly:

> *allocation:* the need to ensure that the productive resources of society are used as effectively as possible;
>
> *stabilization:* to minimize the short-term and long-term fluctuations in the economic system; and
>
> *growth and redistribution:* to see that economic growth continues, that incomes increase, and that social and spatial inequalities are reduced.

These same three functions underlie the objectives of housing policy identified in the following sections.

Others see the increasing degree of government intervention in market-based economic systems as both inevitable and contradictory. One such view argues that that intervention is inevitable because of the symbiotic relationship between government and the capitalist system of production (Harloe, 1978b). In this context, housing becomes part of the capital accumulation process on which the logic of the capitalist system is based, and a means of maintaining the established socioeconomic order. The principal source of conflict is between the need for "efficiency," in maintaining the accumulation process, and the need for "legitimacy" on the part of government in a capitalist state. Legitimacy, in turn, is based on the postulates of a universal participation in consensus formation and of government as an unbiased social arbitrator. The "state," however, in this view, cannot satisfy the latter postulates at the same time as that of efficiency in capital accumulation.

This view has served as a basis for studies of housing policies by an increasing number of geographers, sociologists, and other social scientists (Harvey, 1973; Castells, 1978; Conference of Socialist Economists, 1975; Lambert et al., 1978). Such studies have been particularly valuable in stressing the inherently political nature of housing policy and its internal contradictions. The latter are not, however, unique to any particular economic system.

Differing Concepts of Housing Policy

Given the different concepts of housing summarized in Chapter 2, it might be expected that approaches to housing policy would vary widely. The principal distinction, however, is between differing concepts of the role of housing itself.

Some see housing policy as similar in purpose to those regulatory policies directed to any other economic markets. Thus, it is basically concerned with the regulation of private market initiatives, perhaps supplemented by modest public housing production or shallow subsidies for those least able to cope in the market.

Others, in contrast, see housing policy as one area of social policy. Like health and education, the view is that housing should be provided to all members of society as a social service. This approach can vary in intent from one which simply recognizes the responsibility of government to house those left behind by the market, to one which sees the market as an aberration which the government must recognize but would restrict to serving as a minor contributor in the provision of housing. It is interesting to compare the differing emphases placed on this social service component in the following discussions of housing policies in individual countries.

National Housing Priorities

Regardless of the political philosophy underlying housing provision, most western governments face a relatively similar set of basic issues. The resolution of these issues, in turn, mirrors each society's political and social philosophy, as subsequent sections demonstrate. The major issues include:

> the *relative weight* to be given to housing goals compared to other economic and social goals;

> whether or not to subsidize housing directly or indirectly and if so the *form of subsidy* to employ;

> the *level of intervention*, in terms of the housing value and household income levels at which investment and subsidies are to be concentrated;

> the *location* incentives to be incorporated into housing policy, particularly with respect to low-income households;

> the *administrative* question of what level of government should do what for whom; and

> the question of what administrative *methods* or techniques are needed to achieve defined housing objectives.

Since each country differs so widely in its housing policies and institutions, a separate chapter on each would be a necessity. This following selective review concentrates on the recent experience of two countries, the U.S. and the U.K., but with frequent comparative reference to Canada and western Europe.

HOUSING POLICY REVIEW 1: THE U.S. EXPERIENCE

History of Housing Policy

For the most part, U.S. housing policy effectively dates from the 1930s and particularly from WW II. Even so, these policies represented the outcome of over a century of struggle for improved housing conditions (Wood, 1934). For example, the housing inspector of New York City in 1834 made one of the first public references to inadequate housing in America's congested cities. In 1847, the "Association for Improving the Condition of the Poor" was founded and carried out an initial survey of the appalling housing conditions in some of the city's tenements. Yet it was not until 1857 that even rudimentary municipal controls on privately-built tenements were introduced.[2]

During the rest of the 19th and early 20th centuries, progress was (painfully) slow. Housing standards in cities were gradually raised, primarily by municipal and state governments. Local zoning was introduced and there were some efforts by wealthy individuals, private firms, and housing associations to build housing for the poor. The Board of Housing in New York State actually began construction of low-rent housing in the late 1920s, some 30 years after similar programs of building working class housing began in Britain. It was not until 1918, however, that the federal government undertook to directly provide housing for its citizens; in this case, for returning war veterans.

The great depression and the New Deal period brought the most substantial policy changes. In 1932 the Federal Home Loan Bank Act was passed, facilitating the spread of SLAs and a rapid increase in local sources of housing finance (see Chapter 5). In 1933 the federal government initiated what we now know as public housing through the Public Works Administration, and in 1934 the FHA was created to stimulate residential construction and stabilize the residential mortgage market by insuring private mortgages.[3] Finally, in 1937 the U.S. Housing Authority was created to assist in improving levels of health and welfare through higher housing standards.

World War II brought both sharp policy changes and massive government involvement in housing. Private house-building virtually came to a halt (see Chapter 3). Government then stepped in through the National Housing Agency to build over 850,000 units of "defense" housing. Insurance was also provided to encourage private builders to construct housing for war workers. Moreover, in 1944 the Veterans Administration (VA) was established to assist in housing returning veterans. Since 1944, over 9 million VA housing loans have been extended—worth over $120 billion—the largest single U.S. housing program for a group with "special needs."

Postwar Policies and Programs

The Housing Act of 1949 was an important landmark. It established the goal of "a decent home for every family in a suitable living environment," and initiated what has since become a bewildering array of federal programs and policies. The Act also broadened the concept of housing policy by recognizing the importance of the neighborhood environment and community services and called for a comprehensive approach (i.e., urban renewal) to the solution of housing problems. It also widened the concern of government to include the provision of housing for all, not simply for those of low income; and it initiated federal efforts in urban redevelopment (Title I). In addition, termination of the war presented the nation with a number of economic problems of which housing was both a component as well as a possible solution. There was, for example, a considerable housing shortage and an urgent need to provide jobs in the subsequent transition to a peace-time economy. Increased housing production and mortgage finance became part of this attempt to induce economic growth.

Unfortunately, the 1949 Act was vague in its intent and carried little political weight.[4] No explicit overall targets for housing production were set. Nor was it clear how the objective of a decent home for all would be translated into reality. One interpretation is that the latter was not a policy objective as much as a statement of a desirable state of affairs at some time in the future (Wolman, 1975). Nevertheless, the Act did embrace the concept of government's "responsibility" for housing, a recognition at least of the social service philosophy described earlier.

Since the 1949 Act, we can identify at least five major phases of emphasis in U.S. national housing policy. The dates here are somewhat arbitrary, although most represent points of major revision in national housing legislation.

Urban redevelopment and slum clearance (1949–1960): This was a period of increased public housing construction, slum clearance, and urban redevelopment. Under the provisions of Title I of the 1949 Act, the federal government was empowered to pay up to two-thirds of the difference between the costs of assembling, clearing, and servicing designated slum areas and the market price at which these areas could then be sold to private developers. The objectives were twofold: to stimulate private enterprise in rebuilding older cities and, secondarily, to improve overall housing conditions by removing the worst slums.

The most contentious aspect of the 1949 Act was precisely the public housing component. The Act called for the construction of at least 140,000 units a year for 6 years. Yet less than 250,000 units were actually built during that period. At the same time the stock of low-cost housing was reduced through urban renewal and slum clearance, programs which destroyed three times as many housing units as they built. The combined forces of conservative politicians, federal government indifference, and the unwillingness of many local governments to accept public housing in their midst resulted in a dwindling new supply of such housing throughout the 1950s and 1960s. The reactions of local authorities, and the political problems of locating public housing in cities, are vividly conveyed in Meyerson and Banfield's (1955) study of Chicago.

Urban redevelopment and slum clearance—what soon became known as the federal "bulldozer"—were initially far more popular locally, for obvious reasons. Although the 1949 Act stipulated that cleared lands were to be used for "predominantly" residential purposes, local agencies were not closely regulated and the principle was gradually relaxed. Commercial use of renewal sites was attractive because it helped improve business conditions and added to the local tax base. Moreover, much of the new housing built was not for the poor that renewal initially displaced.

Subsequent acts during this period further deflated the social objectives of the 1949 Act. The Housing Act of 1954 relaxed the emphasis on using renewal lands for residential purposes and extended the financial incentives for private builders.[5] In the 1956 and 1959 Acts, the initial concept of slum clearance was broadened to include neighborhood and community renewal. Although laudable in themselves, these revisions allowed local agencies even more freedom to remove deteriorating housing and replace it with what they saw fit.

The transitional period (1960–65): Subsidizing the private sector: Growing dissatisfaction with the urban renewal bulldozer (in reducing the stock of low-cost housing) and the tendency for public housing to become segregated ghettoes contributed to a gradual shift in attitudes and in housing policy during the 1960s. Although housing was assigned even lower priority as a national policy issue in this period, there was a significant move away from urban renewal towards the pro- vision of subsidies for both low- and middle-income groups.

The 1961 Act brought in subsidized below-market-interest-rate (or BMIR) mortgage loans, through Section 221(d)3, designed for low- and moderate-income households who did not qualify for public housing. While not many units were constructed (about 190,000), most did reach the intended target populations, and some success was achieved in attracting private investment into subsidized housing construction. The purpose of the program was to lower the rent (or less frequently, the ownership costs) for households living in new or rehabilitated housing by subsiding interest charges.[6] This program was also severely hampered, however, by opposing special interest groups, including some banking associations, by limited federal funds, and by management difficulties.

Reflecting a similar philosophy, the 1965 Housing and Urban Development Act introduced a modest rent supplement program. This was, in some ways, a watershed decision, but one which Headey (1978) describes as abortive. Under this program, the federal government was to pay the difference between market rents and one- quarter of the gross income for those households who were below the income limit for public housing but were compelled to rent privately. Although it was initially intended to help moderate-income households, and to "integrate" the suburbs, inadequate funding and fears of competition with the private sector limited the subsidies to a few thousand households of very low income. Nonetheless, it did act to complement Section 221(d)3 and 202 housing, and it introduced the con- cept of linking subsidies to changes in income.

These innovations in housing policy, modest as they were, however, were swamped by other related policy changes and by changing social conditions. Urban renewal not only displaced hundreds of thousands of households, it forced many employers out of business and sent others to the suburbs. The displaced low-income population simply shifted into other low-income neighborhoods, accelerating their decline and spreading blight over even larger areas. At the same time, massive expressway construction wiped out thousands of low-income units and opened the suburbs to a widespread decentralization of middle-income households and jobs.

Social unrest and policy reassessment (1965–68): In the mid-1960s, a number of dramatic events stimulated a major reassessment of housing policy. Most obvious among these events were the social unrest and riots which exploded in cities and on university campuses throughout the country. The subsequent report of the National Advisory Committee on Civil Disorders called for a massive increase in the construction of subsidized housing for low-income families. Parallel housing policy reviews, such as the Kaiser Committee's (1969) report, urged the acceptance of specific production targets based on an assessment of national "housing needs," something which had not been done before. At the same time, the credit squeeze tightened with escalation of the Vietnam war, sharply reducing the volume of private housing construction.

These events were directly reflected in the Housing and Urban Development Act of 1968. Among other items, this Act set a construction target of 26 million new (and rehabilitated) housing units for low- and moderate-income households over the next 10 years. Two new programs were introduced, combining aspects of interest rate subsidies, depreciation benefits, and housing allowances. These programs were Sections 235 for homeowners and Section 236 for renters. The fromer provided subsidies for low-income households in terms of an FHA-insured mortgage. The government was then to make up the difference between actual monthly carrying costs and the households income-related payments. Under Section 236, payments were made to private investors willing to finance low-income rental housing. Tenant rents were limited to a maximum of 25% of gross income for eligible households. The cost difference between the market rent and the rent necessary to cover a fixed low-cost mortgage was to be paid by the government.[7]

The 1968 Act also contained a battery of other housing provisions. It strengthened the secondary mortgage market, designed to reduce the extreme cyclical fluctuations in housing finance, extended insurance coverage for mortgage lenders in high-risk, inner-city areas, expanded funding for public housing, and increased the proportion of low-income housing required on urban renewal sites. Thus, the 1968 Act—as Downs (1975) observes—in combination with new coalitions of liberal politicians and related urban policies (such as the Model Cities program) offered the possible tools to effectuate a major reassessment of housing policy.

The high production period (1968–1974): Initially, at least, things went well. Subsidized housing starts rose from the previous record high of about 160,000 units in 1968 to over 430,000 units in 1970 and 1971. The latter total represented nearly 30% of all housing starts, a peace-time high, and much of it was attributable to the impact of Sections 235 and 236. Unfortunately, most of this housing did not go directly to those for whom it was initially intended.[8]

Private housing starts accelerated in 1971. Total construction rose from 1.9 million units in 1969 to over 3 million in 1972. This boom was in part the result of the collapse of the stock market in the early 1970s. Real estate became a relatively more attractive investment, due in part to the creation of real estate tax shelters (investment trusts, for example). Millions of dollars flowed into housing production and consumption. Widespread mortgage availability and low down payments further stimulated homeownership, particularly of new housing located n suburban areas. At the same time, mobile housing deliveries accelerated from ess than 100,000 in the early 1960s to over 500,000 in 1972.

Some observers have argued that the early success of these programs brought their subsequent downfall. The extent of the subsidies to those of modest incomes alienated many in the private sector. Soon the escalating costs of subsidies, which continued over the length of the mortgage, began to be felt. The default rate on loans to low-income households and marginal landlords also increased. More broadly, the high rate of housing production, as noted earlier, contributed to an accelerated rate of out-migration from the cities. The rate of downward filtering increased, vacancies mounted, the abandonment of older housing became more widespread, and the geographical isolation of the very poor increased. These effects, which as seen in previous chapters (see Chapters 7 and 8) were due to the coincidence of many diverse factors, were no doubt exacerbated by the policy of stimulating new private construction in suburban areas.

Policy consolidation and the recession (1975 on): From 1975 on, substantial changes have taken place in U.S. housing policy and in the environment in which those policies have been introduced. The Nixon administration in 1973 placed a moratorium on Section 235 and 236 and related subsidy programs. Emphasis shifted from supply (building) subsidies, particularly for new construction, to cash assistance (or demand subsidies) for specific target households. We pick up the assistance issue in a later section.

The 1974 Act also abolished individual subsidies for such programs as urban renewal, Model Cities, and parks and sewerage treatment. These were replaced by block grants—notably the community development block grant—to local governments who would then have more discretion in how the money was to be spent. Such monies were to be allocated on the basis of a local plan for the provision of low-income housing and community improvement, but were also related to the relative level of poverty in each area. The Act also reintroduced housing assistance (after the moratorium) through such programs as low-rent public housing, Section 8 (subsidies for new construction and existing housing), and a revised Section 235 program. Each program was directed primarily to low- or moderate-income households, but to a slightly different group of households and income groups in each case.

At the same time as these revisions were taking place, economic and political climates changed. The world recession and inflation reduced the growth of income and jobs and dramatically increased building costs. In 1975 and 1976, the residential building industry almost collapsed as credit tightened and demand slackened. Overall political priorities again shifted away from housing. Governments everywhere subsequently rushed in emergency measures to stimulate construction, bolster demand, and to prevent widespread mortgage default. The recession in new house-building also had several other effects. One, as described earlier (Chapter 7), was to redirect household demand back on to the existing stock. Moreover, house prices rose overall, particularly in locations of continued employment growth.

Current Housing Programs: A Summary

The preceding discussion of the evolution of U.S. federal housing policy may be summarized most succinctly with a simple inventory of current national housing programs (Table 9.1). The right-hand column of the table provides the approximate date at which each program was initiated and the relative size of the program (in 1978) in terms of units produced or improved, households affected, or funds approved. The latter are of course difficult to measure in many instances, so the numbers should be interpreted with caution (see U.S. HUD, 1978). Note that the largest program is still that of traditional public housing. As of 1978, there were 1.15 million occupied units and nearly 200,000 units in various stages of development. Annual production, however (about 40,000 units), remains pitifully low by international standards.

Among those programs of particular interest to geographers and planners are those relating to community services and neighborhood improvement grants. The former, including Community Development Block Grants (CDBG), are designed to provide assistance for building and infrastructure rehabilitation, the costs of local government code enforcement, and household relocation. These have met with modest success. The broader concern for neighborhood revitalization is also suggestive of a growing awareness that improvement is a continuous process and that specific housing rehabilitation grants must be matched by parallel environmental and social programs.[9] Both require careful monitoring by housing researchers.

Reviewing the Objectives of Federal Housing Policy

The objectives of any policy or program include those which are stated and those which are not. This renders both the identification of objectives and an evaluation of the degree to which they were attained extremely difficult. Moreover, these objectives change frequently, either through a process of "natural evolution" or abruptly through a change in government, in the administrators of programs, or in public perceptions of the problems involved.

Nevertheless, the following objectives are frequently cited as underlying recent federal housing policy in the U.S.:

maintaining a high level of new housing production;

reducing the cyclical instability of the house-building industry and thereby encouraging overall stabilization in the economy;

ensuring the availability of adequate (and affordable) housing, particularly for low-income households;

ensuring adequate housing finance by extending the availability of mortgage credit;

encouraging widespread homeownership;

providing housing for households with special needs;

providing equal housing opportunities for all and facilitating racial integration;

improving inner city conditions through community development, neighborhood preservation, and revitalization;

creating "good" new suburban neighborhoods; and

reducing housing costs.

Note that there are clearly different types and "levels" of objectives in this list. Some are targeted to specific problems (reducing costs), others are diffuse (equal opportunities). Still others are little more than good intentions relating to a more ideal world. The relative weight placed on each objective also shifts from time

Table 9.1. A Summary of Current U.S. Housing Programs, 1978

Program description	a) Year introduced b) Number of housing units, projects or $ involved
HOUSING ASSISTANCE PROGRAMS	
Low-Rent Public Housing: Pays development costs and annual operating subsidies for rental projects owned and managed by local public agencies and rented to lower-income tenants at reduced charges.	a) 1937 b) 1.15 million units; 192,000 in process
Section 8 New Construction/Substantial Rehabilitation: Subsidizes rents of lower-income households occupying public and privately-developed projects.	a) 1974 b) 30,000; + 500,000 in process
Section 8 Existing Housing: Provides assistance on behalf of households occupying physically-adequate, moderate-cost rental housing of their own choosing in the private market.	a) 1974 b) 330,000; + 148,000 ready for occupancy
Section 235 Homeownership Assistance: Provides mortgage interest subsidies to lower- and middle-income households purchasing new or substantially-rehabilitated homes.	a) 1968, suspended 1973, revised 1975 b) 287,000 to 1973; 8,000 since; 40,000 in process
Section 236 Rental Assistance and Rent Supplements: Subsidizes mortgages for rental housing projects. Rent supplements make subsidy payments to the owners of private rental housing on behalf of lower-income tenants.	a) 1968 b) 648,000; only 1,600 in process
Section 202 Housing for Elderly and Handicapped: Provides direct loans for the development of rental housing for the elderly and handicapped.	a) 1959, suspended 1970, revised 1974 b) 55,000 (Section 202/8) since 1974
HOUSING-RELATED COMMUNITY PROGRAMS	
Community Development Block Grants (CDBG): Provides grants to local governments, allocated by needs-based formulae. About one-fourth of all CDBG funds go towards housing rehabilitation, building code enforcement and relocation assistance.	a) 1974 b) 3,200 grants (in 1978)
Urban Development Action Grants: Funds development projects involving both private and public investment. Available to distressed cities only.	a) 1977 b) 50 projects (1978 only)
Section 312 Rehabilitation Loans: Provides 3% interest loans for the rehabilitation of privately-owned housing for occupancy by limited-income households.	a) 1968 b) 58,000 loans
Urban Homesteading: Makes federally-held homes available at nominal expense to limited-income persons willing to rehabilitate and occupy units.	a) 1976 (demonstration) b) 2,500 (in 1978)
MORTGAGE CREDIT ACTIVITIES	
Direct Loan Programs: (1) Farmers Home Administration	1a) 1934

Table 9.1. (cont'd)

Program description	a) Year introduced b) Number of housing units, projects or $ involved
provides market-rate and subsidized home loans in credit-deficient rural areas. (2) VA provides market-rate mortgages to qualifying servicemen and veterans.	1b) 825,000 loans outstanding 2a) 1944; 2b) 180,000 loans outstanding
Mortgage Insurance Programs: FHA insures market-rate, single-family and multi-family mortgages and subsidized mortgages on assisted housing projects.	a) FHA 1934 b) 40 active programs
Credit-Market Interventions: (1) Federal National Mortgage Association (FNMA), Federal Home Loan Mortgage Corporation, and (2) GNMA purchase and resell mortgages to encourage use of capital for housing and provide limited financing subsidies. (3) Federal Home Loan Banks (FHLB) provide advances to financial institutions to make up temporary credit shortages and stimulate lending.	1a) FNMA became private in 1968 1b) 1.5 million loans 2a) GNMA–1968 2b) $43 billion 3a) FHLB, $17 billion in advances

HOUSING-RELATED TAX EXPENDITURES

Homeownership Incentives: Permit deduction of (a) mortgage interest and (b) property tax payments for owner-occupied housing; (c) allow deferral of capital gains.	Cost: (1977 est.) a) mortgages–$4.5 billion b) taxes–$4.2 billion c) capital gains–$0.9 billion
Promoting Rental Housing Development: Accelerated depreciation allowances for rental housing and the favorable treatment of construction-period interest and property tax payments for developers.	Cost (1978 est.) $1.0 billion
Tax Benefits for Financial Institutions: Preferential bad-debt deduction allowances for residential credit institutions.	Cost (1978 est.) $0.7 billion

HOUSING AND CREDIT MARKET REGULATIONS

Guaranteeing Equal Housing Opportunities: Prohibitions against discrimination in the sale and rental of most housing and in mortgage lending.	――
Controlling Supply and Cost of Mortgage Credit: Regulations govern maximum interest rates paid on deposits in financial institutions.	――

Source: Adapted and extended from U.S. HUD reports and U.S. Congress (1978).

to time as social conditions, and political realities, dictate. Moreover some of the above objectives are potentially in conflict. For example, the need for overall stabilization of the economy may conflict with several other objectives since it requires a cut-back in housing production during periods of economic expansion.

Since many of these objectives tend to be highly political or ideological, the result has been a lengthy debate on the merits and attainment of various policy alternatives (see Wheaton et al., 1966; Pynoos et al., 1973; Soloman, 1974; Downs, 1975; Wolman, 1975; Headey, 1978). Harvey (1977a), for example, has argued that U.S postwar housing policy has been directed primarily to three broad goals: (1) maintaining the close links between housing finance, economic growth, and capital accumulation; (2) use of the construction industry and housing sector as "Keynesian" regulators through which swings in the economy can be smoothed out; and (3) responding to the relationship between housing supply, the distribution of income, and social unrest. He also stressed the importance of housing construction as a means of creating jobs and preventing widespread unemployment, and the role of expansionary credit policies in facilitating consumer demand for housing. One result of these policies, as suggested above, was the massive postwar suburbanization of housing and jobs.

Housing clearly does play an important role in maintaining the social order, and social status, as defined in Chapter 2. Several authors have argued that the policy of extending homeownership was in part designed to defuse potential social unrest spilling over from the 1930s and from the return of war veterans. Debt-encumbered homeowners, in theory, would be less likely to "rock the boat" of the existing economic order. Most governments would quietly admit that the objective is both present and appropriate.

There is, unfortunately, little empirical evidence on which to base an overall assessment of the relative success of federal policies in attaining their stated or unstated objectives. Nevertheless, it seems reasonable to conclude that such policies have been moderately successful in stimulating new housing construction, in increasing homeownership, in attracting more private capital into the housing sector, and in improving the quality of "new" residential neighborhoods. The objective of stimulating private investment, however, has often meant a parallel reduction in government investment—a further "privatization" of the housing sector.

Such policies have been much less successful in reducing the wide fluctuations in housing production and in targeting housing assistance to families of low and moderate income. They have had no success in reducing overall housing costs and may well have been counter-productive in their efforts at reducing social segregation and in improving conditions in inner city neighborhoods, although both remain to be proven. Equally serious, as demonstrated below, these policies have not significantly reduced the unequal distribution of housing benefits among American society's income classes.

HOUSING POLICY REVIEW 2: THE BRITISH EXPERIENCE

The evolution and current status of housing policy in Britain provide interesting parallels and contrasts with the North American experience. The British experience is, of course, of much longer duration and is more substantial, in terms of the degree of government involvement. It is also relatively better documented; fortunately so, since space only allows for a very cursory review here. Instead, this section seeks only to summarize the contrasts with American housing policies as outlined above and the differing conditions under which those policies have been formulated. Chapter 10 then looks at the public housing experience in Britain in more detail. There are now a large number of comparative studies of British and U.S. policy which provide further background.[10]

Bases of Housing Policies

Housing policy in Britain differs from that in the U.S. in its history and ideology as well as its political machinery and administrative rules. First, public concern over inadequate housing conditions began earlier and more quickly became focused in national legislation than in North America. Second, this concern was more closely related to problems of health and sanitation. The industrial revolution, which began earlier in Britain than anywhere else, when building standards were low, generated rapid, unplanned urban growth and poor-quality speculative housing development in the late 18th and early 19th centuries. The result, as Dickens and other writers so vividly described, was the teeming, polluted metropolis with its congested, working-class terrace housing, often built back-to-back, with little lighting and inadequate or nonexistent basic services. Overcrowding was widespread, and disease was rampant (Alden and Hayward, 1907). These wretched conditions lead to a long series of government (and philanthropic) actions to improve standards of sanitation and housing. Some housing improvement schemes were initiated in the early 1830s and in 1848 the first of a series of public health acts was passed by the central government.

The British experience also emphasizes the importance of public housing and the major role assigned to local governments in providing housing for their residents. The latter principle was recognized as early as the 1850s, and in 1890 the Housing of the Working Classes Act formally authorized local authorities to build and rent working-class housing. Before 1900, several British cities were involved in extensive planning and housing evaluation and some were building houses; and from 1919 on they were obliged to do so. This legislative emphasis has continued to this day. Parallel efforts were also initiated to remove some of the worst 18th and early 19th century slum housing, but such clearance did not get underway on any scale in the major cities until after 1930.

Massive expansion of public sector housing dates from WWI, largely as a response to the acute housing shortage and the need to rehouse returning veterans (homes fit for heroes). Over 720,000 housing units were built by local authorities between 1920 and 1930. Similar efforts were made again after WWII, with considerable success (see Chapter 3). The objective of a decent home for every family clearly became accepted as a national obligation in Britain long before it did in North America.

These efforts reflect not only the relatively serious housing problems inherited by postwar British governments, but also a different prevailing ideology about the role of housing in society. Compared to the North American emphasis on stimulating private investment, housing policy in Britain was seen as filling more of a "welfare" function, with housing acting, at least in part, as a social service—a national obligation—and a higher priority (although still not that high) for government expenditures. The view that "we cannot have a market solution to the housing problem" has generally prevailed (until recently) regardless of the political party in power. The most common translation of this philosophy has been the construction and ownership of housing by local government and by the new town corporations (see Chapter 10).

Current Programs and Priorities

Despite these very important differences in background compared to the U.S., the policy responses, as Wolman (1975) notes, are often surprisingly similar. The major policy objectives, as specified in the 1977 policy review (see U.K. Secretary of State for the Environment, 1977), are not unlike those of American policy cited earlier, but with some important exceptions. Moreover, at the time of writing, and like most other western countries, housing policies are again in a state of flux subject to the search for new objectives by a more conservative government faced with severe economic difficulties.

The 1977 review recommended the following rather broad priorities for housing policy over the next decade, over and above that of a decent home for all: (1) a better balance between new construction and rehabilitation, emphasizing the latter; (2) stability in housing costs, both rental and owner-occupied; (3) meeting the housing needs of special groups (e.g., the elderly, disabled); (4) increasing the access of selected groups to housing of their choice; (5) increasing the scope for geographical mobility, particularly within the public sector; (6) allowing free choice of tenure; and (7) safeguarding the rights of tenants. These objectives, although not new, were to be obtained through revised policies directed primarily at the supply and use of housing.

The Housing and Rent Acts of 1974, the Housing Rent and Subsidies Acts of 1975, building on a series of legislative acts since 1969, provided the basic outline for a new and more comprehensive housing policy. Emphasis shifted from widespread slum clearance and redevelopment to housing conservation and area improvement programs. The role of housing associations was strengthened and funding for cooperative housing was increased.[11] Security of tenure was tightened and extended to the remaining (but rapidly shrinking) unregulated part of the private rental sector—which has added to the financial difficulties of that sector and created some weird anomolies. Legislation was also introduced to increase the flexibility of local authorities in budgeting for their housing programs.[12]

One of the more significant elements of the 1974 Act was the extended use of rehabilitation in dealing with areas of the worst housing "stress." These areas, designated as either Housing Action Areas (HAAs) or Priority Neighborhood (PNs), were those in which both the prevailing social conditions and the physical state of the housing stock were considered unsatisfactory. In both cases, local authorities were given extended powers to deal with housing problems on a broader and more integrated scale.

These housing programs have been supplemented at various times by other land and area-based policies—such as the new towns program, the Community Land Act (1975) and that proposed for the inner cities (1977)—to a much greater degree than in the U.S.; but again not without some negative effects (Headey, 1978). The Community Land Act, designed to facilitate land acquisition and land banking by local authorities, primarily for future residential purposes, has, however, since been repealed. The latter proposed a comprehensive attack on the problems of social deprivation and economic decline—including deteriorated housing—characteristic of the inner areas of many of the larger industrial cities. From this initiative has emerged a "partnership" program designed to help coordinate actions by local, regional, and national governments in these declining inner cities.

Housing policy in Britain has also involved more extensive programs of housing subsidies and assistance and tighter regulation of credit and mortgage lending agencies (notably the Building Societies) than in North America. General housing assistance in Britain has taken three principal forms: (1) tax relief on mortgage interest, as in the U.S.; (2) enormous direct subsidies to public sector housing; and (3) rate (local tax) rebates to individuals and rate support contributions to the housing accounts of local governments. Rent allowances (and rent rebates) are also now available to private as well as public tenants and some low-income homeowners are also eligible for rate rebates. Tenant protection legislation, as noted, is now much more elaborate than anywhere in North America—in fact, tenants are almost granted freehold rights.

More recently the central government introduced new arrangements for local authority housing investment—the Housing Investment Programmes (HIPs). These offer a block grant for all local housing activities—building, maintenance, demolition and clearance, renovation, and loans to households—dependent on the submission of a locally-produced and comprehensive assessment of housing needs. The stated intention of the HIPs is to increase local government flexibility in designing its housing programs and to encourage more efficient financial planning (i.e., lower costs). In outline, the HIPs are considerably broader in scale and intent than the CDBGs in the U.S. (or Canada).

The HIP programs also reflect a changing perception of the nature of housing problems in Britain which roughly parallels that in North America. The prevailing view is that there is no longer a single national housing problem to which a uniform national policy solution is either necessary or appropriate. Instead, it is argued, there are a series of localized problems, which differ in nature and extent by community, and which are best dealt with by local governments and by more spatially sensitive and precise policy instruments.

In summary, recent housing programs in Britain reflect the massive and complex inheritance of housing supply and quality problems. They mirror the particular political mechanisms available for improving that quality and the changing social and economic conditions under which housing policy has been devised and implemented. Equally important is the difference in philosophy about the role of housing in Britain and North American society (a difference in degree perhaps), and the former society's more general adherence to planning practice. The U.S.

has chosen to stimulate private enterprise, while Britain has followed a more explicit course of providing a large stock of housing as a social service and a component of national welfare policy. Both, however, have sought and achieved higher homeownership rates.

SPECIFIC POLICY ISSUES

Previous sections have provided a brief review of the evolution of housing policy but little opportunity to discuss specific policy issues. Here we examine a selection of issues not covered in other chapters in more detail. Each issue is an important policy concern in its own right, but each also reflects some of the dilemmas involved in choosing among alternative policy strategies. Those issues selected for brief review here include: (1) housing (demand) allowances and production subsidies; (2) rehabilitation and conservation vs. new construction and redevelopment; (3) rent control; and (4) the question of who benefits from housing programs. Issues of public housing in general and the housing needs of special groups are discussed in the following chapter.

Housing Allowances vs. Subsidies

A continuing debate in housing policy focuses on the merits of direct-payment housing allowances, relative to those of subsidies for production, in improving housing quality for those of low income. The former, which might be introduced as part of a revised and extended welfare or guaranteed income program, are, for convenience, examined here in isolation.

The concept of housing allowances (or rent supplements) is not recent. They were considered as part of the discussions leading up to the 1937 Housing Act in the U.S. and in the 1964 Act rent supplements were introduced for privately-owned, newly-constructed or rehabilitated units and for local authorities leasing housing to low-income households (Section 23). In the U.K., there has been, as noted above, an even longer history of rent regulation and of subsidies (or rent rebates) to tenants in both the private and public sectors (see Cullingworth, 1978).

Obtaining empirical assessments of the effects of housing assistance is particularly difficult. In 1972, however, the U.S. federal government undertook one of the largest social experiments ever in order to test the impact of direct cash-payment assistance on the use of housing. This test, the Experimental Housing Allowance Program (EHAP),[13] involved some 23,000 lower-income households in 12 locations,[14] who accepted an average monthly cash subsidy for a guaranteed period of 3 to 10 years.[15] The initial purpose of the program was to provide responses to the following kinds of questions. How do households use their allowances? When the use of such funds is unrestricted, do they spend more on housing? Do households subsequently change their housing location and neighborhood? Does the quality of housing improve for participating households and what are the responses of the market itself (e.g., price)?

In general, the results to date have been disappointing. While 90% of eligible households would accept assistance which was not restricted to housing, compared to just 50% when the assistance was so restricted, only 10% of the actual assistance received would be used for housing. When households moved, the amount of housing they consumed increased by roughly 83% of their assistance, but only 40% of that increase could be ascribed to the assistance itself. The corresponding figure for households which did not move was 29%. The principal positive effect was to decrease the average proportion of household income spent on housing (from 40 to 25%).

There were, however, few other effects. Income assistance did not significantly alter household choices, either in housing or neighborhood type (by race or ethnicity). There was no major price effect and no significant new construction resulted. An assessment by the Urban Institute (1979) also concluded that the assistance appears to have done little to promote racial integration, increase production, or stimulate neighborhood revitalization.

One obvious conclusion is that money is not the only prerequisite for an improvement in housing quality. Within the EHAP, non-monetary assistance of two kinds was also provided: (1) better information on the housing market to aid in selecting and evaluating alternatives (see Chapter 2), and (2) equal opportunity and legal assistance to combat discrimination in the market. The former proved to be an important household consideration, while the utilization of legal services in contrast was very low.

More generally, the EHAP (although not yet complete) is not in itself sufficient to offer concrete evidence one way or the other on the relative merits of housing allowances. The impacts were disappointingly small—housing expenditures increased by just 19% and neighborhood effects were negligible—but then there is no way of telling what the effects would be if housing assistance were universally applied. More to the point, the results suggest that a combination of housing allowances and direct subsidies to builders is the preferred alternative. These conclusions are roughly similar to those found in Britain's parallel rent-supplement experiment (see Trutko, Hetzel, and Yates, 1978; and Cullingworth, 1979).

Rent Control

Rent control has become one of the penultimate tools for governments in regulating the private housing market, but it too is not a recent invention. Most European countries have had some form of restriction on housing rents in the private sector since the 19th century. Britain, for example, introduced rent restrictions in 1914 as a temporary war-time measure and they have persisted ever since, although in varying forms (Wolman, 1975).

In North America, on the other hand, rent controls have not been a continuing feature of government housing policy. The U.S. introduced temporary controls during WWI, but these were quickly removed, and again during WWII (1942). The latter were continued after the war and during the Korean conflict. All federal controls on rent were finally lifted by 1954, only to be briefly reimposed in 1971–72 under phases I and II of the anti-inflation program.

Among individual cities, only New York, which extended the WWII controls under state authority, has had a significant experience with rent control. In fact, New York has evolved a rather complex system combining rent control and rent stabilization in which the latter depends in large part on self-regulation by an association of landlords.[16] From 1969 on, other cities including Washington, D.C., Baltimore, Boston, and smaller centers in Massachusetts, Connecticut, New Jersey, and most recently California, have enacted forms of rent control, or what is often more accurately described as rent "review." In Canada, the provinces of Ontario, Manitoba, and B.C. have also introduced mild forms of rent control, and Quebec has had rent review for some time.

The arguments for and against rent control have filled volumes (Hayek et al., 1978). Basically, those in favor of controls argue that renters in the private market must be protected from excessive rent increases and unfair exploitation by landlords, particularly when housing supply is limited. Normally controls are imposed during periods of rapidly escalating rents, inflation, or during national emergencies. The arguments against are many: that rent control discourages adequate maintenance in the existing stock and reduces investment in new construction; that it is inequitable because it benefits renters at the expense of owners and some renters at the expense of others; that it encourages dishonest practices (e.g., key money); and that it presents a regulatory nightmare for housing authorities. Both sets of arguments are true, in part.

The effect of rent control depends essentially on the nature of the controls and the way they are applied. Some have simply frozen rents, others allow increases equivalent to some base, while others allow full cost (pass-through) rent increases. Still other areas have only rent "review" which may or may not specify a limit on rent increases, but which does provide a forum for tenant complaints.

Nevertheless, most studies, such as the Rand Institute's review of the New York City experience (Lowry et al., 1972), have concluded that controls, while often preventing "unfair" rent increases, do distort the market in undesirable ways. They have also left some owners with few alternatives but to reduce building maintenance and services (if not, in extreme cases, to abandon the structure). New construction also suffered. On the other hand, there is also little doubt that the declining real income of many tenants in older inner cities has reduced the owners' revenues and encouraged deterioration, quite independently of rent controls (Harloe, 1979).

One other long-term side-effect ascribed to rent controls is the decline of private rental housing. The rental sector in North America has declined in recent years in relative size, largely for reasons other than locally-imposed rent controls, but such controls have not helped. In Britain, the massive drop in the private rental sector has paralleled the tightening of rent restrictions, but again in combination with other and perhaps more significant factors (e.g., tax benefits from homeownership).[17] In any case, even if rent control is not a permanent fixture, procedures for rent review and tenant forums will be increasingly common.

Conservation and Redevelopment

Part of the debate on urban renewal has focused on the merits of conserving older housing (through increased maintenance and rehabilitation) in comparison to those of demolishing and building anew. Since this topic was discussed earlier in the chapter on supply (Chapter 5), it can be dealt with here relatively briefly.

It has already been noted that systematic cost figures on rehabilitation and maintenance are seldom available and are inconsistent when available (Bagby, 1974; Kirby, 1979). Thus most discussion has centered on noneconomic arguments and on political whims. Nonetheless, the clear trend of recent years has been away from those policies which encouraged widespread housing demolition in the 1950s and 1960s to those in the 1970s which encourage reuse and improvement of the existing stock. In many cities, demolitions by public authorities have virtually ceased, replaced by a series of loans and grants for housing rehab and neighborhood revitalization. Both the U.S. and Canada now have such schemes, while the U.K. again has a similar but much more extensive system of improvement grants.[18]

Even when a decision has been made to increase the emphasis on rehabilitation, however, several thorny problems remain. These include the kinds of subsidies to be extended; the restrictions placed on the use of those subsidies; and the problem of defining the criteria by which grants are distributed among people, houses, and locations. There are also a number of important side-effects to consider. In the private market, rehabilitation grants almost inevitably lead to higher housing prices and thus to increased profits for speculators, landlords, and individual homeowners when the property is subsequently sold (Hamnett, 1973; Balchin, 1979). Attempts to control resales, or to capture that proportion of the price increase attributable to the rehabilitation grant, have generally failed. Moreover, determining which housing units warrant rehabilitation poses severe administration headaches for local authorities, including opening new opportunities for discrimination and corruption.

Despite these difficulties, it is likely that more effort will be made in the next decade to improve the quality of the existing stock through private investment, insured loans, self-help and co-op programs and outright government grants. It is increasingly recognized that aggregate housing quality can often be improved faster and at less cost through conservation and selective improvement than through an exclusive emphasis on redevelopment and new construction. This is particularly true when one considers the social costs of destroying existing communities through massive redevelopment and the benefits in terms of improvements in neighborhood quality which result from rehabilitation. Clearly, however, housing rehabilitation in older urban areas needs to be judicious in the choice of houses and locations. Again, the challenge is one of finding an appropriate balance in each local housing market.

Who Benefits from Housing Programs?

Any review of the success or failure of housing policies in general leads inevitably to the specific question of who benefits from such programs and who loses. The distribution of benefits and costs in housing is, of course, such a vague and complex issue, and one which has been the subject of intense debate for decades, that clearly there are no simple answers. Nonetheless, the prevailing view is that U.S. federal policy initiatives have primarily benefitted the private building industry, existing homeowners, financial intermediaries, and middle- to upper-income households. Those who have benefitted least have been the poor, renters, and minority groups.

Since the latter groups tend to live in different locations and neighborhoods, such programs also have had a differential spatial impact within the city. The emphasis on new construction, as noted, has benefitted the suburbs at the expense of areas of older housing in the central city. This bias has acted to reinforce that which flows from the concentration of renters, the poor and minority groups in those central areas. The image and reality of the urban ghetto is all too obvious evidence.

The overall level and social distribution of housing subsidies is suggested in Table 9.2. Most people, in most countries, are unaware of the scale of subsidies provided by government through indirect measures–largely tax relief. In the U.S., for example, of a total estimated housing subsidy of $20.56 billion in 1972. nearly two-thirds represented tax relief of various kinds.[19] Most of this subsidy went to households with above-average incomes. Direct housing subsidies (e.g., public housing), on the other hand, totalled an estimated $7 billion. Even assuming that all of the latter subsidy went to households of below-average income, which is unlikely, the combined result is heavily in favor of those households who are better off. In the U.K. the same conclusion is applicable, although the balance is less heavily weighted to indirect tax subsidies.

Each of the indirect or tax-related also has a somewhat different distributional effect across the scale of household income (Fig. 9.1). Most such benefits tend to

Table 9.2. Direct and Indirect Housing Subsidies to Households
By Income Level in U.S., 1972

Source of subsidy	Total benefits	
	Household income above median	Household income below median
Tax relief[a]	$11,370 million	$2,090 million
Direct subsidies[b]	–	$7,100 million
Total	$11,370 million	$9,190 million
Per household subsidy (66,676,000 households)	$341	$275

Notes: [a]Interest and property tax deductions, tax-free capital gains, etc.
[b]Rent rebates, public housing, allowances, etc.
Source: U.S. HUD (1973b).

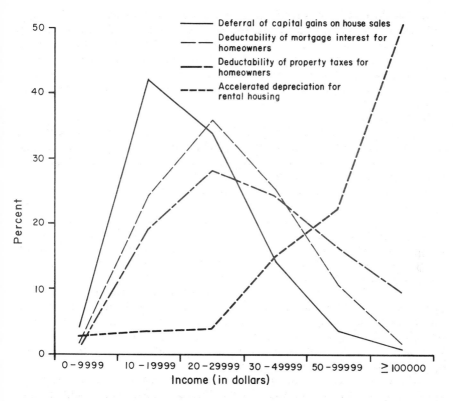

Fig. 9.1. The distribution of benefits from housing-related tax provisions, by income group, U.S., 1977.
Source: U.S. Congress, 1978.

fall to the middle-income homeowner, except for the accelerated depreciation allowance for owners of rental housing which increases with income. The least regressive of the tax-related provisions appears to be the deferral of capital gains on house sales while the most inequitable is the tax deductability of local property taxes for homeowners.

Finally, if we examine the distribution of direct housing subsidies by income group, we find both an impact which is in total limited and a distribution which has not been of pronounced benefit to the very poorest. Overall, less than 3% of households nationally received direct housing subsidies. Even in the lowest income groups (<$6,000 in 1972), less than 7% of households benefitted directly from subsidy programs.

The obvious implication from the above statistics is that housing subsidy programs in the U.S. have reached relatively few people among those in real need.

Moreover, the largest proportion of subsidies to housing have been in the form of tax credits, most of which have gone to middle-income households. On this basis, one can conclude that such programs have not been particularly successful, measured *in social equity terms*, in part because housing policy has been dominated by financial incentives and economic objectives.

The Housing Impacts of Non-Housing Policies

The preceding selective review of housing policies and issues has stressed the importance of policies which do not have housing as one of their principal objectives. To put together elements of the above discussion, Table 9.3 lists examples of the wide variety of non-housing sectoral policies which impinge on housing and

Table 9.3. Some Examples of the Housing Impacts of Non-Housing Policies

Policy sector	Example(s) of policies	Possible impacts on housing
Transport	Emphasis on highway construction rather than public transit	Encouraged decentralized new suburban housing construction
Taxation	Exemption of personal residence from capital gains tax	Shifts personal investments into housing, increasing the consumption and price of housing
	Tax deductability for mortgage interest	Encourages greater housing consumption, particularly among higher income groups, and stimulates household relocation
Investment	Depreciation allowances and investment tax shelters	Encourages new housing (rental) construction, devalues what is old
Industry and employment	Incentives to "rationalize" industry, and to stimulate high technology industries	Encourages geographical concentration and reduces the demand for housing in disadvantaged areas
Fiscal and monetary	Regulating the economy through restrictions on credit	Leads to excessive cyclical fluctuations in housing supply
Social services	Returning institutional patients to the community	May create medical ghettoes in private housing market
Environmental conservation	Environmental assessment of development projects	May delay new building and add costs through higher standards
Education	Locating new schools and closing old ones	Adds to or substracts from the price and quality of housing in a school district
Welfare	Federal transfer payments	May encourage a concentration of poor households in older housing in central cities

their possible impacts. In aggregate, the most obviously relevant policies are, first, the housing-related tax incentives and subsidies described above, and, second, those relating to local fiscal and national credit practices. Housing, and urban real estate in general, are particularly sensitive to both (see Case and Mittelbach, 1976).

Among other policies which impact on the geography of housing, perhaps those relating to transportation, employment (and economic) growth and local service provision are most crucial. Decisions on the location of new centers of employment and on whether to subsidize old industries, for example, drastically alter the demands placed on existing housing and on the location of additions to that stock. The siting of a new urban transportation facility cannot only wipe out large areas of housing, but it can and does shape geographical variations in neighborhood attractiveness and housing prices within cities. The effect of the interstate highway system in the U.S., in particular, has been one of the single most important factors in determining what housing has been built (or demolished) and where, and who has physical access to it. Other perhaps less dramatic impacts result from policy decisions on social services, welfare, school location and/or conflicts with environmental conservation legislation (see Babcock and Callies, 1973).

This inventory may be obvious to most readers, and could of course be extended in great detail. The point is, however, that what one must consider as housing policy is nothing less than the *summation of all spatial and sectoral decisions* which shape the geography of housing production and consumption in a city or country. In these terms, it is not surprising that direct housing policies, narrowly-defined, are often inadequate in scale, diffuse in their intentions, and misdirected.

NOTES

[1] See, for example, the reviews of the economics of housing in Stafford (1978), Headey (1978), and R. Robinson (1979); also comparative reviews on housing policy in the U.S. and Britain (Wolman, 1975; Headey, 1978), and Sweden (Kemeny, 1978). Useful edited collections on U.S. housing policies are provided in Wheaton, Milgram, and Meyerson (1966), Pynoos et al. (1973), and Phares (1978). British housing experience is summarized in detail in Merrett (1979), Cullingworth (1979), and Lansley (1979). Similar summaries are readily available on U.S. policy initiatives (U.S., HUD, 1973b, 1978; U.S. Congress, 1978 and on Canadian policy (see Dennis and Fish, 1972; L. B. Smith, 1977; Rose, 1978).

[2] Wood (1934) notes that it was not until 1879, for example, that legislation required that new tenements be built with a window to the outside. More than 350,000 windowless rooms had been constructed in New York City before that date.

[3] Unfortunately, the apparent emphasis of the FHA on racially-exclusive neighborhoods was to contribute to subsequent problems of racial segregation and discrimination in housing in American cities.

[4] Federal housing policy in the 1950s was largely vested in the Housing and Home Finance Agency (HHFA), which did not enjoy departmental status.

[5] In particular, the FHA under Section 220 of the 1954 Act was allowed to extend liberal mortgages to those who would invest in housing for middle-income households in cleared areas. Section 221 was to provide similar incentives for those displaced by renewal.

[6]For example, mortgage funds were provided through conventional financial institutions at roughly 3% interest, the BMIR rate set in the 1959 Act, Section 202, for housing provided by nonprofit groups for the elderly. The Federal Government National Mortgage Association (GNMA) would then purchase the mortgage at the rates of interest prevailing at the time.

[7]Subsidies were to be based on the difference between the rent necessary to cover the monthly service charges on the mortgage debt at current market rates and the rent based on a fixed 1% interest rate.

[8]It was estimated that the major benefits of Section 235 housing went to families in the moderate-income group ($5–10,000) rather than the low-income group ($3–8,000). Section 236 showed a lower bias, but subsidies in both programs tended to increase with income.

[9]Similar trends are evident in Canadian housing policy. The National Housing Act (amended by Bill C-29 in March, 1979) included measures to extend the range of nonprofit and co-op housing which could receive subsidies on interest rates or government insured mortgages, and replaced several existing programs of NHA aid to municipalities with a broader Community Services Contribution Program.

[10]See Wolman (1975), Headey (1978), Cullingworth (1979) and the 1977 Consultative Document on Housing Policy (Cmnd 6851).

[11]Nonprofit housing associations play a relatively large role (some 30–50,000 units annually) in housing supply in the U.K. Some 2,700 such associations build, rehabilitate, and manage rental housing for specific client groups. Most receive direct financing from the central government's Housing Corporation (see M. Smith, 1977).

[12]Each local authority maintains a Housing Revenue Account for its publicly-owned stock which contains its revenues from local property taxes (rates), rents from tenants, subsidies from central government (about 50% of revenue), and other sources (such as sales of council houses).

[13]Authorized under Section 504 of the HUD Act of 1970, as amended by Section 804 in 1974. The EHAP in fact consists of three sub-programs: (1) a demand experiment, to examine how households respond; (2) a supply experiment, to analyze how housing markets responded to demand; and (3) an administrative agency experiment to provide information on conducting a housing allowance program.

[14]The sites included both large cities (Pittsburgh) and small cities (Green Bay) as well as rural areas (North Dakota).

[15]Calculation of the actual amount of the allowance is complex, and varies by the specific program involved, but is generally based on the gap between that household's income and the cost of renting an appropriate housing unit in that local housing market.

[16]Rent stabilization is even more complicated, in both concept and administration, than traditional rent controls (see Harloe, 1979). Basically it imposes codes of practice and required standards of services on apartment owners and provides procedures for setting fair rents and for hearing complaints from tenants. In 1975, roughly 30% of all rental units were under controlled rents and 32% were in the rent-stabilized sector.

[17]At present, both the U.S. and U.K. allow the deduction from taxable income of interest paid on mortgages (Canada introduced a tax credit scheme in 1979). This cost the governments involved some $4.2 billion and £1.2, respectively, in 1978.

[18]Improvement grants in the U.K. increased from an annual average of 100,000 at the beginning of the 1960s to over 300,000 in the early 1970s, but have declined since then. Roughly two-thirds of these grants are to the private sector, the rest go to local authority (council) housing or housing associations.

[19]Some observers argue that the largest component in these indirect subsidies, and the most difficult to measure, is the absence of a tax on "imputed rent"—i.e., the rent which homeowners do not pay.

Chapter 10

Public Sector and Social Housing

One of the most common responses of government to the apparent inability of the private market to produce housing for all, in sufficient quantity, quality and at reasonable prices, is to intercede directly by constructing "public" housing. Traditionally this has meant housing built, owned, and managed by national or local governments (or nonprofit housing associations), but increasingly the term "public" has given way to the concept of "social" housing. The latter refers broadly to all housing directly subsidized by governments or institutions, but including conventional public (or council) housing.

This chapter examines the role of public housing in policies of national and local governments, and in urban real estate markets, as well as the behavior of the state as landlord and landowner. Given the earlier emphasis on the allocation process in the private housing market (see Chapters 2 and 4), an extended discussion is included here of the parallel allocation mechanism within the public sector. The second part of the chapter examines the increasing public attention paid to "special purpose" housing, i.e., housing primarily intended for social groups with special needs, taking as one example the purposes, politics, and locational requirements of housing for the elderly. The chapter concludes with a discussion of alternative strategies for locating housing for the poor, within the city.

THE STATE AS LANDLORD

The Size and Scope of the Public Sector

The degree of reliance of western capitalist countries on directly provided public sector or social housing varies widely. As Chapter 3 demonstrated, traditional public housing accounts for only a very small proportion of the housing inventories in the U.S., Canada, and Australia (see Chapter 3). For example, in the U.S. the figure is less than 2%. In Britain and most of western Europe, on the other hand, the proportions are much higher, although usually not over 40%. In Britain, in 1977, over 35% (or nearly 6 million units) of the housing stock was in the public sector (primarily owned by local authorities, new town corporations, local trusts, and nonprofit associations). All of these figures, of course, stand in sharp contrast to those for countries in the Socialist bloc where the vast majority (but not all) housing is owned by the state or by nonprofit cooperatives.[1]

Among western countries, the contrasting roles of public housing reflect not only ideological differences but the diverse historical origins of land and housing policies in each country. Differences in ideology and in attitudes to the public ownership of housing and land, particularly in urban areas, are well known, but the importance of the historical roots of housing policies is not so obvious. Each country is in some sense a prisoner of its past policy decisions, or frequently its non-decisions.

These differences are directly mirrored in the populations served by public sector housing. Taking the U.S. and Britain as examples, the contrast is striking (Fig. 10.1). Given the proportionally much larger size of the public sector in Britain compared to the U.S., it might be expected that the former would serve a much broader spectrum of the nation's population. Even so, the income distribution of households who are resident in council housing in Britain is wide indeed. Over 40% of such residents had gross incomes (in 1972) above the national median, while a negligible percentage in U.S. public housing had similarlily high incomes. In the latter, as might be expected, almost all tenants had incomes less than the national average, and the majority had incomes of less than one-half that average.

This single index illustrates the contrasting histories and philosophies which underlie the current contribution of public sector housing in the two countries.[2] In the U.S., as in Canada and Australia, public housing is obviously only intended for a few of the very poor. It is provided, often reluctantly, as a minimal element in the national welfare system. More specifically, public housing in the U.S. (at least that within the low-rent program) is overwhelmingly occupied by those on unemployment insurance or welfare, by minority households, problem families, and by those with children and only one parent at home (many of these, of course, are the same households). In 1977, for example, nearly 63% of public housing tenants were members of minority groups, over 43% received some form of welfare, and 36% were elderly (U.S. HUD, 1978). And these proportions are increasing. Of those moving in during 1976–77, however, over 70% were receiving some form of social assistance.

It is not surprising, therefore, that traditional public housing has such an unfavorable image in most of North America. The historic emphases in American policy have combined to limit public housing to a small and unusually disadvantaged population. In most instances, such housing is so "stigmatized" in the public view that any proposal for a substantial increase in its numbers is now unlikely to succeed. The result is obvious: the images of, and policies for, public housing become mutually reinforcing.

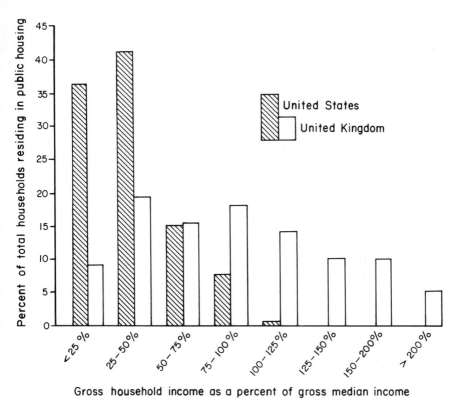

Fig. 10.1. A comparison of the distribution of public housing tenants by income, U.S. and U.K., 1972 (after Wolman, 1975).

In Britain, as in much of western Europe, council housing has traditionally been seen as a necessary and integral part of the nation's social system. Although views differ on what is the appropriate size of that sector, there is little disagreement on the need for such housing. The wide range of incomes in council housing shown above also reflects a desire to maintain a social mix in such housing, particularly in the new towns, and the absence of rigid upper limits on the incomes of tenants. Housing policy objectives are also aided by tighter land use planning controls. A long history of public acquisition of urban land by local authorities for parks, historical restoration, land banking, and slum clearance has facilitated the construction of large-scale public sector housing. This is especially evident in the dominance of public housing in the postwar new towns in Britain and in the suburban planned communities in Sweden and other western European countries.[3]

It is also important to reiterate who provides and manages the public housing sector. Recall from the preceding chapter that in Britain local governments take the principal responsibility in building and subsequently managing public housing—subject to central government guidelines and financial regulations. In fact, local authorities are compelled to provide housing for their own residents (although some refuse to house the poor). Nonprofit housing associations also tend to be more locally based and administered. In North America, local governments are not under any similar obligation, although an increasing number have assumed that role. In most instances, however, it is the state, provincial, or national governments (if any) which take the initiative, a factor which often encourages benign neglect.

Arguments Pro and Con Public Sector Housing

This is not the place to debate at length the arguments in support of or against a large public sector in housing, in light of the privatization trend in housing policy noted earlier, but it is instructive to summarize these arguments as a means of responding to two distinct but interrelated questions: one is concerned with attitudes to public ownership in general and the other with the best method (public of private market) of providing adequate housing for all. Here we concentrate on the latter question, using the British and U.S. approaches as examples.

U.K. approach: possible advantages	*U.S. approach: possible disadvantages*
(1) bring housing directly to those in most need;	(1) directly affects very few of the needy;
(2) discourages the formation of ghettoes;	(2) usually ensures the creation of low-income ghettoes;
(3) serves a wider range of housing needs and encourages some social mixing; and	(3) discourages social mixing; and
(4) allows for some economies in the provision of public services.	(4) fragmentation adds to the cost of public services.
possible disadvantages	*possible advantages*
(1) shifts resources from private to public sector, without necessarily increasing the total resources available for housing;	(1) may increase total resources allocated to housing by encouraging private investment;
(2) may create a large and costly bureaucracy;	(2) avoids expansion of public bureaucracy;
(3) often subsidizes those who do not need it;	(3) serves only those who are in severe need;
(4) reduces geographical mobility, perhaps adding to labor market imperfections; and	(4) applies to those who have little mobility; and
(5) may destroy the private rental sector.	(5) maintains a large (perhaps healthy) private rental sector.

This listing is highly overgeneralized and of course does not exhaust the arguments. Moreover, it is often other factors which intercede to determine whether it successfully meets housing needs not met by that market. The disadvantages frequently attributed to public sector housing, however, often have more to do *with the way such programs are designed and administered* than with the underlying philosophy itself.

Neither is it possible to say which approach has produced the most housing benefits at the least social cost. In Britain, publicly built housing was widely viewed as the most efficient and humane way to overcome the housing problems left by the industrial revolution and two wars. Because it is now well established, a large public sector in turn creates a demand for its continuation and further expansion: visibly it is seen as serving an obvious social need and as playing a major role in the national welfare system. Older, well-built public housing, on which the initial construction debt has been retired, may also be an important revenue producing asset for local housing authorities. In North America, on the other hand, without such an historical inheritance, the costs and political difficulties of mounting large-scale public programs now seem prohibitive.

The debate over public sector housing is, however, much broader than that between publicly owned housing and the private sector. The more general issue, as described in Chapter 9, is one of the size and distribution of *social housing*, of which purposefully built government housing is but one dimension. The most common substitutes for traditional public housing as such are threefold, usually appearing in combination. These three include policies to subsidize tenants in order to provide them with sufficient income to rent or purchase housing at current market levels, to encourage housing associations and other nonprofit groups to build and manage housing for needy groups, or to subsidize private builders in constructing low-cost housing for those of modest means. Thus, even when there is agreement on ends—that of improving the quality of housing available to the poorest in our society—there is an inevitable difference of opinion on the most efficient and just means and on who is the most appropriate landlord.

Other Impacts of Public Sector Housing

The provisions of public housing in urban areas dominated by the private market can and does alter the operation of that market. It may have impacts on overall levels of prices and rents, on the choices open to consumers, on the kinds of social services required, and on real estate in general. The extent and direction of these impacts depends primarily on the size and character of the public housing stock and its occupants and on its location. The latter we examine in more detail in subsequent sections, although it should be stressed here that since the provision of public housing also means the design of communities in which real people are to live, its major impacts are on social relations and living conditions.

The size of the public sector is perhaps the most crucial variable in measuring its effects on housing prices and choice. If that sector is large, and well managed, it may serve as a means of holding down price increases in the private sector and of increasing choice. If it is large but poorly designed or located, it may have the exact opposite effect: of shifting demand to the private sector and thereby increasing prices. In the former case, the public sector stock can become a means of indirectly regulating the private sector. In the latter case, it may only make matters worse. In Britain, as noted, it has also contributed to the emasculation of the privately rented sector.

The influence of the public sector on housing choice, in turn, depends on the types of housing provided, the locations selected, and on public attitudes to different kinds of tenure. As noted in Chapter 3, some countries have been able to provide a public (or nonprofit) sector which can compete with the private sector for middle-income tenants. Where the two sectors are distinct, in quality and image, the effect is (as in the case of prices) to create separate sub-markets and thus to effectively reduce choice. When the public housing sector is also geographically distinct, and concentrated in isolated or unattractive locations, cut-off from jobs or services, the effect on choice can be even more severe.

A related policy question is that of the impact of selling (privatizing) publicly owned dwellings. This issue is not new (see Nevitt, 1966), and although it has arisen at various times in most countries including the U.S.,[4] it is perhaps most pronounced in those with large stocks of public housing. In Britain the tendency to sell off council housing has varied with the party in power, and has also generated a long academic debate (see Murie, 1975; Duncan, 1977; Cullingworth, 1979). Although the amount of housing involved is only a small fraction of the total stock, it is a highly visible issue.[5] It has little, if anything, to do with improving the quality of housing available to the poor, however. In fact, the reverse is likely to be the case.

ALLOCATION IN THE PUBLIC SECTOR

There are as many variations in the process by which housing is allocated to households within the public sector as there are agencies involved. This section examines only two of the many possible dimensions of this issue: (1) the objectives and administrative criteria by which households are assigned to housing units, and (2) the spatial and social outcomes of that process. This example is valuable here, even if traditional public housing is in decline, since it illustrates the dilemmas facing all housing systems.

The Allocation Process

The process by which households are assigned to dwelling units in the public sector is in some ways remarkably similar to that in the private sector, although the institutional context as well as the criteria and objectives of allocation clearly differ. Essentially, public sector housing is allocated to those households who are known to be in most immediate *need*, and those for whom the political system assumes some responsibility. The criteria of individual needs, however, are in theory modified to take into consideration community-wide objectives relating to maintaining "equity" among different social groups and urban subareas.

The mechanism of allocation is through a public agency—i.e., a housing commission, association, local authority, or similar agency—whose responsibility it is to match households to available units in the housing stock. Unlike the private market, however, allocation is carried out on a one-to-one basis. To illustrate the process here we draw on a number of recent empirical studies of the public sector allocation process in Britain (see Gray, 1976; Housing Services Advisory Group, 1978; Lambert et al., 1978; Taylor, 1978). The details are, of course, unique to the specific city under study, but the process is not.

Figure 10.2 summarizes the components in a typical allocation process. As in the previous example of the private market, one begins with a stock of available or vacant housing units and an inventory of demand (needs). The stock of available units derives from three sources: (1) new construction, (2) acquisition of existing units from the privately owned stock (through purchase or expropriation), and (3) relets within the public sector resulting from household departures (due to death, out-migration, or eviction). These units in turn are cross-classified in terms of their "suitability" for different types of households according to varying sets of criteria: the age and type of structure, its size, condition, accessibility to jobs and services, and general environmental quality, as well as the image or reputation of the neighborhood or estate of which that unit is a part.

For households, the housing authority undertakes to identify the various sources of "demand" for public sector housing. Such households are ranked according to their needs and in relation to the alternative housing choices, if any, open to them (see Cullingworth, 1972, 1979; Harloe, 1977). In most instances the principal measure of demand is the housing register, or waiting list, of people who have expressed their needs. Some local authorities also undertake to access the extent to latent demand through surveys within their jurisdictions of households currently living in overcrowded or unsatisfactory conditions.

The five principal populations—or sources of demand—for public sector housing, ranked in a typical order of priority, are: (1) the *homeless* (although some local authorities oppose taking in the homeless); (2) those requiring *rehousing* because of slum clearance and renewal, for which that local authority assumes "special" responsibility; (3) those in urgent need because of *medical* or social problems, or because they represent "key" workers; (4) those requesting *transfers* within the public sector for reasons other than the above, often to move to a more preferred unit or location; and (5) those on the regular *waiting list*. Strictly speaking, the first three of the above categories represent "needs" as the term is traditionally defined, while the latter more frequently reflect "demand" in the conventional sense discussed earlier. As in the private sector, there is also a demand schedule for public sector housing, representing the obvious fact that tenants differentiate between good and bad units and preferred locations.

How does this listing conform to the actual situation, i.e., who exactly is on the waiting list for public housing? What kinds of housing are they currently in? Although this varies widely between housing authorities, and over time, a 1977 national survey in the U.K. estimated that nearly 1.5 million persons were on council house waiting lists (an exaggeration, no doubt). The present tenures of

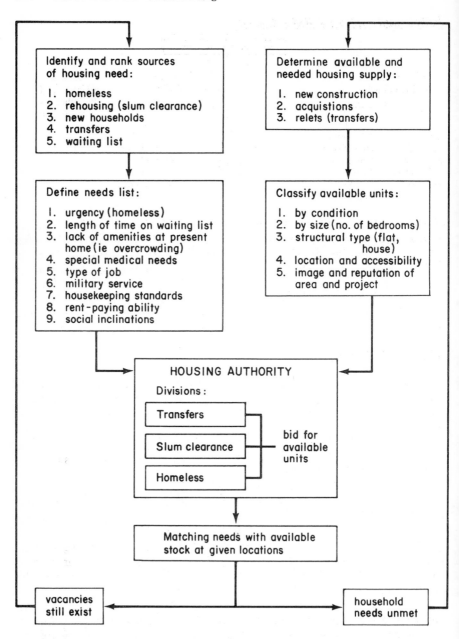

Fig. 10.2. The allocation process for public sector housing.

these people were distributed as follows:

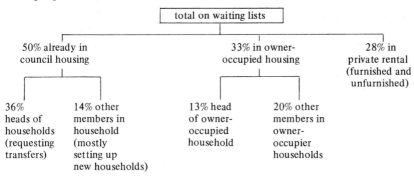

Perhaps most surprising is the size of the owner-occupier category. Since the survey does not provide cross-tabulations, we do not know exactly who these people are, although the owner-occupier heads are likely to be elderly and the "other" members are likely to be young and setting up their own household for the first time. Equally surprising, the survey also shows that only about 15% were in housing which was classified as lacking one or more basic amenities. What clearly has happened recently is that the clients have changed and there has been a shift from those "in need" to those "demanding" better accommodation.

Allocation Objectives

In undertaking to assign people to housing, the authority has to balance a number of competing objectives.[7] It has to be seen to be allocating housing as fairly and as equitably as possible. They must undertake to get the best use of the available stock and to meet social needs and preferences, while avoiding geographic polarization by age, race, or family structure. They must also remember that they are the "architects" of communities, through their decisions on where to locate individual households.

The scale and complexity of this allocation process should not be underestimated. First, there is the difficult trade-off between meeting individual household needs and responding to the collective interests of the larger community. The latter might include the desire of members of one racial group to live together, or the desire of no one to live near problem families; or it might involve locating public housing in a way which conforms to a larger land use or transport plan, the community-wide benefits of which in turn might be viewed quite differently by the people who are to live in that housing.

Second, in allocating housing the responsible authority has to solve essentially the same decision problems—of investment, distribution, and location—that the private sector leaves largely to the market, except that it has to do so for each individual household in the system. To be done effectively, this requires an immence amount of information, in fact much more than the private market requires. Without that information, allocation decisions can often be costly, inequitable and perhaps socially disruptive. Thirdly, as W. F. Smith (1970) argues, the allocation process must in theory be simultaneous, since the assignment of a given household *i* to unit *j* should consider the impact of that decision on the welfare of all other households previously allocated in that sector in order to maintain overall equity. This kind of continual reassessment and reallocation is in practice impossible, and generally a universal "welfare" equilibrium is ignored even as a long-term objective.

Allocation Criteria

Perhaps the most difficult and contentious issue in public sector housing allocation is to establish the criteria for defining needs and priorities, and thus a rank-ordering of households. In situations where the supply of public sector housing is less than total demand, which is almost always the case (but decreasingly so in recent years), the allocation process itself also contains a myriad of internal contradictions. Contrary to popular impressions, however, this problem does not disappear even when public sector housing is not in short supply. All that happens in such situations is that the poorest and most unattractive units—the "difficult-to-let" units (Taylor, 1978)—remain unoccupied. The basic allocation problem, that of deciding who should have the largest and most preferred of the units in the rest of the inventory, still exists—and in some ways becomes more difficult.

Figure 10.2 also provides a rough (hypothetical) listing of the criteria on which housing needs might be determined and households ranked. Points may be assigned to each household in a manner not unlike that of some immigration departments. Since in both the housing and immigration examples there is usually an upper limit on the number let in, the ranking process is clearly competitive. Usually the most important criteria identify those households who require immediate accommodation (the homeless and refugees from slum clearance), their length of time on the waiting list, the degree of deprivation in a household's current living situation, and increasingly those persons with special needs (e.g., medical). Some units may also be reserved, especially in depressed areas, for "key" workers who may require housing as part of the incentives deemed necessary to attract new industry, and simply to facilitate the geographic mobility of labor.[8]

If the above criteria define priorities for "access" to public housing, most local authorities also have "restrictive" entry criteria. Most insist on some minimum length of residency in that community (from 6 months to 5 years) and many have upper limits, or "bars," on the incomes of tenants. Others exclude or give low priority to very young households, singles, students, lodgers, previous rent debtors, and the cohabitation of unrelated individuals.

In addition, housing authorities frequently employ purely subjective criteria in selecting households and then in allocating these households to specific units and locations. The results are often inequitable and perverse. Such criteria may, for example, assign points to the "suitability" of the prospective tenant—in general or for particular kinds of units—including their housekeeping standards and rent-paying ability. Points may also be subtracted for households with what are perceived to be social or behavioral problems. Other households are excluded, or allocated to the least favored units and estates, because of racial, ethnic, or religious discrimination. Consequently, there is some evidence that problem families are housed last and that the poorest are allocated to the oldest and lowest quality units in the worst locations (Cullingworth, 1972; Gray, 1976; Duncan, 1977).[9]

In effect, different households have differing degrees of "power" to influence or control the allocation process as it applies to them. Their attributes define a position with respect to the public system which plays the same role as income does in the private sector. For example, those households with no alternative in housing, those who have no special medical problems or job priority, and who also have a problem reputation, have virtually no power. In contrast, those households already residing in the system can be more selective in their choice of housing by simply refusing to move from their present unit until a more preferred alternative is offered.

These problems in turn raise a number of issues regarding the behavior of housing institutions, whether public or private, which have been stressed throughout this book. One such issue is that public housing authorities or agencies, like other institutions, have their own internal structure and managerial objectives. They also operate within a larger "organizational" framework which conditions their attitudes and behavior (Donnison, 1967; Harloe, Issacharoff, and Minns, 1974). This behavior is expressed in several ways. First, in large local authorities where there are divisions concerned with different types of tenants, these divisions often compete for units on behalf of waiting tenants. In a sense they "bid" for units, using as arguments their ability to maximize the use of existing housing resources and the length of their particular queues. Second, as institutions needing to justify their continued existence within a larger system, housing authorities, like any landlord, prefer to minimize their costs and management difficulties and to run an expanding and efficient operation.

This presents all housing managers with a real dilemma. The obvious way to achieve the latter objectives is to discriminate among tenants, to select those who are least likely to cause trouble or to increase maintenance costs, and those who pay "fair" rents. On the other hand, by sticking closely to criteria on needs, and the length of time on the waiting list, they may discourage households from improving their housing condition through other means while encouraging some to "compete" with others in establishing their claim (merit) for public housing.[10]

There are several other interesting questions which the student of housing must address with reference to public sector housing allocation. How, for example, given a priority list based on need, does one avoid geographical concentrations of the most disadvantaged families? Conversely, how far does one go in circumventing the needs list in a desire to achieve some degree of social mixing in a housing project? What degree of self-selection in public residential location is possible and desirable and what weight should be given to locational needs and preferences, relative to those of physical housing needs and priorities?

SPECIAL PURPOSE HOUSING

The Diversity of Special Needs

Most governments in recent years have broadened their emphasis from housing for the poor to include providing housing for specific groups in society with special needs (see U.N., E.C.E., 1977). This includes housing for such diverse groups as the elderly, single people, transient workers, immigrants, the physically handicapped, and the mentally ill. The kinds of housing provided vary from single units and group homes to large estates. In part, this policy emphasis is long overdue; these groups have generally been ignored by public authorities or left entirely to the vagaries of the private market.

Most of these groups have specific requirements in both the design and location of their housing, and in addition many are also poor. Here we examine one such group, the low-income elderly, an increasing proportion of most national populations. We can address essentially the same kinds of questions of housing allocation for this diverse group as to other groups: How much housing is needed and of what type? How much has been or should be provided and by whom? What are the location requirements for such housing?

In most developed countries, the elderly (>65) now account for at least 8% and as much as 15% of national populations. These proportions have increased rapidly and will increase still further in the 1980s as the effects of greater longevity and previous demographic bulges exert their impact. Further, an increasing proportion of the elderly appear to prefer, or have no choice but to live on their own, as our concepts of extended family responsibility and the desire for autonomy change.

As a consequence, the aggregate demand for housing for the elderly has also grown rapidly. Moreover, many of the elderly, particularly those on fixed incomes and pensions, have been severely affected by the recent escalation of housing prices and costs described earlier. A recent survey in Canada, for example, showed that many elderly spend over 50% of their limited incomes on housing (Andreae, 1978). Elderly homeowners, even with their accumulated equity, are often house-poor because of rising operating costs, especially taxes, heating, maintenance, and debt service changes. Equally, elderly renters are often crushed by the rising real costs of private rental.

The government response to these trends has been to initiate or expand a wide range of housing programs, each of which could be the subject of a book. These include: (1) the direct provision of housing assistance and supplements, (2) property tax and rent rebates, (3) rehabilitation grants, (4) the delivery of "at home" services, and (5) the construction of special purpose housing. The latter approach, the direct provision of housing, by public and private means (excluding institutions), specifically for "senior" citizens, is selected for discussion in the following section.

Housing for the Elderly

The elderly are both a visible (although not yet politically powerful) and growing component of housing demand (Struyk, 1977). They represent a population which in aggregate is relatively easily defined but whose housing needs are not. They are, however, a group whose housing problems are becoming more evident and apparently more serious, a reflection of the recent trends in demography, housing costs, and negative attitudes to shared housing with older relatives, noted above.

The actual volume of housing constructed for the elderly, although still numerically small, has increased dramatically in recent years. These units, at least in the U.S. and Canada, are of three principal types: (1) low-rent public housing, (2) assisted housing provided by nonprofit associations under federal loans (such as Section 202 housing), and (3) private market construction. The latter in turn may be combined with rent assistance or rent-geared-to-income subsidies to builders. In the U.S., the number of units intended specifically for the elderly under the low-rent public housing program alone rose from only 18,000 units in 1960 to 360,000 in 1977, or from just 3% to nearly 27% of the entire public housing stock.

Thus it seems that the increase in housing for the elderly has come, in part, at the expense of public housing for families. In both the U.S. and Canada, this shift has reflected a growing political dissatisfaction with, or disinterest in, family housing (Rose, 1978). The latter is more expensive to build, more difficult to manage, and seems to produce numerous problems for public authorities: vandalism crime, high turnover, and neighborhood spill-over effects. Senior citizen housing, in contrast, is administratively more convenient. The elderly tend to stay put and to pay their rent on time. They usually do not vandalize property, abuse local services, or bother other tenants. Consequently, they are more acceptable to the local authorities as clients, as well as to the neighbors in residential areas in which they are located.

Locational Criteria

Despite pressures to build more senior citizen housing as quickly as possible, increasing attention is now given to the locational and environmental needs of housing for the elderly (see Davis, 1973; Golant, 1975; Grigsby and Rosenburg, 1975; Andreae, 1978; Mercer, 1979). The reasons are fairly obvious: with lower incomes and levels of geographical mobility on average, the elderly are simply more dependent on the structure of their immediate environment and on their accessibility to services and friends. They also are more likely to feel the psychological stress of being uprooted from a familiar environment and moving to a new one. From the point of view of local government, the location question is also of considerable importance since it must allocate social services more closely to the spatial distribution of the elderly than is necessary for other more mobile population groups.

There are at least three major dimensions to this question. One is the problem of location within an urban area in combination with the need to select the most appropriate design of the immediate residential environment. A second is whether housing for the elderly should or should not be segregated from housing for other age groups. The third question is what services should be available to the elderly within a given range of "critical" distances from each project or community.

Table 10.1. Ranking of and Critical Distances to Selected Services in Housing Projects for the Elderly

Type of service/facility	Ranking in importance	Critical distances
Grocery store	1	2 to 3 blocks
Bus stop	2	1 to 2 blocks
Place of worship	3	1/4 to 1/2 mile
Pharmacy/chemist	4	3 blocks
Clinic or hospital	5	1/4 to 1/2 mile
Bank	6	1/4 mile
Social center	7	indeterminate/ on site if feasible
Library	8	1 mile
Newsagent/tobacco shop	9	1/4 mile
Restaurant	10	1/4 to 1/2 mile
Cinema	11	1 mile

Source: Adapted from Niebanck and Pope, 1965, and from Andreae, 1978.

The response to the first question is generally that the elderly should be provided with a choice of locations and, if they so desire, a choice of living in segregated buildings, but preferably buildings located as an integral part of a familiar and mixed neighborhood. Most studies indicate that the elderly, when moving to senior citizen housing, prefer to remain within communities they know and have resided in. That being so, the location question becomes not primarily one of where to provide such housing, in the sense of choosing between downtown and suburban locations, but rather one of ensuring that each community has its own "fair-share" of such housing to ensure a degree of social mix and choice (Mercer, 1979).

In terms of the accessibility provided by the location of senior citizen housing, it is evident that several factors—such as lower automobile ownership rates and greater physical immobility—necessitate a redefinition of standard measures of geographical proximity. The availability of public transport is particularly important, if not a prerequisite, in locating such projects. Unfortunately, public transit, notably urban rapid transit, is often neither convenient nor practical for many elderly (and for others not physically agile).

Perhaps more crucial is the question of what social services are, or should be, available within a given walking distance. Niebanck and Pope (1965), for example, have provided estimates of the "critical distances" within which a range of public and commercial services for the elderly should be available (see Table 10.1). Here the ranking of each service is determined by their frequency of mention in the survey. The critical distances are the actual distances at which the elderly expressed serious dissatisfaction with their current level of accessibility to services.

Clearly these distances will vary with the city and environment under study, as well as between groups of the elderly, but at least they provide a set of benchmarks on which the interested student or practitioner can undertake to evaluate the quality of a given location and environment for senior citizen housing. Although housing location is obviously not the most important issue facing the elderly in our society, it is too important to be ignored.

LOCATION WITHIN THE CITY

A great deal has been said already about the problems of locating social housing, particularly housing for low-income and minority groups, within an urban area. In this section we need only pull these various strands together. First, we undertake to reiterate the nature and scale of the problem and second, to examine—albeit briefly—alternative strategies for altering the existing geographical patterns of public housing.

The Problem Restated

It is by now painfully obvious that siting public housing within urban areas, at least in societies in which most land is privately held and discrimination is pervasive, remains one of the most serious obstacles to improving the quality and environment of low-income housing (Meyerson and Banfield, 1955). Many innovative national policies have been scuttled at the local level precisely because of the inability or unwillingness of local governments to find suitable locations for public sector housing. Many such projects which are actually built are assigned to unattractive locations either in the inner city or in remote suburban estates. The resulting high degree of concentration of such housing has frequently lead to the creation of new "public" slums and racial ghettoes, in which both housing and neighborhood quality rapidly deteriorate.

The origins of the problem are many and complex, but lie essentially in a fear of the unknown, discrimination, and local self-interest. There are reinforced by a real estate market and property tax system which render the acceptance of public housing as a social burden for the immediate neighborhood and a financial liability for the wider community. Local governments, even local resident organizations, often resist the intrusion of public housing (and other forms of low-income and/or racially mixed housing) into their midst on these same grounds, even those who argue that they are only trying to maintain the existing social character and property values of that area. The view of the existing community, as described in Chapter 8, derives from a fear that the residents of public housing (with the possible exception of the elderly) will reduce the quality of life in their neighborhoods, lower housing prices, overburden local services, increase rates of crime and vandalism, and threaten the quality of local schools. These fears are reinforced by the uncertainties created by the "prisoners dilemma" which discourages investment in housing in areas undergoing a rapid social or racial transition.

Perhaps the most blatant expression of the siting problem is the existence of *restrictive covenants* in many suburban municipalities in American cities, and to a lesser extent in Canada, Britain, and other western countries. The origins and nature of these restrictions are now well known (Soloman, 1974; Downs, 1975; Kain and Quigley, 1975; Phares, 1978). By various means, such as minimum restrictions on the size of a residential lot or house, by setting high servicing standards or by outright refusals to accept public housing, suburban municipalities are often able to exclude those of lower incomes and of a different race or class from living in higher status areas. They become "gate-keepers" of the suburban social order. This has occurred even in urban areas with a metropolitan-wide government, such as London, and in which that government has sought to distribute public housing more widely.[11] Efforts at "opening up the suburbs" to those of lower incomes in both the U.S. and Britain have generally failed.[12] In the U.S., racial discrimination is cited as a principal explanation for such restrictions, but given the experience of other countries which do not have a large racial minority, it is likely that the same restrictions would apply without the racial problem simply because of income or class differences.

Alternative Spatial Strategies

The likely outcome of such restrictions, and of the private market processes of land use competition and neighborhood decline described earlier, is the creation of distinct ghettoes, or concentrations of low-income and disadvantaged households as well as deteriorated residential structures. There is considerable recent evidence that the situation in most U.S. cities has not improved and may well have grown worse (McKay, 1977; Yinger et al., 1978). Thus any housing policy intended to help low-income and minority households must contain a component which not only recognizes this geographical pattern but attempts to alter it.

One provocative summary of alternative strategies for dealing with these issues is provided by Downs (1975). The alternatives he proposed address the combined issues of spatial concentration (of poor people and poor housing), of poverty in general, and of the type and location of new housing required. He differentiates the policy alternatives on the basis of whether they:

> act to *disperse* low-income households to the suburbs or to simply *contain* the deterioration;
>
> emphasize *capital enrichment* (building and neighborhood improvements) or income maintenance and social services (noncapital enrichments);
>
> encourage a slower or faster rate of *filtering* (trickle-down) of the existing stock;
>
> encourage a high or low rate of *new housing production*;
>
> encourage the *insertion* of new housing production at low-to-moderate or middle-to-high *price levels*;
>
> encourage *immediate* or *delayed redevelopment* of decayed inner city areas.

Taken together with traditional anti-poverty programs, these alternative approaches produce some 49 different policy combinations, many of which are internally contradictory.[13]

To date the overall strategy applied to U.S. cities (if there can be said to be a single strategy) has been one of attempting to contain decay while maintaining high overall levels of housing production (at middle to upper price levels), combined with minimal programs of housing assistance and income maintenance. One result of this approach is that the filtering process has been accelerated with the resulting exaggerated decay of inner city neighborhoods.

Although there is no single optimal strategy, Downs' preference is for a mixture of different approaches. This mixed strategy might involve greater efforts at spatial dispersal, increased noncapital enrichment programs, delayed redevelopment of inner city areas, a blending of demand and production subsidies, and an emphasis on low and moderate price levels of new construction. He assumes that an all-out effort on all fronts at once is infeasible. Even so, his modest proposals have not been translated into a coordinated polity response nor, in most cases, into specific programs.

A much simpler spatial strategy has, however, been widely adopted. This is the proposal for *"fair-share"* housing allocation. In this approach, each local area is required to take its "fair" share of housing for households of low and moderate income (Listokin, 1976), in much the same way as described above for housing for the elderly. The criteria for determining each area's fair share could be either of: (1) proportionally *equal shares*; (2) actual housing *need*; (3) spatial *equity* and *social mix*—allocating low-income housing to those areas which do not have such housing; (4) *suitability* to absorb additional housing (e.g., availability of vacant land and existing services); (5) the availability of employment nearby; (6) the *past performance* of each area in being able to accommodate such households; and (7) the simple need for a greater geographical *dispersal* of inner city low-income residents.

None of these alternative strategies is sufficient in itself. The first approach has the attractive of simplicity, but it ignores most or all of the other environmental conditions which influence housing needs and preferences. The needs criterion does little to expand housing opportunities for the low-income where such housing is presently limited, and thus may increase geographical segregation. The equity and social mix criterion ignores the fact that building sites may physically not be available, and the suitability criterion would most likely identify the environmentally most attractive areas where community resistence to housing for the poor is strongest. Consequently, most fair-share proposals require (or allow for) a combination of criteria in allocating social housing to urban subareas, combinations which in theory permit the allocation process to reflect local conditions and constraints as well as different housing needs.

Even so, neither fair-share plans nor theoretical arguments will necessarily result in different patterns of low-income housing on the ground. That goal necessitates a degree of government control and a consensus on criteria which are all too rare in western countries and within large complex urban areas. As long as many local governments find it an economic and fiscal penalty to accept low-income housing in their midst, and individuals or groups of households refuse to accept some community-wide responsibility for those less fortunate than themselves, and as long as our property tax system discourages them from doing so, the problem of locating housing for low-income households will persist. Clearly, the location question in social housing remains a critical dimension of housing policy and an issue which is far from being adequately understood or resolved.

NOTES

[1]Cooperative ownership of housing can mean either public (state) or private ownership, depending on specific local arrangements (see Chapters 3 and 5). The critical difference is that it is not "individual" private ownership.

[2]For detailed discussions see Fuerst (1974), Wolman (1975), Stafford (1978), Headey (1978), and Merrett (1979).

[3]In Sweden, for instance, nearly 80% of new suburban housing in recent years has been built on publicly-owned land. Much of this land was brought into the public domain through a far-sighted policy of municipal land-banking which began before WWII.

[4]The U.S. government very quickly sold most of the public housing constructed under its war-time housing programs.

[5]To date council house sales in Britain have seldom exceeded 50,000 units in a single year (the peak was 61,957 in 1972). Geographically most sales have taken place in areas with newer housing stocks, few apartments, which are in suburban locations and have Conservative-controlled councils. In 1979, however, the new Conservative government in Britain announced its intention to provide substantial incentives for local housing authorities to sell thousands of council houses to sitting tenants at discounted prices.

[6]Under this "pooling" system, rent levels in the public sector are based on the historic average costs of building (and maintaining) all housing units owned by a local authority. Since the costs of construction and interest debt retirement for many older units are low in current terms, rent "surpluses" from these units can be pooled in order to lower the rents on new high-cost units.

[7]Detailed reviews of the objectives of and procedures for allocation within the council house sector in Britain are provided in: U.K. Central Housing Advisory Committee (1969), U.K. Secretary of State for the Environment (1977), U.K., Central Housing Advisory Committee (1978), and Cullingworth (1979).

[8]It is generally agreed that mobility in the public housing sector is lower than in the private sector. This might be expected for no other reason than the practice of local authorities to assign people on the basis of the length of time they have been on that authority's waiting list. It is not clear, however, how much of the difference is due to a lower propensity to move, and to the different populations which are in the public sector.

[9]Geographic concentrations of the most disadvantaged families in the poorest quality council housing can occur even when the allocation process is entirely equitable through differential rates of out-migration. Such families often find it more difficult to leave their present units and to secure accommodation in more attractive housing and neighborhoods.

[10]Taylor (1978), for example, has noted that higher rates of reported medical problems occur in large blocks of flats (apartments) which are "difficult-to-get-out-of" on other grounds.

[11]Young and Kramer (1978) provide a fascinating account of the struggles between the Greater London Council and suburban boroughs (Bromley in particular) in reference to the location of public housing for low-income tenants who were being moved out of the inner city. They conclude that these efforts failed in part because the strength of suburban resistance was grossly underestimated.

[12]The term "opening up the suburbs" is taken from the title of a classic book by Downs (1973).

[13]For example, high levels of new housing construction and noncapital enrichment are not compatible with a strategy of contained decay. The former would pull or push more people out of the inner city while the latter would require some dispersal of population (in Downs' view) because of the limitations on living conditions posed by deteriorated inner city neighborhoods.

Chapter 11

Alternative Housing Systems: Quasi-Market, Socialist, and Third World

No review of housing would be complete without at least a formal recognition that very different housing conditions and systems of allocating housing arise in countries with diverse political systems and at different levels of socioeconomic development. Despite an attempt in previous chapters to maintain a broad international perspective, most of the examples thus far have been drawn from North America and Western Europe, with an emphasis on the U.S., Britain, and Canada. Here we turn our attention to selected examples of other housing systems within different political contexts.

Alternative Types of Housing Systems

As argued in earlier chapters, patterns of housing production and consumption reflect the level of economic development, social attitudes, institutional structures, and political ideologies of each country. As background, Table 11.1 suggests one possible ordering of the housing systems of developed countries, an ordering based primarily on the presence and degree of public control over the private market sector. These systems are given conventional political labels: unregulated market or "laissez-faire," liberal interventionalist, social democratic, and socialist. Within the latter, a differentiation is made between systems which do or do not contain a major private market sector. Other political classifications could, of course, be developed based, for example, on the principal ideological objectives of the housing systems involved (Headey, 1978). Nevertheless, the important point to remember is that there are no "pure" models of either state-controlled or market-based systems.

Table 11.1. Alternative Types of Housing Systems and Degrees of Government Involvement in Housing in Developed Countries

Type of system	Example(s)	Locus of control	Nature of housing production
Laisséz-faire	U.S. Canada Australia	Private market, little public sector housing or control	Housing provided by market, private ownership dominates, government intervention tied to specific problems
Liberal interventionalist/ social welfare	U.K.	Private market, but important public sector	Housing largely provided by market, but with large public (35%) sector, and substantial subsidies
Social democratic	Sweden	Private market within a system of public controls	Dominant government control in land ownership and financing
Socialist: dominant state control	Poland	Public system but with large private sector	Housing provided by the State or through public or private cooperatives
Socialist: pure state control	U.S.S.R.	Public system with little or no private sector	Housing provided by the State, allocated according to needs and status, rents are are usually low

Two examples from outside the English-speaking world are selected for discussion in the following sections to illustrate the above range of housing systems. The first is Sweden, where a long-standing social-democratic political partnership has developed a relatively unusual and high quality housing system. Since much has already been said about Sweden in previous chapters, only a brief synthesis is necessary here. The second example, Poland, serves to illustrate the housing problems and policy priorities of a relatively recent socialist state, but one with a vibrant private sector. Finally, we briefly acknowledge the differences and similarities in the housing problems facing countries in the Third World, particularly in their burgeoning cities.

THE SOCIAL DEMOCRATIC MODEL

The label "social democratic" is commonly used to describe those capitalist systems in which social welfare legislation is given relatively high priority and housing in particular is more likely to be seen as a social service rather than strictly as an economic commodity. They differ from the traditional socialist model in that the private market in housing is allowed to operate, if not flourish, and from more laissez-faire systems in that state intervention is seen as a permanent necessity, not a short-term imperative.

The Example of Sweden: A Socialist Market?

So much has been written about housing and planning systems in Sweden that in many ways we already know how these systems operate. The interested reader is referred to the extensive literature on Sweden in the English-language press.[1] One reason that the Swedish experience is of such widespread interest is the view that Sweden appears to have solved the traditional problems of housing supply and finance, of coordinating housing policies with those for other land uses, and of limiting class differences between tenure types which still throttle most other developed nations. Here we look briefly at the evidence.

Policy innovations: Sweden is essentially a capitalist country with about the highest per capita income in the world. It was not always so wealthy, however, and its housing policies reflect its earlier agrarian and relatively weak economy. A number of basic characteristics which distinguish that system of policies can be summarized briefly as follows:

Some 80% of all new housing is constructed on lands purchased well in advance by public agencies at their then current predevelopment value.

Expansion of housing finance was facilitated by the creation of state mortgage banks in the early 1930s, which helped to smooth out the usual fluctuations in building, and by the use of national pension funds for mortgages.

A massive construction program in the postwar period was designed to reduce the extreme housing shortages and poor condition of housing inherited from the prewar period.

Alternative forms of housing tenure have been encouraged (see Chapter 3), including cooperatives and nonprofit housing, with the result that tenure in Sweden is relatively neutral in terms of class and income (Kemeny, 1978).

Mortgage-interest deductions are at least partially balanced by production subsidies for rental accommodation. About 90% of all house building since 1950 has received state loans.

Building costs and rents in the private sector were strictly controlled (both have now been removed), allowing the public sector to compete with the private sector for middle-income households.

Neighborhood quality, and the level of local services provided, are high and much less variable across an urban area than is the case in much of North America.

The consequences: The results of these initiatives, and other related government policies, are clearly evident in the housing market. The public sector has tended to lead rather than follow the private sector. The private market has in the past been tightly controlled, creating what Headey (1978) calls a "socialist market," speculative profits in land development and financing have been held down, and the costs of housing for those of low and moderate incomes have remained at relatively low levels while housing quality has improved.[2] We cannot, however, divorce housing policy from the context of Sweden as a highly developed welfare state in which per capita subsidies for social programs are roughly twice those of North America.

Some of these trends are conveyed in Table 11.2. Public and quasi-public agencies or companies are responsible for some 50% of all housing production in

Table 11.2. Sources of Housing Production, Sweden, 1951–55 and 1971–75
(percent)

Years	State and local communes	Public companies	Cooperatives	Private sector
1951–55	a	a	18	42
1971–75	3	36	11	51

Note: [a]35% by state and local communes *and* public companies.
Source: Swedish Government, Housing and Construction Statistics.

Sweden (see Chapter 5 for mortgage totals) and fully 90% is subsidized one way or another. Owner-occupation, while still generally low by North American, Australian, and British standards, is clearly more evenly distributed among social and occupational groups (or classes) and between income levels, but it too is now increasing.[3] Whether this latter trend leads to a return of wide differences in housing consumption between tenure groups remains to be seen.

The Swedish house building record and its innovative ability in setting new policies are obviously impressive. Both have been facilitated by rapid growth in the economy and in national wealth, by an enlightened political bureaucracy, and by the acceptance of a long-term planning horizon. Nevertheless, Sweden is not without many of the contemporary housing problems common to other western countries. Housing costs have increased dramatically during the 1970s and new construction has slowed. Inequalities in tax treatment for different tenures remain and appear in recent years to be increasing. Overcrowding is a persistent problem, particularly among the low-income and especially among recent immigrant groups in the large cities. The figures here are surprisingly high. Moreover, there is growing dissatisfaction with some of the large suburban public housing estates, notably high-rise developments built in the 1960s. Vacancies and vandalism are increasing. All of this sounds vaguely familiar.

HOUSING IN SOCIALIST SOCIETIES

The housing situations in socialist, or more accurately "centrally planned," economies within the developed world differ at least as much from each other as they do from those in capitalist or mixed economies. There are two obvious reasons for these differences. One is that the countries themselves vary in their standard of living, the degree of collective or state ownership of the economy and of housing, and in terms of the condition of the historical inheritance of housing. It should also be remembered that most Eastern European countries, except the USSR, went through the transformation to socialism only after the second world war, and even then the process was invariably slow, incomplete and inconsistent.

The Role of Housing

The second reason for this wide variability is that classical Marxist writings are rather ambivalent on the role of housing in general, and of owner-occupied housing specifically, within a socialist state. It is certainly true, as noted earlier, that that "housing question" was seen as part of the manifestation of structural and social contradictions in capitalist societies. Thus, the housing question could only be resolved after the broader process of extending direct social control over the means of production and through the redistribution of social resources inherent in the transition to socialism had been implemented. This social redistribution in part involved the reallocation of existing housing, to eliminate extreme inequalities in consumption, and in part it meant ensuring that the large-scale accumulation of capital which came from rents on housing would go to the state rather than private landlords.

These attitudes did not, however, preclude *individual* owner-occupation; certainly it was not considered as important as large-scale ownership by capitalists of both land and housing. Private ownership of land was viewed with much more scepticism than that of housing, but in most East European countries the traditional political strength of large numbers of land-owning peasants and rural homeowners discouraged outright nationalization of all land and housing.[4]

Given this ideological uncertainty and the realities of existing ownership patterns, it is perhaps not surprising that political attitudes and policies directed to housing tenure differ so widely in the socialist world (Donnison, 1967). Each country has more or less sought its own compromise. Many did undertake, as Engels suggested, a massive redistribution of the existing stock of housing, particularly through the subdivision and reallocation of large units. Moreover, in most postwar construction programs, tight controls have also been maintained on the size of units produced to prevent overconsumption and to ease the overall housing shortage. Production was largely nationalized, while existing owners have been treated differently and a rather surprising diversity of tenure types has been encouraged in new housing. At the same time, it must be remembered, most East European countries were forced by the need to rebuild war-devastated economies to trade-off housing production goals against needed capital investment in other economic sectors.

In this section we take a brief look at the recent policy experience of one socialist country in the developed industrial world—Poland. Several other countries might seem to some readers as better choices, such as the Soviet Union. However, the housing situation in the latter country is somewhat better known abroad (DiMaio, 1973), and in any case the scale and complexity of Soviet housing precludes even a cursory examination here. The obvious drawback of Poland as an example of socialist housing policies is that the economy is still very much a mixture of state ownership and private market, more so than in most of eastern Europe. Nonetheless, it provides a useful illustration of the similarities and contrasts in housing provision between centrally-planned and market economies.

The Example of Poland: A Market Within

Poland has been among the most liberal of East European socialist governments with respect to housing. Not the least important reason for this was the staggering housing shortage inherited after WWII. A relatively poor country with an inadequate housing stock prior to 1939, Poland subsequently lost some 20 to 25% of its housing stock during the War (not to mention the loss of over 6 million people). Losses due to destruction were followed in the immediate postwar period by an increased housing demand due to rapid population growth as well as massive movements of population from her former eastern territories and from rural to urban areas, placing additional severe strains on housing supply.

Historical evolution: The initial policy response to these problems was to stimulate rapid construction of new housing units of modest size and quality, blending both public and private investment.[5] Any intention to build state housing for all, however, was soon abandoned (if it ever existed).[6] Also, a comprehensive policy of socialization (i.e., nationalization) of existing housing was not implemented after the war in rural areas, except in western Poland in those lands formerly belonging to Germany.

The detailed evolution of housing policies in Poland is of course as complicated as that of any other country, and can only be touched on here. Immediately after the war, and the change in government, state housing policies were introduced, as in most other eastern European countries, to redistribute—more or less equally—a scarce housing stock. Fixed floor area standards and occupancy densities were established, to which new construction also had to conform. Over time, however, as incomes and living standards rose, attitudes and policies changed. Restrictions on housing supply were relaxed and later were completely rewritten. People were to be given more choice in housing, as they were in other consumer goods, but within certain limits. Fixed standards were changed into minimum standards, but at the same time maximum space restrictions were introduced to limit the differences in housing consumption which would surely emerge.

Housing construction has traditionally been undertaken, at least in urban areas, primarily by the state and by building cooperatives, but increasingly by the latter (see below). These new units are then assigned to either local municipalities for their own internal distribution, to state industrial enterprises for use by their workers, and to local cooperatives; a small but growing proportion are now sold directly to individual households as well. Local municipalities generally no longer build for themselves. Both state produced and cooperative housing are now subsumed under the general heading of "social" housing.

It is also interesting to note the gradual shift in emphasis from housing as a form of social consumption (i.e., with little or no direct payment) to housing as an individual consumer good. The latter implies the existence of a private market. This shift is reflected in the distribution of households within the existing stock. Households with the lowest incomes are allocated to state, municipal, or industrial housing; those with middle incomes receive their housing primarily through cooperatives and those with the highest incomes through individual means. Moreover, state housing is often sold to sitting occupants at price discounts which are based on their length of residence, income, and social "achievements."

Table 11.3. Trends in Housing Construction, By Source and Tenure in Poland, 1950–76

Year	Number of dwellings completed (in 000's of units)	Percent of all dwellings constructed by:			Housing investment as % of national investment
		State	Housing cooperatives	Private	
1950	60	60	–	40	–
1960	142	48	10	42	20
1965	171	55	19	26	15
1970	194	23	49	28	16
1972	202	23	51	26	14
1976	273	20	57	23	–

Sources: Selected from "Housing, Building and Planning in the Polish People's Republic," Warsaw, 1973; Ball and Harloe, 1974; and *Bulletin*, Institute of Environmental Management (Instytut Ksztaltowania Srodowiska), Warsaw, 1977.

Tenure policies: Table 11.3 illustrates the diversity of sources in new housing construction. State housing has declined rather remarkably as a proportion of total starts, as has the private sector although the latter still remains important (23%). Part of this switch in emphasis from direct state housing since the early 1960s has clearly been into cooperatives, which are primarily for tenants, but in which the cooperative itself may own the building. Most cooperatives are financed by a combination of interest-free state bank loans and tenants' down payments, but are otherwise self-financing in the sense that rents must cover debt repayment and maintenance costs. By 1976 over 57% of all new units were financed in this way, although they still constituted only about 16% of the total stock.

Owner-occupied housing in Poland is financed in part by "sweat-equity" (building one's own home) and in part by methods similar to those for tenant cooperatives. The down payment requirement is generally higher than for cooperatives and a real rate of interest is charged on loans. The latter also serves as a form of rationing not unlike that of the price mechanism in capitalist markets.[7] State controls remain tight, however, on the size and distribution of these loans. Interestingly, over 50% of private individual house building has been in rural areas, particularly in those areas in which households have several income sources, although it is now increasing in urban areas.

As the result of these trends, the housing stock in Poland's urban areas (in 1972) consisted of five basic tenure types distributed as follows (from Ball and Harloe, 1974):

State housing	39%
Housing provided by state-owned industrial firms	12%

Private rental housing	14%
Owner-occupied housing	19%
Cooperatives–tenant (14%)	16%
–owner (2%)	

The vast majority of these units are in flats or apartments, although the traditional single-family unit typical of rural areas and small towns is now reappearing in the fringes of cities. The small sector of private rental housing is a prewar relic, much of which is old and often of relatively poor quality. The State effectively manages, but does not (bother to) own such units.

Housing allocation: How then is state and cooperative housing allocated? In fact, it is allocated in much the same way as in the previous example of public housing allocation in capitalist societies, subject to the obvious constraint of limited available housing. State housing is allocated according to need, the length of time on the waiting list, and job priority. The latter reflects both the overall housing shortage and the demands of national planning to accommodate the workers required for specific industrial developments in a given city or region. Although people are in theory free to change jobs, the availability (or nonavailability) of housing acts as the major incentive (or constraint) to geographical mobility. Housing, in fact, is a major planning instrument.

The allocation mechanism is primarily the responsibility of the central housing agency, which is now increasingly decentralized, and of the various cooperatives and state-owned industries which manage other tenure types. Considerable weight is given to maintaining a balanced social and occupational mix in each new housing estate, as well as in rebuilt housing in the inner cities. One obvious result is that there is not the same distinct spatial segregation of socioeconomic groups as there is in most western cities.

Relatively little weight, on the other hand, appears to be given to other locational considerations in housing allocation, although the available evidence here is very thin. In part, this may be because the State planning bodies can ensure greater uniformity of local services, particularly in outlying suburban areas, than would likely be the case in western countries where such services are often provided by the private sector. In part, location is also less significant again because of the overall housing shortage—some housing is clearly better than none—and the relatively homogeneous character of the systems—made apartment blocks which have dominated the recent housing stock.

Another revealing element of Poland's housing policy evident in Table 11.3 is that, despite a continued housing shortage, the level of investment in housing has actually declined as a proportion of total national investment. Since the State largely controls the means of housing supply, this trend suggests an explicit policy decision to accelerate economic production in other sectors. Housing is but one of many consumer goods which remains in short supply. One obvious reason for the increase in cooperatives and the persistence of a viable private housing sector, and the heavy down payments both require, is that both depend on savings. Encouraging households to save has the additional advantage of skimming off excess wages, which would otherwise be chasing other consumer goods in limited supply, and it provides capital funds for other State investments.

In reviewing recent Polish housing policy initiatives, Ball and Harloe (1974) raise the additional question of whether the increasing reliance on the ability to pay and the encouragement of private-ownership will lead to widening inequalities in access to and in the consumption of housing—inequalities which are too obvious in market-based societies. Further, and despite severe State controls over the sale or transfer of private housing and the prices which can be charged, it is possible that individual wealth accumulation will reappear through the private ownership of housing. This trend in turn may (almost inevitably will) lead to the emergence of geographic zones of very different social status within Polish cities. Only time will tell.

Summary: Poland has clearly made most impressive gains in new housing construction, historical reconstruction, in removing some of the serious prewar problems, and in the redistribution of housing resources. Nontheless, overall shortages, quality problems, and a differential consumption of housing still exist. Through a combination of historical conditions and the imperatives of encouraging economic growth, Poland has chosen a path which sanctions a diversity of housing tenures and encourages substantial investment in, and private ownership of, housing.

The point to stress here is not that these policies are misplaced or necessarily inequitable. Rather they are one response to the problems of housing supply and allocation, and of managing the public sector generally, while at the same time satisfying other policy objectives which all governments—regardless of political ideology—must face. Nor is this conclusion meant to imply that all housing systems in centrally-planned economies operate in the same way as Poland's does. They do not. In fact, few systems operate as they were intended to.

THE THIRD WORLD[8]

Housing conditions and housing problems in the Third World (less developed countries or LDCs) are quantitatively and qualitatively different from those in the developed world. Although beyond the scope of this volume in any detail, it is essential that we at least acknowledge the dimensions of these differences. As noted in the introduction, it is in these countries that what Abrams (1964) called man's global struggle for adequate shelter will be won or lost in the long term. The housing problems facing the more developed industrialized countries, both capitalist and socialist, as discussed in the preceding text, pale in comparison to those of the developing countries.

The purpose of this brief review is threefold: first, to provide selective examples of the range and scale of housing problems in the Third World; second, to illustrate some of the alternative policies for dealing with these problems; and third, to demonstrate the importance of comparative studies of housing systems in different parts of the world. If in so doing this review can awaken readers in the developed countries to the staggering housing problems of the LDCs, and at the same time remind those readers of the inherent limitations of imposing concepts and planning strategies from the developed world on housing situations in the Third World, it will have served its purpose. There is now a large and expanding literature on housing in the Third World on which the interested reader can draw for further details (e.g., Dwyer, 1975; Burns and Grebler, 1977; Mabogunje, Hardoy, and Misra, 1978).[9]

Scale and Diversity in Housing Conditions

There is much more diversity in housing conditions among Third World countries than there is in the developed world. These countries vary from small and newly rich (the oil states) to large and very poor; from those whose economy has some highly advanced sectors to those which are almost entirely subsistence. Their housing systems vary accordingly: from those in which housing is rural and noncommercial to those in which it is predominantly urban and a market good. Their housing policies reflect all combinations from centrally-planned models to those more strictly laissez-faire approaches based on the private market. Their housing stocks also vary in composition and quality from the massive apartment blocks of Seoul, Hong Kong, or Sao Paulo to the more basic African or Asian hut.

Perhaps the only common denominators are (excluding the oil states) low levels of income, a limited inheritance of quality housing, inadequate investment in residential infrastructure, and continued high levels of urbanization. The latter process has overwhelmed even the most extensive programs for housing construction and the improvement of social and health services, particularly in the rapidly growing major urban centers. The statistics are sobering. The 1976 United Nations Conference on Human Settlements (Habitat), for example, estimated that over 200 million people moved into the cities of Asia, Latin America, and Africa during the 1960s. Within those cities, birthrates have remained high and death rates have dropped. Combined, these trends are likely to take the total population of the Third World from 3.0 billion in 1975 to 5.0 billion in the year 2000, and their urban populations from about 800 million to over 2.1 billion.

The scale of the problem is reflected in United Nations housing statistics, such as those in Table 11.4. Since no one knows how many housing units there are in most LDCs, these figures can only be taken as very crude indices indeed. Nonetheless, it is evident that variations in housing quality among the latter are even wider than among developed countries. Dwellings vary in size from 1.3 rooms in African countries to 2.4 in Latin America, as against 5.1 in North America. Persons per room vary from 1.7 in Latin America to nearly 3.0 in Asian countries (0.6 in North America). The proportion of dwellings with piped water, an index of housing quality as well as health standards, is only 24% in the LDCs compared to 83% in the developed world. Within the LDCs, the distribution of housing quality is unequal in the extreme, reflecting the greater inequalities in those societies generally. Those inequalities are especially evident where the economy is polarized around a foreign-dominated modern sector and a traditional or indigenous sector.

Most disturbing is that the situation seems to be deteriorating, although this varies with the country in question. The LDCs as a whole, with 73% of the world's

Table 11.4. Housing Quality and Rates of New Housing Construction in Developed and Developing Countries, 1970 and 1975

Region	Quality: % dwellings with piped water	Rate of housing construction (per 000 pop.)	Number of dwellings built (000s)	% of total world building	% of total world population
Developing countries	24	2.3	5,830	40	73
Africa	19	1.3	451	3	10
Asia (excl. Japan)	23	2.4	4,703	32	54
Latin America	36	2.4	671	5	8
Developed countries	83	8.0	6,468	44	21
Australasia	93	10.7	165	1	0.4
Europe (excl. USSR)	73	7.5	3,471	24	12
North America	98	5.9	1,347	9	6
Japan	95	14.3	1,485	10	3
USSR	na	9.4	2,286	16	6
WORLD TOTAL[a]	61	4.0	14,579	100[b]	100[b]

Notes: [a]Total population = 3,967,000,000; [b]Total may not sum due to rounding error; na = not available.

Source: United Nations, Compendium of Housing Statistics (1974–1978); Burns and Grebler, 1977.

population (in 1975), received only 40% of the world's new housing units. This discrepancy is even greater, of course, when the quality of the housing produced is taken into account. We do know, as shown in Chapter 6, that housing investment does tend to vary systematically with the level of development in any given country. It is lower in the early stages of development, as investment is concentrated on more "productive" sectors, then starts to grow rapidly as incomes rise and the demand for better housing increases (Lakshmanan et al., 1978). However, the increasing size of the housing deficit in these countries leads one to conclude that the transition will come too late. When the expected growth in population to the year 2000 is taken into account, the magnitude of the deficit becomes almost incomprehensible.[10]

Urbanization, Spontaneous Settlements, and Housing

The most glaring expression of the population explosion and the housing deficit is in the so-called "squatter" settlements which typify many of the cities in the Third World. These settlements, which Turner (1973) and others prefer to call "autonomous urban settlements," but are more commonly known as barrios, favellas, bidonvilles, or simply shack towns, have generally sprung up without, or in defiance of, government approval. Many are located on the periphery of such cities, but others develop in close proximity to centers of unskilled employment wherever there is vacant land (steep hill sides, ravines, etc.). Some are temporary, others are more permanent and better organized; but most are unplanned, with low quality housing, high unemployment, and nonexistent social services. In some areas, these spontaneous residential settlements represent from one-third to one-half of the total population of the metropolitan area.

In the minds of the migrants to these settlements, housing is likely to be, at least initially, a relatively minor consideration. They come for jobs and for higher standards of living, which they perceive to be available in the cities, and to escape rural poverty and overcrowding. Housing is a place to sleep; it can be put up quickly and cheaply, and taken down as easily. Despite its apparent inadequacies, there is evidence that such primitive housing is considered sufficient for the time being (Burns and Grebler, 1977). It is, in part, the simple numerical scale of this in-migration and the settlements it generates which produces the real problems.

The planning approach to these settlements has traditionally been to define them as slums and then to tear them down. The residents are relocated to new high-rise public housing projects, or more frequently left to fend for themselves. Only limited public resources (and local resistence) have prevented more widespread disruption and relocation. The parallel with the urban renewal experience of developed countries is striking. It only became obvious later that these settlements were in fact communities, serving different needs for a wide diversity of households. People, it seemed, often preferred to remain where they were, even in tin shacks which by conventional standards were substantially deficient.

The alternative approach is more modest, but likely to be more productive in the long run. It involves not demolition but making such settlements better places in which to live. This can be done, as shown below, by adding to or introducing local health and social services and by coordinated self-help schemes for housing improvement. By removing the threat of demolition, the blanket of uncertainty which hangs over such settlements is removed and individual households are encouraged to invest their time and resources in improving their existing homes (the principle of "sweat equity"). Although such efforts have achieved some success in a few countries, they are swamped by further in-migration, high levels of poverty and unemployment and by bureaucratic ineptness.

Contrasting Policy Approaches

Even the preceding cursory review of housing conditions and problems in the developing countries should leave readers in no doubt that these problems require rather different combinations of policies than those reviewed in previous chapters. Again, the range of possible examples is extremely wide, but perhaps three distinct approaches stand out. The first two essentially follow the policies and programs adopted in the industrial world—drawing from either or both of the capitalist and socialist worlds—but adapted in varying degrees to local circumstances. The rate at which such policies have been introduced since WWII has been quite dramatic, particularly when one considers that most developing countries have initiated such policies at a much earlier stage in their economic development than did most industrial countries.

The range of policies introduced is broader than one might expect. Many countries have established systems of financial institutions to subsidize construction, launched insured mortgage schemes for home purchase, and encouraged companies to provide housing for their workers. Some have established relatively large social housing sectors, based on the traditional European model. Factory-built housing designs have been widely adopted and modern construction techniques and equipment have been imported on a massive scale. In most cases, however, state intervention in housing is considerably greater than in most western countries at comparable stages in their development.

The limitation of the adoption of policy models from the developed world, whether the model is the private market or state control, is the tendency to transfer procedures and standards which are inappropriate given the level of income, rates of growth, social structure, and accumulated housing needs of the developing countries. New building standards, if set to the levels of developed countries, can severely restrict the aggregate number of housing units produced and thus the number of people who benefit. Modern construction techniques ignore the most common local resource in the LDCs—labor—and large-scale housing programs require a pool of technical expertise and political coordination which is seldom available. Moreover, as Burns and Grebler (1977) note, the adoption of housing standards from the developed world often necessitates the import of materials and personnel which the LDCs cannot easily afford.

The third option, and the one which has attracted the most interest, particularly in the poorest and most densely populated countries, involves the use of more locally-based housing strategies. These fall under several headings, such as local initiatives or "sites and services" schemes, or more generally as "self-help" programs (Turner, 1973). Essentially, these programs reflect the need for more modest, partial, and incremental approaches to housing improvement which reach a larger proportion of the population. They draw on local resources and materials, and accept the need for housing standards more in line with local income. Under the sites and services approach, for example, public authorities may provide the site, plan the layout of the settlement, construct the infrastructure, and manage the community services. The actual construction of housing is then left to the residents. Similar methods can be applied to improve existing squatter settlements. Organized self-help schemes may also provide assistance, in the form of building materials or technical advice, to the home-builders themselves or to community groups.

The advantages of these methods should be obvious. The quality and cost of housing is geared more closely to the ability of poor societies to pay; more housing can be produced more cheaply than by conventional methods; and thus housing benefits are spread more widely. Self-help schemes are also labor intensive, less demanding of scarce capital and costly imports, and less prone to bureaucratic restrictions. Perhaps the greatest attraction, according to Burns and Grebler (1977), is their flexibility. Labor can be used when and where it is available. Households can vary their investment in housing over time depending on their income and needs. Rooms can be added as needed. Governments can modify their provision of services accordingly and material shortages can be more easily accommodated then in large-scale, integrated housing construction. Nevertheless, most observers see the need to combine more mechanized housing production systems with self-help schemes in order to take advantage of the benefits of both.

Conclusion

The Third World clearly adds another important dimension—in aggregate, an overwhelming dimension—to the study of housing and housing policies. Developing countries contain the bulk of the world's serious housing deficit, and that deficit appears to be widening. Their attempts at ameliorating these problems attest both to the diversity of housing strategies which are possible and to the importance of linking housing programs to those for social service provision, urban infrastructure, and economic development generally. In many instances, despite the scale of the housing problem, developed nations can also learn from some of the more imaginative schemes used in Third World countries—notably of trying to achieve more with less, through the logic of "second-best" solutions, when resources are limited and the future so uncertain.

NOTES

[1] Excellent contemporary reviews of housing policy in Sweden are provided in Duncan (1978), Kemeny (1978), Burns and Grebler (1977), and Headey (1978).

[2] Unlike North America and the U.K., the proportion of income needed for housing has declined in Sweden, at least until the early 1970s. The proportion of average after-tax income required to rent a two-bedroom apartment declined from 28% in 1945 to 24% in 1970 (quoted in Duncan, 1978).

[3] One obvious reason for the relatively low level of homeownership in Swedish cities is that much of the housing built since 1945 has been in flats, which are more frequently rented. The recent shift toward homeownership again is due partly to government policy and partly to a shift to lower density single-family units.

[4] Nor did Engels preclude the continuation of rent payments in their traditional sense following the revolution. In fact, all socialist regimes charge "rents" on state housing, although they are usually relatively low.

[5] Equally high priority was given to rebuilding housing of historical and architectural value, in such war-ravaged cities as Warsaw, Crakow, and Gdansk, a policy which also reduced the investment available for new construction.

[6] In this regard at least, Poland followed the initial course of housing policy in post-revolutionary Soviet Union.

[7] The interest rate is also higher for units over a given minimum size, a further reflection of the desire to limit excessive housing consumption or at least to increase the marginal costs of such consumption.

[8] The Third World is only a label of convenience; it does not imply a uniformity of either housing problems or approaches.

[9] A particularly valuable compilation of materials on housing and urbanization in the Third World was prepared as part of the United Nations Conference on Human Settlements (Habitat) held in Vancouver in 1976.

[10]The United Nations has estimated (in 1974) that developing nations were building only 2 to 3 housing units per thousand population annually, creating an overall deficit which they estimate is accumulating at 4 to 5 million units annually.

Chapter 12

Summary and Prospects

The major objective of this book has been to provide an introduction to the geography of housing, set within the context of urban real estate markets, neighborhood change, and public policy. It has stressed definitions and conceptual frameworks as a means of helping us to organize and understand the diversity and complexity of housing conditions and patterns which we observe in our cities. It has also emphasized the analysis of process, and the debate on housing conditions, rather than the description of those conditions. In so doing, it may assist the reader in making sense of a myriad of housing policies which are complicated, volatile, and, at times, contradictory.

Real world examples of housing conditions and policies have been drawn from several different countries in the developed world, both socialist and capitalist. The purpose of this approach is not to construct an international geography of housing as such, but rather to show the diversity of processes which can produce similar results in terms of housing conditions—or conversely, that similar circumstances can produce quite different results in other countries. It is important that we frequently move outside our own local or national context in order to evaluate which of the relationships in one housing system are unique or transitory and which seem to be persistent features of all systems.

CONCEPTS AND TRENDS

Throughout the text, emphasis has also been placed on the importance of studying housing in its appropriate contexts—i.e., the historical, political, sociocultural, economic, and neighborhood environments which define the *external relationships* through which housing is produced and consumed. This emphasis, in turn, led to the identification of a number of imperatives which lie behind the study of housing in contemporary society:

> as a highly durable commodity, housing must be interpreted within a long-term historical perspective;

> that housing is of such importance for both individuals and society, it must reflect prevailing social attitudes and political persuasions as well as economic realities;

> that housing supply is so dependent on sources of capital, it essentially becomes one sector of financial and investment markets;

> that housing is so enmeshed in institutional regulations, it can only be fully examined in relation to the rules created by those institutions; and

> since housing is fixed in location, it draws much of its utility and value in urban areas from the character of the immediate neighborhood and the local environment.

Each of these imperatives necessitates that we look beyond housing as shelter, as a physical facility and an economic good, to include the housing system in general and the broader implications for housing of elements in the social and economic organization of our urban society.

The Changing Environments of Housing

Equally important, these contexts are continually changing. Housing ages. People move. Attitudes and policies shift over time regarding what is necessary and desirable in housing standards. Life-styles change. The financial situation can and does fluctuate widely, altering both the basis for investment in housing supply and the costs of occupying that housing. Governments still use the housing sector as a means of regulating the rate of growth in the economy as a whole, leading to even wider swings in housing production, prices, and costs. Changes in tax legislation, in housing policy, building standards, design, and land development practices tend to be frequent and often unpredictable in timing and impact.

Equally important for the urban focus of this volume are changes in the physical environment, social character, and relative attractiveness of urban neighborhoods. Almost any change in the urban fabric—in the transportation system, the distribution of jobs and social services, the social mix of in-migrants and in local planning policy—alters the patterns of housing supply and demand within urban areas. In some cities, neighborhood transition is a way of life, a continual source of uncertainty for households and planners, and an element in generating cumulative social and housing problems. When these changes are accompanied by intense racial or ethnic segregation and . discrimination in the market, the resulting inequalities are intensified. Certain disadvantaged groups become trapped in rotten and deteriorated housing. All too often otherwise adequate housing becomes inadequate, if not uninhabitable, because of deterioration of the external environment.

Housing Conditions: The Paradox

In almost all developed countries, housing standards have improved substantially in the postwar period. The stock of available housing has increased at a rate equal to or faster than population growth, and the quality level of that stock has risen dramatically. There are now relatively few seriously physical deficiencies in the occupied urban housing stock, at least according to traditional definitions. But it is also clear that such definitions—(e.g., the absence of full plumbing facilities, insufficient wiring or heating facilities, and overcrowding)—are now of decreasing relevance for policy. They, in turn, have been replaced by new concepts of housing services, by new standards of quality and new definitions of housing needs and problems. We often seem to solve one problem simply by creating others.

The paradox we now face is one of generally high housing standards but with an apparently increasing dissatisfaction with the current stock and distribution of housing opportunities. One obvious explanation for this apparent paradox, aside from the usual exaggerations in the popular press, is that of *rising expectations*. Our expectations as to what quality of housing we will accept and, more important, our anticipations of attaining an "ideal" housing type, seem to have exceeded both our willingness to pay for that housing and the ability of society to produce it. Robson (1979), for example, also notes that housing expectations have now become "socialized," i.e., incorporated into the mythology and value systems of our society as a common good, while the economy in general and housing production in particular have remained "privatized"—oriented to and dependent on the whims of the private market.

The basic issue, then, is not primarily one of the physical inventory of housing but of *the distribution of that inventory among people and places*. Continued inequalities have now become more obvious. Our standards and expectations are increasingly set by what others, our immediate neighbors or those in the next neighborhood or city, currently occupy. This has, of course, always been the case to a certain extent. Yet it seems that the intensity of interactions through which expectations are set and standards raised—the flood of government reports, pressures from the advertising media, and extended sources of information on housing opportunities—is now much greater than in the past. At the same time, we know that society begins to worry about questions of inequalities primarily during prosperous times.

The darkest side of these trends, and perhaps what should be the real concern of the student of housing, is the persistent gap in standards between those households living in what is now considered to be adequate and affordable housing and those who are not. While national or aggregate housing problems may have diminished, local problems in turn have become more serious. They are now more concentrated geographically and they impact most severely on specific groups in society. These groups include not only the poor but those who are disadvantaged in other ways—the elderly, transients, one-parent families, the handicapped and mentally-ill, minorities, recent immigrants, and those otherwise unable to cope with the system (or who are prevented from doing so because of discrimination).

When we consider that these people also tend to live (or perhaps simply survive) in urban neighborhoods which are often dirty, polluted, decaying, poorly-serviced, and dangerous, if not demoralizing, only then do the inequalities in housing costs, standards, and living conditions become fully appreciated. The location factor then takes on increasing importance as a component in future housing research and social policy. It should again be stressed, however, that location and environment are essentially conditioning factors, which add to or subtract from the quality of living conditions in our cities and which influence certain kinds of social relations and socially constructive (or destructive) behavior. But, they do not in themselves predetermine such conditions or behavior.

Themes Reiterated

Despite our primary interest in this text with housing as a social concern and a policy problem, the bulk of the discussion has concentrated on concepts and on underlying processes of change: for example, what is housing, how is it distributed or allocated, how do supply and demand interact, what spatial patterns and problems does this interaction produce, and who benefits and loses? It is worthwhile here restating several of the more important of these concepts and themes which run through the text.

One such theme is that housing must, at the outset, be defined as a complex, multidimensional entity or bundle. It is clearly both an economic or merit good and a social necessity, which (in both cases) delivers to its owners and occupants a wide range of benefits (and disbenefits) or services. These services, for households, include not just shelter but satisfaction, security, status, and the tax-free capital gains and inputed rent which flow from occupance of the housing unit itself. The location of housing, in turn, provides the key to a given basket of neighborhood and environmental goods (e.g., schools, a property tax rate, parks, etc.). Combined, house and location also help to define the networks of social relationships between groups of people and between those groups and society as a whole.

This diversity and complexity in what is meant by the term housing, and in the roles it plays in our lives, implies that housing is not the sole province of any single approach or discipline. It does not submit to an all-embracing research paradigm, nor to a deterministic methodology or ideological stance. To argue that it does is to obscure the diverse origins and complex current interdependencies which characterize housing in modern societies. The disciplines of economics, sociology, architecture, planning, political science, and geography, for example, all have important contributions to make to the study of housing, but not in isolation.

The mechanism by which housing is distributed to people and among locations has been succinctly described as an "allocation" process. The two principal expressions of housing allocation are the private market and public (social) sector or collective allocation. It must be recognized, however, that there are varying combinations of these systems within most countries in both the capitalist and socialist worlds. The concept of allocation provides an underlying unity to the discussion. It allows one to identify when and where the two systems operate in a similar way and when they do not, and what contradictions and problems arise from both. It also provides a single framework within which one can examine the allocation of resources to housing at a national level as well as the allocation of houses to locations and people to houses at a local level.

Within urban areas, particularly large and diverse metropolitan conurbations, we must recognize that the housing stock and households are segmented spatially. Clearly, there is not a free trade-off or substitution of houses by households across an urban area, even when differences in the value of housing and the costs of commuting to work are taken into account. Thus, the adjustment of the stock to changing demands, and new policies, is inevitably slow and spatially inconsistent. Otherwise well-intentioned research designs and policy initiatives often fail in the face of two simple questions: whether separate spatial sub-markets in housing do or do not exist; and if they do, what is the extent of their influence on prices and quality and on restricting the access of some groups to housing of their choice. These questions are further complicated by the fact that subdivisions of the housing stock by type and price, and geographical concentrations of different social groups, seldom remain constant for long. This ebb-and-flow of social boundaries renders any assessment of the consequences of market segmentation extremely difficult.

The basic components and determinants of housing supply and demand must also be examined within differing time frames and at both aggregate and disaggregate (local) levels. In the longer term, the housing inventory is primarily shaped by supply conditions at the national level, whereas in the short run, and in small areas, it is demand which alters that inventory and the movement of prices. There is now ample empirical evidence which illustrates just how different trends in housing supply and demand can be between and within metropolitan areas. It is also only at the local level, and with disaggregated data, that we can see how the various actors involved in housing (and land) development come together, and what factors influence their behavior. Furthermore, it is only at this level that we can adequately "*monitor*" the critical outcomes of the market process: property transactions, occupancy turnover, prices, household relocation decisions, and neighborhood change.

The negative outcomes of this process may also be interpreted in several ways: (1) as failures of the private market allocation mechanism itself, (2) as the consequence of excessive or misdirected government intervention, or (3) as the inevitable side-effects of continual changes which affect all housing systems (e.g., the aging of housing, shifting demand and needs, transport innovations). The latter point, in turn, suggests that housing systems are in a perpetual *state of disequilibrium*, since supply seldom if ever matches demand (or needs) in aggregate and even less so when location is considered. It will not please the reader looking for simple answers to read here that all three of these interpretations are valid, to some extent, but in varying degrees at different times and places. Whatever perspective one takes, however, it is clear that housing problems are made worse when all three sources appear in concert.

Housing Policy: From Where and for Whom?

Housing policy, as developed in most western countries (as previous discussions have confirmed) tends to be vague, confused, even contradictory and in a continual state of flux. In fact, rather than a single housing policy as such, there are instead a plethora of policies and programs directed to housing and to groups of households, deriving from different levels of government. Each has its own historical origins, objectives, and means of delivery, which are seldom coordinated. They are best described, according to Dennis and Fish (1972), as programs in search of a policy. Frequent changes in policy, whether for better or worse, add another element to an overall picture of uncertainty and confusion—what has often been called the "housing mess".[1] This makes any attempt to assess the impacts of housing policies on people and on the supply of housing at best a tenuous exercise.

This situation contributed to our earlier assertion that many of the more important policy decisions affecting housing are not made within the housing sector, or with reference to housing. These policy decisions relate to the regulation (or deregulation) of the national economy, to taxation and investment legislation, to the balance between transport systems, to local land use planning practices and public service provision, and the like. The influence of the Interstate Highway System in the U.S., and of extensive tax subsidies for owner-occupied housing in most countries, are but two better known examples. Thus, "housing policy" effectively becomes the sum total of all public and private policies which directly or indirectly affect housing patterns and occupancy.

The above inconsistencies in housing policy in part reflect the undeniable complexity of the issues involved, and in part they mirror our ambiguity about the role of housing in our society: whether it is strictly an economic good to be bought and sold for profit, or a social good, more like education. This ambiguity in turn confuses the precise purpose of housing policies. To whom should such policies be directed; and by what means? Should, housing policies undertake to augment the incomes of households so they can purchase more housing or should they be directed to increasing new construction and improving the housing stock? Or both? Such inconsistencies in policy also reflect the inherent *conflicts and contradictions* involved in increased state intervention in a market in which the commodity—housing—is largely privately-owned and financed; and which is tied to land and fixed to a location and environment.

Despite this instability, there are a number of distinctive trends in recent housing policies. During the 1970s, the emphasis has shifted from widespread slum clearance and redevelopment to conservation and improvement of the existing stock. Programs of housing assistance have been extended and the range of public subsidies for both new construction and rehabilitation has increased. Housing for special groups, notably the elderly but also for transients, the mentally-ill and the handicapped, has also increased (although unfortunately often at the expense of housing for large and/or problem families). At the same time, legislation regarding tenant security, controls on speculation, rights to access and real estate information, mortgage disclosure and antidiscrimination laws and rent control (or rent review) has been widely introduced or extended. Average citizens have demanded and in some cases received a greater voice in the production and management of their housing, notably in the public sector.[2] Other initiatives, designed to deal more comprehensively with specific problem areas—such as community block grants, homesteading or housing stress and community action areas—have been introduced with varying success. Greater emphasis has also been given to neighborhood revitalization and to noncapital (service) enrichment and self-help housing programs.

In addition to designing appropriate programs and policies, the question still remains as to what level of government should do what in housing. If the preceding assertion is correct (see Chapter 10), that the "national housing problem" is in fact now a series of localized problems which differ in nature and degree by community, then this question of level of responsibility takes on renewed significance. Localized problems are best dealt with by policies and instruments which are both flexible and more spatially-sensitive than those of the past. This conclusion, in turn, makes the link between national housing and financial policies and the *implementation* of those policies at the local level all the more critical. Local governments thus increasingly hold the key to the success or failure of housing programs.

Another important element in the recent policy debate is the question of what constitutes a *social housing policy*, and how such a policy is to be achieved. Generally, the term refers not only to a housing policy which is at least as sensitive to social factors as it is to economic and financial considerations, but to one which includes a large component of social housing, i.e., subsidized (or nonprofit) housing for groups with special needs. Most readers would probably agree on the objective of more socially-sensitive housing policies, but that still leaves a number of unanswered questions. How large should the social sector be? Who should produce and who should receive that housing? How should rents or prices be set? What is the role of cooperative housing? If private profits are restricted, how do we ensure a continued flow of investment into the housing sector?

Given that there seems to be no limit to the amount of housing we as a society can consume, there must be some constraints on housing use in both the private and social sectors. At present, price is allowed to act as the constraint in the private sector, with limited supply, waiting lists, and poor quality construction as constraints in social housing. But are these really the constraints we want to employ? If not, what are the alternatives? Does a social housing policy require publicly-owned or simply nonprofit housing, and if so, how much? If there is to be a large social sector, how do we make it responsive to changing needs and priorities—in a humane way—and avoid creating additional inequalities in the distribution of housing opportunities? Finally, we must stress that it is one matter to build housing but quite another matter to design viable communities.

PROSPECTS

There are sufficient signs in the literature and in data on recent housing trends to suggest that the future context of housing production and consumption will be markedly different from that in the past. We have already referred to the recent and dramatic changes in demographic structure and their potential effects in restructuring housing demand (through slower growth, aging, and life-style changes). In addition, one must look to the critical effects on housing of a continued economic recession and inflation, of changing preferences and cultural values, of employment redistribution, migration shifts and increased energy costs, and of realignments in political ideologies (both of the right and the left) regarding the degree of government intervention in housing and tightening fiscal constraints on public expenditures.

Housing and the Post-Industrial Society

To illustrate some of the major directions of change, Table 12.1 provides a selective summary of several commonly quoted attributes of what we typically consider to be industrial and post-industrial urban societies. Examples suggestive of the transition from an industrial to post-industrial state include shifts in the economic base (from productive to service sectors), in politics and culture and the changing locus of social control, and the likely expression of these trends in new urban forms and patterns of housing use. Although overgeneralized, and perhaps optimistic in light of recent economic troubles, these characteristics do serve as useful indicators of our perceptions of what are the important variables which will shape future patterns of urban land use and housing needs.

In the emerging post-industrial society (leaving aside the debate on what is or is not post-industrial), housing supply and demand and policy will take on different priorities. We have already cited evidence of a shift from production (new construction) to an emphasis on conservation, and to questions of the distribution of benefits and costs deriving from specific housing policies. Further, the concern for achieving minimum standards of quality (physical) has been replaced by standards based more on aesthetics and tastes, as the role of housing itself moves from one of providing shelter to one of enhancing an individual's social status (the post-shelter era?). At the same time, as we have seen in previous chapters, the mix of housing types (structural forms), designs and forms of tenure (e.g., non-profit and cooperative housing) have also increased. Finally, increases in real income and the extension of the life-styles of the leisure class to an ever larger proportion of the population have expanded the use of second homes and created entire communities of retirement and recreational housing. In this sense, the post-industrial or *post-shelter society* is already here, at least for some fortunate people.

Most of the literature on the post-industrial society and the future city, however, conveniently overlooks those who are left behind. With reference to housing, we might ask, what will happen to the social problem described in detail in previous chapters—such as those of segregation and discrimination, physical decay, price and affordability and limited choice? More generally, will current levels of inequality in the amount and quality of housing consumed (including location and neighborhood services), by different classes and income groups, increase or decrease? And what will happen to the neighborhoods in which the most disadvantaged people choose, or are forced, to live? Will the current fiscal problems of local governments lead to still further spatial differences in the provision of services to households? Will state intervention in the housing market generally, increase or decrease?

Table 12.1. The Changing Context of Housing in a Post-Industrial and Post-Shelter Society: A Summary

Factor	Industrial	Post-Industrial
Population and demographic structure	Rapid population growth and urbanization; in-migration to cities; youthful populations; families dominant	Slow population growth and perhaps urban decline; out-migration from cities; aging populations; small, nonfamily households increasing
Economy	Production sectors, manufacturing dominant; nonrenewable resources, low-cost energy	Service sectors and high technology industries; growth of self-help and informal sectors; renewable resources, high cost energy
Politics and culture	Laissez-faire philosophy; business control; growth ethic dominant	Growth of public intervention; shifting social control; amenity ethic dominant
Urban spatial structure	Concentrated, monocentric form; regular channels of interaction; spatially-based communities	Dispersed, mult-centred form; multiple channels of interaction; aspatial communities
Housing	Emphasis on production and new construction; overall housing shortage; minimum-quality building standards; housing as shelter; limited housing forms; high-rise/low rise contrast; densities declining; distinct types of tenure and ownership; increase in homeownership rates	Emphasis on conservation, distribution and rehabilitation; overall housing surplus; aesthetic standards, diverse preferences dominant; housing as status; diverse housing forms, mixed high and low-rise; densities may increase; alternative types of tenure and mixed ownership; increase in retirement and recreational housing

The answer to each of these questions is that we do not know. Yet we can venture some opinions, as dangerous as that is, on the basis of limited evidence on recent trends. First, and most obvious, it is clear that as long as income and wealth in our society are unevenly distributed there will be *continued inequalities* in the distribution of housing. One's position in the housing system is primarily (but not exclusively) determined by one's position in that society's socioeconomic order. Equally important, to the extent that neighborhood quality and the provision of social services reflects the revenues derived from local neighborhoods, then, the *location of one's residence* acts to exaggerate inequalities in housing due to income differences. The latter can be ameliorated somewhat by revenue sharing among urban municipalities, by the creation of metropolitan-wide governments or special boards. Changes in the former, however, require at least a partial restructuring of the existing social order.

Special problems, such as housing deterioration and abandonment, are thus reflections of more deeply rooted problems. Racial discrimination, greedy and absentee landlords, a regressive tax system, and the uncertainties created by neighborhood transition have combined with low incomes to generate a vicious cycle of poverty and housing deterioration. That cycle will not be broken through programs of housing rehabilitation or neighborhood preservation alone, as valuable as these are, unless the underlying societal causes are also treated. Although it is unlikely in the near future that housing policy itself will have much effect on these causes, other factors, such as slower growth, energy shortages, and demographic change, may help to alter the pressures on many older neighborhoods.

Problems of escalating house prices (and rents) and the affordability of housing are, as we have argued previously, in part, problems of rising aspirations and supply difficulties during the 1970s. As and if these aspirations are curtailed and development restrictions are streamlined or relaxed, some of these price pressures may decline. They are also, however, typical of those trends which impact most severely on particular groups of households who are in disadvantaged positions with respect to the housing market. These households may be simply poor, or they may be tenants in uncontrolled rental buildings, those on fixed incomes, members of minority groups, those who are not yet in the homeownership sub-market, or those who live in the wrong location. Existing homeowners, of course, have no interest in seeing prices come down, and they are also comfortably shielded from many of the effects of price inflation. It is important in this regard that we examine the origins of the inflation psychology in housing.

At the same time, the kinds of new housing produced in the future will also likely be different. We will, almost certainly, see fewer massive and monotonous high-rise towers built, particularly in the public sector. Instead, emphasis will be placed on the production of low-rise, multi-family and clustered single-family housing, both as *in-fill* within already built-up urban areas and as part of new suburban developments which have a greater *mix of tenures* and housing styles than in the past. Traditional public housing may decline. Nonprofit and co-op housing may increase. Service and building standards may also be relaxed to lower start-up costs for new households entering the housing market. New developments will also likely be of *higher density*, at least in North America, in response to the substantially greater costs of servicing low-density suburbia, increased property taxes (rates), life-style inclinations and the need for *energy conservation*. The latter ironically may bring an end to urban sprawl: higher energy costs may necessitate shorter journeys to work and the growth of higher-density housing developments clustered closer to centers of employment.

It is less likely, however, that residential mixing in social terms will increase. There is little evidence that racial segregation in U.S. cities is decreasing, although this varies with the area involved. In western Europe, on the other hand, there is some evidence that ethnic segregation, both voluntary and involuntary, is increasing, especially of recent immigrant groups, and that the contrast between the public and private housing sectors also appears to be increasing. These depressing conclusions do not necessarily mean that housing conditions will not subsequently improve for all groups—even for the poor—but it does mean that maintaining a social balance will be much more difficult.

How Will Demography Alter Our Housing Problems?

One area in which we are able to chart with some reliability the impact of future events on housing is that of changes in demographic structure. We have already noted several recent and important demographic trends: (1) slower rates of population growth, (2) a sharp reduction in average household size, (3) parallel changes in household mix, particularly the growth of one-parent, childless, and single-person households, (4) a gradual aging of the population, and (5) the increase in two-income households.

What impact will a continuation of these trends have on housing in the future? Ironically, this is not a new question. Wood (1934), writing during the depression of the 1930s, called for attention to the emerging housing problems in a society (the U.S.) which she predicted would soon have a stable or declining total population. She was not wrong, but somewhat premature. Nevertheless, the first impact of slow growth will be to reduce the aggregate demand (or need) for new housing in the 1980s and 1990s to a level substantially below that of the 1960s and 1970s, even allowing for the construction of replacement units for those now badly housed and for further improvements in standards. The entire building and real estate industry will need to adapt to lower levels of housing production, as will local governments.

Even more dramatic effects will be felt in the distribution of housing demand. Smaller households call for smaller units (although per capita space consumption may still increase); different life-styles require alternative housing forms, designs, and tenures; and the location of housing demand will change. The mix of physical and social infrastructure and services required to support those units and life-styles will also likely be different. Finally, given such demographic shifts, which makes population migration proportionally a more important factor in growth, it is possible that geographic *inequalities in housing stress* may widen. Some urban areas undergoing persistent population decline may witness an increasing housing surplus, abandonment, and physical deterioration, while other areas may show continuing shortages and price increases.

Will this demographic transition, combined with the economic and life-style changes noted earlier, also alter the pattern of housing opportunities within urban areas? Our response is that it really depends on what else happens. It is possible (as argued in Chapter 8) that lower growth rates will reduce the demand pressures on housing in some inner city areas occupied by minority groups, and thus permit some reductions in price and improvements in the amount and quality of housing consumed. But if the local neighborhood is also deteriorating, these gains in housing may be small and short-lived. Equally plausible, however, is the argument that a reduction in aggregate housing demand, combined with an overall housing surplus (created by continued high rates of new housing construction in suburban areas or in other growing regions), will contribute to continued out-migration from the inner cities and in turn further deterioration of older housing.

The countervailing trend—the tendency for more middle-class families or childless households to take up residence in the inner cities (gentrification)—has increased in recent years, but is still numerically small. Whether it expands further depends again on the alternatives provided through new construction, on relative increases in the costs of commuting to work, preference changes and the progress made in improving the character of the physical environment and social services in the inner city. It is also possible that more residents will combine a small city house or flat with a second home in the rural countryside, particularly if the work-week is shortened, and early retirements increase. Neither of these trends, however, would help the poor. In fact, both are likely to further reduce the low-cost housing inventory presently available in the inner city.

Further Housing Research

In each of the earlier chapters, it has been evident that there is much we need to know about the mechanisms by which housing is distributed in our society and about the changing conditions and occupancy of that housing. Although this is not the place to write a research agenda, and the list of outstanding questions is very long indeed, a number of specific topics stand out as warranting further investigation.

First, there is considerable merit in the earlier suggestion of an increased number of comprehensive case studies of housing conditions, household movements and market behavior—that is, the *urban housing system*—in individual urban areas. There have to date been relatively few such studies, particularly ones which provide a spatial and environmental dimension (see Grigsby, 1963; Murie et al., 1976; Berry, 1979). Second, we need to systematically examine spatial variations in housing price changes over space and time. To what extent, for example, are there *premiums*, or *quasi-rents*, for housing in certain locations and why do they appear? How permanent are these premiums and who pays them? These questions lead, in turn, to a third set of issues: how spatially segmented is the housing stock in an urban area? That is, do spatial sub-markets exist? And, if so, what attributes differentiate these sub-markets? Which households find their locational choices and residential mobility restricted by the presence of such sub-markets? Aside from their value in understanding how a housing market works, these questions are also relevant to the task of assessing how the effects of housing policies are transmitted through an urban housing system.

Fourth, there is scope for further case studies of the choices, levels of satisfaction, and changing housing needs of particular social groups, at different stages in their *housing career plans*, and living in very different kinds of urban environments (see Michelson, 1977). The poor elderly are one such group discussed earlier in the text; others include single-parent households, the handicapped, and immigrants. What are the real and perceived *constraints* on the housing choices open to such groups? What needs are not now being served, in terms of housing conditions and neighborhood services? Fifth, we need more careful assessments of the social and spatial impacts of alternative public policies—including those not designated as housing policies—and of the behavior of our financial institutions. The former requires initially that we link housing policy decisions made by national (senior) levels of government with those of regional and local authorities. This is, of course, an immensely complicated area, with a notorious lack of hard information. Nevertheless, there are specific topics within this general area on which systematic research is practical (e.g., mortgage insurance; the experimental housing allowance program).

Sixth, and perhaps the weakest component in the geography of housing, is that of supply. Here we need research on the nature of the building and construction sector and the property industry in general, as well as the factors behind decisions made on the location and timing of land purchase and housing development. When, how, and at what rate is vacant land released for residential purposes? Again, comparative studies of housing developments in different cities would be valuable. Within cities, we have very little idea of how the supply of housing produced by (or flowing from) the existing stock changes over time or why those changes vary spatially across the city. As society places more and more emphasis on conserving and reusing the older housing stock, on neighborhood revitalization, and on the preservation of existing communities, questions of how the flow of services from that stock is altered—or could be altered in desired directions—take on increasing importance.

To respond to such questions, research will also be required to address the explicit links between housing occupancy and changes in the spatial structure of urban areas. This involves relating changes in housing supply to recent trends in the location of jobs, community organization, land prices and ownership, transport improvements, and the provision of social services. Housing quality should also be linked to such specific issues as energy costs and urban form, continued neighborhood racial transition, crime, social unrest, and vandalism. Since the list of possible research topics is clearly endless, priorities for research must reflect the problems facing particular local communities, not just those facing national governments.

Finally, and in tandem with an improved base of housing information and descriptive studies, our existing theoretical frameworks and conceptual designs need to be modified and extended, and in some cases replaced, in the face of the new and different conditions affecting our cities and housing systems—e.g., slow growth and aging, inflation, and fiscal problems. Without such concepts and theories, empirical studies and statistical series, although necessary, can become but shallow mirrors of isolated situations. But theory, in turn, must be firmly grounded in the reality we observe around us, if its purpose is eventually to change and improve that reality as well as to understand it.

Postscript

This book has overlooked a great deal of what is relevant to the study of housing. After absorbing all that has preceded this conclusion, readers will still not know how to build, buy, rent, mortgage, or maintain a house, flat, or apartment. Nor will they know much more than they already do of what housing looks like in different areas or countries. But these were not the initial purposes. Instead the objective has been to provide an outline—a skeleton—of basic information, ideas, conceptual frameworks, and tools of analysis which can be used to study housing and its changing socioeconomic characteristics in widely diverse geographical and political contexts. The book poses and debates questions, undoubtedly far more than it answers, but questions which hopefully will stimulate more and better research, a greater social awareness of the complexity of housing issues and more sensitive policy decisions during the 1980s. Adding the flesh to this skeleton is left to the interested reader.

NOTES

[1] See for example, the special issue on U.S. housing policy in the *Journal of Public Interest*, Vol. 57, Fall, 1979, which bears this title.

[2] Examples of the latter include citizen membership on rent review forums or tribunals, designed to monitor rent increases in the private sector, and tenant management boards or committees for both private and public sector rental housing.

References

Aaron, H. J. 1972. *Shelter and Subsidies*. Washington, D.C.: The Brookings Institute.

Abrams, C. 1964. *Mans Struggle for Shelter in an Urbanizing World*. Cambridge, Mass.: M.I.T. Press.

Adams, J. S. 1970. "Residential Structure in Midwestern Cities," *Annals, Association of American Geographers*, **60**, 1-37-62.

_____. 1973. *New Homes, Vacancy Chains and Housing Submarkets in the Twin Cities Area*. Center for Urban and Regional Affairs, University of Minnesota, Minneapolis.

Alden, P. and Hayward, E. E. 1907. *Housing*. London: Headley Brothers.

Alonso, W. 1964. *Location and Land Use*. Cambridge, Mass.: Harvard University Press.

Ambrose, P. 1976. "The Land Market and the Housing System," *Working Paper No. 3*, Urban and Regional Studies, University of Sussex, Falmer, Brighton, U.K.

Ambrose, P. and Colenutt, R. 1975. *The Property Machine*. London: Penguin.

Andreae, A. E. 1978. *Senior Citizens' Housing: Locational Considerations and Social Implications*. Major Report No. 14, Centre for Urban and Community Studies, University of Toronto, Toronto, Canada.

Apgar, W. C. Jr. 1977. "Census Data and Housing Analysis: Old Data Sources and New Applications," in G. K. Ingram, ed., *Residential Location and Urban Housing Markets*. Cambridge, Mass.: Ballinger, 139–172.

Apps, P. F. 1973. "An Approach to Urban Modeling and Evaluation: A Residential Model, 2: Implicit Prices for Housing Services," *Environment and Planning*, 5:705–717.

Babcock, R. F. and Callies, D. L. 1973. "Ecology and Housing: Virtues in Conflict," in M. Clawson, ed., *Modernizing Urban Land Policy*. Baltimore: R.F.F., 205–220.

Bagby, G. D. 1974. *Housing Rehabilitation Costs.* Lexington, Mass.: Lexington Books.

Balchin, P. 1979. *Housing Improvement and Social Inequality.* London: Saxon House.

Ball, M. J. 1973. "Recent Empirical Work on the Determinants of Relative House Prices," *Urban Studies,* 10:213–223.

Ball, M. J. and Harloe, M. 1974. *Housing Policy in a Socialist Country: The Case of Poland.* Research Paper 8, Centre for Environmental Studies, London.

Ball, M. J. and Kirwin, R. M. 1975. "The Economics of an Urban Housing Market, Bristol Study Area," *Research Paper 15,* Centre for Environmental Studies, London.

_____ and _____. 1977. "Accessibility and Supply Constraints in the Urban Housing Market," *Urban Studies,* 14:11–32.

Barlev, B. and May, J. 1976. "The Effects of Property Taxes on the Construction and Demolition of Houses in Urban Areas," *Economic Geography,* 52:304–310.

Barrett, F. A. 1973. *Residential Search Behavior.* Geographical Monographs No. 1, York University, Toronto.

Barrett, S., Stewart, M. and Underwood, J. 1978. *The Land Market and Development Process. A Review of Research and Policy.* School of Advanced Urban Studies, University of Bristol, Bristol, U.K.

Beckmann, M. J. 1974. "Spatial Equilibrium and the Housing Market," *Journal of Urban Economics,* 1, 1:99–107.

Berry, B. J. L. 1975. "Short-Term Housing Cycles in a Dualistic Metropolis," in G. Gappert and H. Rose, eds., *The Social Economy of Cities.* Beverly Hills, Calif.: Sage Publications, 165–182.

_____. 1976. "Ghetto Expansion and Single-Family Housing Prices: Chicago, 1968–1972," *Journal of Urban Economics,* 3:397–423.

_____. 1979. *Race and Housing: The Chicago Experience, 1960–1975.* Cambridge, Mass.: Ballinger.

Berry, B. J. L. and Bednarz, R. 1975. "A Hedonic Model of Prices and Assessments for Single-Family Homes: Does the Assessor Follow the Market or the Market Follow the Assessor?", *Land Economics,* 51, 1:21–40.

Berry, B. J. L. and Kasarda, J. D. 1977. *Contemporary Urban Ecology.* New York: Macmillan.

Birch, D. L. 1971. "Toward a Stage Theory of Urban Growth," *Journal of the American Institute of Planners,* 37, 2:78–87.

Bird, H. 1976. "Residential Mobility and Preference Patterns in the Public Sector of the Housing Market," *Transactions, Institute of British Geographers,* New Series No. 1:20–33.

Boddy, M. J. 1975. "Theories of Residential Location or Castles in the Air?" *Environment and Planning A,* 7:109–111.

_____. 1976. "The Structure of Mortgage Finance, Building Societies and the British Social Formation," *Transactions, Institute of British Geographers,* New Series, Vol. 1:58–71.

_____. 1979. *The Building Societies.* London: Macmillan.

Boddy, M. J. and Gray, F. 1979. "Filtering Theory, Housing Policy and the Legitimation of Inequality," *Policy and Politics,* 7:39–54.

Bonham, G. S. 1973. "Discrimination and Housing Quality," *Growth and Change,* 3:26–34.

Bossons, J. 1978. "Housing Demand and Household Wealth: Evidence for Home-Owners," in L. S. Bourne and J. R. Hitchcock, eds., *Urban Housing Markets.* Toronto: University of Toronto Press, 86–106.

Bourne, L. S. 1969. "Location Factors in the Redevelopment Process: A Model of Residential Change," *Land Economics*, XLV, 2:183–193.

_____. 1976. "Housing Supply and Housing Market Behavior in Residential Development," in D. Herbert and R. Johnston, eds., *Social Areas in Cities, Vol. 1*. London: John Wiley, 111–158.

_____. 1977. "The Housing Supply and Price Debate: Divergent Views and Policy Implications," *Research Paper No. 86*, Centre for Urban and Community Studies, University of Toronto.

_____. 1978. "Perspectives on the Inner City," *Research Paper No. 94*, Centre for Urban and Community Studies, University of Toronto.

Bourne, L. S. and Berridge, J. D. 1973. "Apartment Location and Developer Behavior: A Reappraisal," *Canadian Geographer*, 17:403–411.

Bourne, L. S. and Hitchcock, J. R., eds. 1978. *Urban Housing Markets: Recent Directions in Research and Policy*. Toronto: University of Toronto Press.

Bourne, L. S. and Simmons, J. W. 1978. "On the Spatial Structure of Housing Submarkets." Paper presented to the Annual Meetings of the AAG, New Orleans, April 13, 1978.

Bradbury, K. 1977. "Changes in Urban Housing Supply Through Conversion or Retirement," *Discussion Paper 417*, Institute for Research on Poverty, University of Wisconsin-Madison, Madison, Wisconsin.

Bradford, C. 1979. "Financing Home Ownership: The Federal Role in Neighborhood Decline," *Urban Affairs Quarterly*, 14, 3, 373–336.

Brown, W. J. 1972. "Access to Housing: The Role of the Real Estate Industry," *Economic Geography*, 48, 1:66–78.

Brown, L. and Moore, E. 1970. "The Intra-Urban Migration Process: A Perspective," *Geografiska Annaler*, Series B, 52B: 200–209.

Brueggeman, W. B. 1975. "An Analysis of the Filtering Process with Special Reference to Housing Subsidies," in *Housing in the Seventies*, Vol. 2. Washington, D.C.: HUD.

Buckley, R. M., Tucillo, J. A. and Villani, K. E., eds. 1978. *Capital Markets and the Housing Sector: Perspectives on Financial Reform*. Cambridge, Mass.: Ballinger.

Burnett, J. 1978. *A Social History of Housing, 1815–1970*. North Pomfret, Vt.: David and Charles.

Burns, L. S. and Grebler, L. 1977. *The Housing of Nations*. London: Macmillan.

Byler, J. W. and Gale, S. 1978. "Social Accounts and Planning for Change in Urban Housing Markets," *Environment and Planning A*, 10:247–266.

Canada, Central Mortgage and Housing Corporation, 1978. *Canadian Housing Statistics*. Ottawa: CMHC.

Canadian Council on Social Development, 1977. *A Review of Canadian Social Housing Policy*. Ottawa: CCSD.

Carlson, D. and Heinberg, J. 1978. *How Housing Allowances Work*. Washington, D.C.: The Urban Institute.

Carvalho, J., Hum, D., Sahay, H. and Falconer, D. 1976. "On the Determinants of Residential Property Values," *Plan Canada*, 16:190–197.

Case, F. E. and Mittelbach, F., eds. 1976. *Public Sector Impacts on Housing and Real Estate*. Los Angeles: University of California.

Cassidy, R. G. 1975. "Urban Housing Selection," *Behavioral Science*, 20:241–250.

Castells, M. 1972. *La Question Urbaine*. Paris: Maspero.

_____. 1975. "Advanced Capitalism, Collective Consumption and Urban Contradictions," in L. N. Lindberg et al., eds., *Stress and Contradiction in Modern Capitalism*. Lexington, Mass.: D. C. Heath, 175–198.

_____. 1978. (trans. by E. Lebas). *City, Class and Power*. London: Macmillan.

Central (Canada) Mortgage and Housing Corporation. 1978. *Housing Requirements Model: Projections to 2000*. Ottawa: CMHC.

Centre for Environmental Studies, 1978, 1979. *Housing Review* No. 4, No. 5, No. 6. London: C.E.S.

Chapin, F. S. 1976. *Household Activity Patterns*. Chapel Hill, N.C.: University of North Carolina.

Chinitz, B., ed. 1978. *Central City Economic Development*, Cambridge, Mass.: Abt. Books.

Clark, W. A. V. 1964. "Markov Chain Analysis in Geography: An Application to the Movement of Rental Housing Areas," *Annals, Association of American Geographers*. 55:351–359.

Clark, W. A. V. and Cadwallader, M. 1973. "Locational Stress and Residential Mobility," *Environment and Behavior*, 5, 1:29–42.

Clark, W. A. V. and Moore, E., eds. 1978. *Population Mobility and Urban Change*. Studies in Geography No. 25, Northwestern University, Evanston, Ill.

Clawson, M. 1971. *Suburban Land Conversion in the United States. An Economic and Governmental Process*. Baltimore: Johns Hopkins.

Colton, K. W. 1978. "The Future of the Nation's Housing Finance System: Reform or Paralysis," *Journal of the American Institute of Planners*, 44:306–316.

Conference of Socialist Economists, 1975. *Political Economy and the Housing Question*. Vol. 1. London: Housing Workshop.

Courant, P. N. 1978. "Racial Prejudice in a Search Model of the Urban Housing Market," *Journal of Urban Economics*, 5:329–345.

Cox, K., ed. 1978. *Power and Conflict in Market Economies*. London: Methuen.

Cullingworth, J. B. 1960. *Housing Needs and Planning Policy*. London: Routledge and Kegan Paul.

_____. 1966. *Housing and Local Government*. London: Allen and Unwin.

_____. 1972. *Problems of an Urban Society*. Vol. 2. London: Allen and Unwin.

_____. 1978. "Housing Allowances: The British Experience. A Brief Review of the Background to and Provisions of the British Housing Allowance Program," *Research Paper No. 95*, Centre for Urban and Community Studies, University of Toronto.

_____. 1979. *Essays on Housing Policy: The British Scene*. London: George Allen and Unwin.

Cybriwsky, R. A. 1978. Social Aspects of Neighborhood Change, *Annals, Association of American Geographers*, **68**, 1:17–33.

Davis, J. T. 1965. "Middle Class Housing in the Central City," *Economic Geography*, **41**, 3-238-251.

Davis, O. and Whinston, A. B. 1966. "The Economics of Urban Renewal," *Law and Contemporary Problems*, XXVI, 5:105–117.

Davis, R. H., ed. 1973. *Housing for the Elderly*. Los Angeles: University of California Press.

Dear, M. J. 1976. "Abandoned Housing," Chap. 3 in J. S. Adams, ed., *Urban Policy-Making and Metropolitan Dynamics: A Comparative Geographical Analysis*. Cambridge, Mass.: Ballinger, 59–99.

de Leeuw, F. and Struyk, R. J. 1975. *The Web of Urban Housing*. Washington, D.C.: The Urban Institute.

Dennis, M. and Fish, S. 1972. *Programs in Search of a Policy: Low Income Housing In Canada*. Toronto: Hakkert.

Di Maio, A. J. 1973. *Soviet Urban Housing: Problems and Prospects*. New York: Praeger.

Dingemans, D. 1979. "Redlining and Mortgage Lending in Sacramento," *Annals, Association of American Geographers*, 69, 2:225–239.

Doling, J. 1976. "The Family Life Cycle and Housing Choice," *Urban Studies*, 13:55–58.

Donnison, D. V. 1967. *The Government of Housing*. London: Penguin.

Downs, A. 1973. *Opening Up the Suburbs*. New Haven: Yale University Press.

_____. 1975. *Urban Problems and Prospects*, 2nd ed. Chicago: Rand McNally.

_____. 1978. "Public Policy and the Rising Cost of Housing," *Real Estate Review*, 8:27–38.

Drewett, R. 1973. "The Developers' Decision Processes" in P. Hall et al., *The Containment of Urban England*, Vol. 2. London: Allen and Unwin, 163–193.

Duncan, G. and Newman, S. 1975. "People as Planners: The Fulfillment of Residential Mobility Expectations," Chap. 8, in G. Duncan and J. Morgan, eds., *Five Thousand American Families: Patterns of Economic Progress*. Vol. 3. Ann Arbor, Michigan: Institute of Social Research.

Duncan, S. S. 1977. "The Housing Question and the Structure of the Housing Market," *Journal of Social Policy*, 6, 4:385–412.

_____. 1978. "Housing Provision in Advanced Capitalism: Sweden in the 1970s," *Working Paper No. 10*, Urban and Regional Studies, University of Sussex, Farmer, Brighton, U.K.

Dwyer, D. J. 1975. *People and Housing in Third World Cities*. London: Longman.

Edel, M. 1972. "Filtering in a Private Housing Market," in M. Edel and J. Rothenberg, eds., *Readings in Urban Economics*. New York: Macmillan, 204–215.

Engels, F. 1844. *The Condition of the Working Classes in England*. Moscow: Progress Publishing. (reprinted 1973)

_____. 1872. *The Housing Question*. Moscow: Progress Publishing. (reprinted 1954)

Ermisch, J. forthcoming. "Demographic Change, Housing and Infrastructure Investment," in D. E. C. Eversley, ed., *Population Change and Social Planning*. London: Edward Arnold.

Evans, A. W. 1973. *The Economics of Residential Location*. London: Macmillan.

_____. 1975. "Rent and Housing in the Theory of Urban Growth," *Journal of Regional Science*, 15, 2:113–125.

Eversley, D. 1979, forthcoming. *The Politics of Housing*.

Firestone, O. J. 1951. *Residential Real Estate in Canada*. Toronto: University of Toronto Press.

Firey, W. 1947. *Land Use in Central Boston*. Cambridge: Harvard University Press.

Fishman, R. F., ed. 1978. *Housing for All Under Law: New Directions in Housing, Land Use and Planning Law*. Cambridge, Mass.: Ballinger.

Forrest, R. 1976. "Monitoring: Some Conceptual Issues in Relation to Housing Research," *Working Paper No. 42*, Centre for Urban and Regional Studies, University of Birmingham, U.K.

Fried, M. and Gleicker, P. 1961. "Some Sources of Residential Satisfaction in an Urban Slum," *Journal of the American Institute of Planners*, 27:303–315.

Fuerst, J. S. 1974. *Public Housing in Europe and America*. London: Croom Helm.

Gad, G., Peddie, R. and Punter, J. 1973. "Ethnic Differences in the Residential Search Process," in L. S. Bourne et al., eds., *The Form of Cities in Central Canada: Selected Papers*. Toronto: University of Toronto Press.

Gale, D. E. 1979. "Middle Class Resettlement in Older Urban Neighborhoods," *Journal of the American Planning Association*, **45**, 3:293–304.

Gilbert, G. 1972. "Two Markov Models of Neighborhood Turnover," *Environment and Planning*, 4:133–146.

Gillingham, R. 1973. "Place to Place Rent Comparisons Using Hedonic Quality Adjustment Techniques," *Discussion Paper No. 7*, U.S. Bureau of Labor Statistics, Washington, D.C.

Gittus, E. 1976. *Flats, Families and the Under Fives*. London: Routledge and Kegan Paul.

Golant, S. M. 1975. "Residential Concentrations of the Future Elderly," *The Gerontologist*, **15**, 1:16–23.

Goldberg, M. A. 1977. "Housing and Land Prices in Canada and the U.S.," in L. B. Smith and M. Walker, eds., *Public Property: The Habitat Debate Continued*. Vancouver: Fraser Institute, 207–254.

_____. 1978. "Developer Behavior and Urban Growth: Analysis and Synthesis," in L. S. Bourne and J. Hitchcock, eds., *Urban Housing Markets*. Toronto: University of Toronto Press, 181–227.

Goodman, A. C. 1978. "Hedonic Prices, Price Indices and Housing Markets," *Journal of Urban Economics*, 5:471–484.

Goodman, J. L., Jr. 1978. "Causes and Indicators of Housing Quality," *Social Indicators Research*, 4:195–210.

Gottlieb, M. 1976. *Long Swings in Urban Development*. New York: National Bureau of Economic Research.

Gray, F. 1975. "Non-explanation in Urban Geography," *Area*, 7, 4:228–235.

_____. 1976. "Selection and Allocation in Council Housing," *Transactions Institute of British Geographers*, **1**, 1:34–46.

Grebler, L. et al. 1956. *Capital Formation in Residential Real Estate*. Princeton: University Press.

Greendale, A. and Knock, S. F., Jr., eds. 1976. *Housing Costs and Housing Needs*. New York: Praeger.

Grigsby, W. 1963. *Urban Housing Markets*. Philadelphia: University of Pennsylvania Press.

Grigsby, W. and Rosenburg, J. 1975. *Urban Housing Policy*. New York: A.P.S. Publications.

Guest, A. M. 1977. "Residential Segregation in Urban Areas," Chap. 5, in K. P. Schwirian, ed., *Contemporary Topics in Urban Sociology*. Morristown, N.J.: General Learning Press, 268–336.

Hallett, G. 1977. *Housing and Land Policies in West Germany and Britain*. London: Macmillan.

Hamnett, C. 1973. "Improvement Grants as an Indicator of Gentrification in Inner London," *Area*, 4:252–261.

Hanushek, E. A. and Quigley, J. M. 1978. "The Dynamics of the Housing Market: A Stock Adjustment Model of Housing Construction," *Journal of Urban Economics*, 5:411–429.

Harloe, M., ed. 1977. *Captive Cities: Studies in The Political Economy of Cities and Regions*. New York: John Wiley & Sons.

_____. 1978a. *Housing Management and New Forms of Tenure in the U.S.* Policy Series 2, Centre for Environmental Studies, London.

_____. 1978b. "Housing and the State," *International Social Science Journal*, XXX, 3:591–604.

_____. 1979. "The Private Rental Sector in the United States," unpublished report, Centre for Environmental Studies, London.

Harloe, M., Issacharoff, R. and Minns, R. 1974. *The Organization of Housing.* London: Heinemann.

Harvey, D. 1972. "Revolutionary and Counter Revolutionary Theory in Geography and the Problem of Ghetto Formation," *Antipode*, 4, 2:1–13.

_____. 1973. *Social Justice in the City.* London: Edward Arnold.

_____. 1977a. "Government Policies, Financial Institutions and Neighborhood Change in United States Cities," in M. Harloe, ed., *Captive Cities.* New York: John Wiley, 123–139.

_____. 1977b. "Labor, Capital and Class Struggle Around the Built Environment in Advanced Capitalist Societies," *Politics and Society*, 6:265–295.

_____. 1978. "The Urban Process under Capitalism: A Framework for Analysis," *International Journal of Urban and Regional Research*, 2, 1:101–131.

Harvey, D. and Chatterjee, L. 1974. "Absolute Rent and the Structuring of Space by Governmental and Financial Institutions," *Antipode*, 6, 2:22–36.

Hayek, F. et al. 1978. *Rent Control: A Popular Paradox.* Vancouver: Fraser Institute.

Headey, B. 1978. *Housing Policy in the Developed Economy.* London: Croom Helm.

Herbert, D. 1972. *Urban Geography: A Social Perspective.* Newton Abbot: David and Charles.

Herbert, D. and Johnston, R. eds. 1976. *Social Areas in Cities*, Vol. 1. London: John Wiley.

Holmans, A. E. 1979. "Housing Tenure in England and Wales: The Present Situation and Recent Trends," in Central Statistical Office, *Social Trends*, Vol. 9. London: HMSO, 10–19.

Holmes, J. 1976. "Urban Housing Problems and Public Policy," Chap. 17, in M. Yeates and B. Garner, *The North American City*, 2nd ed. New York: Harper and Row, 400–420.

Housing Services Advisory Group. 1978. *Allocation of Council Housing.* London: Department of the Environment.

Hoyt, H. 1933. *A Hundred Years of Land Values in Chicago.* University of Chicago Press.

_____. 1939. *Structure and Growth of Residential Neighborhoods in American Cities.* Washington, D.C.: FHA.

Hughes, J. W. and Bleakly, K. D., Jr. 1975. *Urban Homesteading.* New Brunswick, N.J.: Rutgers, The State University.

Hyman, G. and Markowski, S. 1979. "Speculation and Inflation in the Market for Housebuilding Land in England and Wales," *Working Note CES WN537*, Centre for Environmental Studies, London.

Ingram, G. K., ed. 1977. *Residential Location and Urban Housing Markets.* Cambridge, Mass.: Ballinger.

Institute of Economic Affairs. 1972. *Verdict on Rent Control.* London: The Institute.

Isard, W. 1942. "A Neglected Cycle: The Transport-Building Cycle," *Review of Economics and Statistics*, 24, 4:149–158.

Isler, M. 1970. *Thinking About Housing.* Washington, D.C.: Urban Institute.

James, F. J. 1977. "Back to the City: An Appraisal of Housing Investment and Population Change in Urban America," *Working Paper 241-01*, The Urban Institute, Washington, D.C.

Johnson, J., Salt, J. and Wood, P. 1974. *Housing and the Migration of Labour in England and Wales.* London: Saxon House.

Johnston, R. J. 1971. *Urban Residential Patterns.* New York: Bell.

————. 1972. "Activity Spaces and Residential Preferences: Some Tests of the Hypothesis of Sectoral Mental Maps," *Economic Geography*, 42:137–160.

Jones, C. 1978. "Household Movement, Filtering and Trading Up Within the Owner-Occupied Sector," *Regional Studies*, 12:551–561.

Jones, E. and Eyles, J. 1977. *An Introduction to Social Geography.* London: Oxford University Press.

Journal of the American Planning Association, Vol. 45, Oct., 1979. "Symposium on Neighborhood Revitalization," pp. 460–559.

Kain, J. and Quigley, J. 1970. "Measuring the Value of Housing Quality," *Journal of the American Statistical Association*, 65:532–548.

————. 1975. *Housing Markets and Racial Discrimination.* New York: National Bureau of Economic Research, Columbia University Press.

Kaiser Committee. 1969. *A Decent Home.* Report of the Presidents Committee on Urban Housing: Washington, D.C.: U.S. GPO.

Kaiser, E. J. 1972. "Decision Agent Models: An Alternative Modeling Approach for Urban Residential Growth," in D. C. Sweet, ed., *Models of Urban Structure.* Lexington, Mass.: D. C. Heath, 109–122.

Kemeny, J. 1978. "Urban Home-ownership in Sweden," *Urban Studies*, 15:313–320.

————. 1979, forthcoming. *The Myth of Home Ownership.* London: Routledge and Kegan Paul.

Kern, C. R. 1977. "High Income Neighborhoods in the City: Will the New Demography Guarantee Their Future?" Paper presented to the Annual Meetings of the Regional Science Association, Philadelphia.

King, A. T. and Mieszkowski, P. 1973. "Racial Discrimination, Segregation and the Price of Housing," *Journal of Public Economy*, 81:590–606.

King, L. and Golledge, R. 1978. *Cities, Space and Behavior.* Englewood Cliffs, N.J.: Prentice-Hall.

Kirby, A. M. 1975. "Housing Market Studies: A Critical Review," *Transactions, Institute of British Geographers*, 1:2–7.

Kirby, D. A. 1979. *Slum Housing and Residential Renewal: The Case of Great Britain.* London: Longmans.

Kirwin, R. and Ball, M. 1973. "The Microeconomic Analysis of a Local Housing Market," in *Papers CES Urban Economics Conference*, Vol. 1, Centre for Environmental Studies, London.

Kristof, F. 1972. "Federal Housing Policies: Subsidized Production, Filtration and Objectives, Part 1," *Land Economics*, 48:309–320.

Lakshmanan, T. R., Chatterjee, L. and Kroll, P. 1978. "Housing Consumption and Level of Development: A Cross-National Comparison," *Economic Geography*, 54, 3:222–233.

Lambert, J., Paris, C. and Blackaby, B. 1978. *Housing Policy and the State: Allocation, Access and Control.* London, Macmillan.

Lansing, J. B. et al. 1969. *New Homes and Poor People: A Study of Chains of Moves.* Ann Arbor: University of Michigan Press.

Lansley, S. 1979. *Housing and Public Policy in Britain.* London: Croom Helm.

Lapham, V. 1971. "Do Blacks Pay More for Housing?" *Journal of Political Economy*, 79:1244–1257.

Lee, T. R. 1977. *Race and Residence.* Oxford: Clarendon Press.

Lett, M. R. 1978. *Rent Control: Concepts, Realities and Mechanisms.* New Brunswick, N.J.: Rutgers University.

Leven, C. L. et al. 1976. *Neighborhood Change: Lessons in the Dynamics of Urban Decay.* New York: Praeger.

Leven, C. L. and Mark, J. H. 1971. "Revealed Preferences for Neighborhood Characteristics," *Urban Studies*, 14:147-159.

Lewis, J. P. 1965. *Building Cycles and Britain's Growth.* London: Macmillan.

Ley, D. 1974. *The Black Inner City as Frontier Outpost: Images and Behavior in a Philadelphia Neighborhood.* Washington, D.C., Association of American Geographers.

_____. 1979. "Liberal Ideology and the Post-Industry City," School of Geography, Oxford. (mimeo.)

Lindberg, L. N. et al., eds. 1975. *Stress and Contradiction in Modern Capitalism, Public Policy and The Theory of The State.* Lexington, Mass.: D. C. Heath.

Lipton, S. G. 1977. "Evidence of Central City Revival," *Journal of the American Institute of Planners*, 43, 2:136-147.

Listokin, D. 1976. *Fair Share Housing Allocation.* New Brunswick, N.J.: Rutgers University.

Listokin, D. and Casey, S. 1979. *Mortgage Lending and Race: Conceptual and Analytical Perspectives on the Urban Financing Problem.* New Brunswick, N.J.: Rutgers, Center for Urban Policy Research.

Little, J. T. 1976. "Residential Preferences, Neighborhood Filtering and Neighborhood Change," *Journal of Urban Economics*, 3:68-81.

Lorimer, J. and Ross, E. 1976. *The City Book.* Toronto: J. Lorimer Publishers.

Lowry, I. 1960. "Filtering and Housing Standards: A Conceptual Analysis," *Land Economics*, 36:362-370.

Lowry, I. et al. 1972. *Rental Housing in New York City Volume II.* New York: Rand Institute.

Mabogunje, A. L., Hardoy, J. E. and Mista, R. P. 1978. *Shelter Provision in Developing Countries.* New York: John Wiley.

Maher, C. A. 1974. "Spatial Patterns in Urban Housing Markets: Filtering in Toronto, 1953-71," *Canadian Geographer*, 18, 2:599-611.

Maisel, S. J. 1963. "A Theory of Fluctuations in Residential Construction Starts," *American Economic Review*, 53, 3:359-383.

Mandelker, D. R. 1974. *Housing Subsidies in the U.S. and England.* New York: Bobbs-Merrill.

Markusen, J. and Scheffman, D. 1977. *Speculation and Market Structure in Urban Markets.* Toronto: University of Toronto Press.

Mayers, D. G. 1979. *The Property Boom.* London: Martin Robinson.

McKay, D. 1977. *Housing and Race in Industrial Society. Civil Rights and Urban Policy in Britain and the United States.* London: Croom Helm.

Meadows, G. R. and Call, St. T. 1978. "Combining Housing Market Trends and Resident Attitudes in Planning Urban Revitalization," *Journal of the American Institute of Planners.* 297-305.

Mendelsohn, R. 1977. "Empirical Evidence on Home Improvements," *Journal of Urban Economics*, 4:459-468.

Mercer, J. 1972. "Housing Quality and the Ghetto," in H. Rose, ed., *Geography of The Ghetto: Perspectives in Geography Vol. 2.* Dekalb, Ill.: Northern Illinois University Press, 143-168.

_____. 1979. "Locational Consequences of Housing Policies for the Low-Income Elderly: The Case of Vancouver, B.C.," in S. M. Golant, ed., *Location and*

Environment of the Elderly Population. Washington, D.C.: V. H. Winston & Sons.

Mercer, J. and Hulquist, J. 1976. "National Progress Toward Housing and Urban Renewal Goals," Chap. 4, in J. S. Adams, ed., *Urban Policy-Making and Metropolitan Dynamics: A Comparative Geographical Analysis.* Cambridge, Mass.: Ballinger, 101–162.

Merrett, S. 1979. *State Housing in Britain.* London: Routledge and Kegan Paul.

Merton, R. K. 1966. "The Social Psychology of Housing," in W. Wheaton et al., eds., *Urban Housing.* New York: Free Press, 20–29.

Meyerson, M. and Banfield, E. 1955. *Politics, Planning and the Public Interest.* New York: Free Press.

Michelson, W. 1974. "The Reconciliation of 'Subjective' and 'Objective' Data on Physical Environment in the Community," in M. P. Effrat, ed., *The Community: Approaches and Applications.* New York: Free Press, 147–173.

———. 1977. *Environmental Choice, Human Behavior, and Residential Satisfaction.* New York: Oxford University Press.

Mills, E. S. 1967. "An Aggregate Model of Resource Allocation in a Metropolitan Area," *American Economic Review,* 57:197–211.

Moore, E. G. 1972. *Residential Mobility in the City.* A.A.G. Resource Paper 13, Association of American Geographers, Washington, D.C.

———. ed. 1973. *Models of Residential Location and Relocation in the City.* Evanston, Ill.: Northwestern University.

———. 1975. "The Dynamics of Overcrowding," *Working Paper No. 8*, Research on Metropolitan Changes and Conflict Resolution, University of Pennsylvania, Philadelphia.

Moore, E. and Clatworthy, S. 1978. "The Role of Urban Data Systems in the Analysis of Housing Issues," in L. S. Bourne and J. R. Hitchcock, eds., *Urban Housing Markets.* Toronto: University of Toronto Press, 228–258.

Morris, E. W. and Winter, M. 1978. *Housing, Family and Society.* New York: John Wiley & Sons.

Morris, R. S. 1978. *Bum Rap on America's Cities: The Real Causes of Urban Decay.* New York: Prentice-Hall.

Morrison, P. S. 1977. "Data Sources on Residential Change and the Housing Market: A Guide to Contemporary Sources and Tests of Bias," *Major Report No. 10*, Centre for Urban and Community Studies, University of Toronto.

———. 1978. "Residential Property Conversion, Subdivision, Merger and Quality Changes in the Inner City Housing Stock: Metropolitan Toronto, 1958–73." Unpublished doctoral dissertation, University of Toronto, Department of Geography, 1978.

———. 1979. "Mortgage Lending in Canadian Cities" *Research Paper No. 111*, Centre for Urban and Community Studies, University of Toronto.

Murie, A. 1975. "The Sale of Council Housing: A Study of Social Policy," *Occasional Paper No. 35*, Centre for Urban and Regional Studies, University of Birmingham, Birmingham, U.K.

Murie, A., Ninar, P. and Watson, C. 1976. *Housing Policy and the Housing System.* London: Allen and Unwin.

Muth, R. F. 1961. "The Spatial Structure of the Housing Market," *Papers of the Regional Science Association,* 7:207–220.

———. 1969. *Cities and Housing.* Chicago: University of Chicago Press.

———. 1974. "Moving Costs and Household Expenditures," *Journal of Urban Economics,* 1, 1:108–125.

_____. 1976. "The Effect of Constraints on House Costs," *Journal of Urban Economics*, 3:57–67.

_____. 1978. "The Allocation of Households to Dwellings," *Journal of Regional Science*, 18:159–178.

Myers, D. 1975. "Housing Allowances, Submarket Relationships and the Filtering Process," *Urban Affairs Quarterly*, 11:215–240.

Needleman, L. 1965. *The Economics of Housing*. London: Staples Press.

Nevitt, A. A. 1966. *Housing, Taxation and Subsidies. A Study of Housing in the U.K.* London: Nelson.

Niebanck, P. and Pope, J. B. 1965. *The Elderly in Older Urban Areas*. Philadelphia: University of Pennsylvania.

Nutt, B., Walker, B., Holliday, S. and Sears, D. 1976. *Obsolescence in Housing: Theory and Applications*. London: Saxon House.

O'Loughlin, J. and Munski, D. C. 1979. "Housing Rehabilitation in the Inner City: A Comparison of Two Neighborhoods in New Orleans," *Economic Geography*, 55, 1:52–70.

Olsen, E. 1969. "A Competitive Theory of the Housing Market," *American Economic Review*, 59:612–622.

_____. 1974. "Do the Poor or the Blacks Pay More for Housing?" in G. M. von Furstenberg, B. Harrison and A. Horowitz, eds., *Patterns of Racial Discrimination, Vol. 1. Housing*. Lexington, Mass.: D. C. Heath.

Ozanne, L. and Struyk, R. J. 1976. *Housing from the Existing Stock*. Washington, D.C.: The Urban Institute.

_____ and _____. 1978. "The Price Elasticity of the Supply of Housing Services," in L. S. Bourne and J. R. Hitchcock, eds., *Urban Housing Markets*. Toronto: University of Toronto Press, 109–138.

Pahl, R. 1976. *Whose City?* 2nd ed. Harmondsworth, U.K.: Penguin.

_____. 1977. "Managers, Technical Experts and the State: Forms of Mediation, Manipulation and Dominance in Urban and Regional Development," in M. Harloe, ed., *Captive Cities*. New York: John Wiley, 49–60.

Palm, R. 1976. "Real Estate Agents and Geographical Information," *Geographical Review*, 66:266–280.

_____. 1977. "Homeownership Cost Trends," *Environment and Planning A*. 9:795–804.

_____. 1978. "Spatial Segmentation of the Urban Housing Market," *Economic Geography*, 54, 3:210–221.

_____. 1979. "Financial and Real Estate Institutions in the Housing Market: A Study of Recent House Price Changes in the San Francisco Bay Area," in D. Herbert and R. Johnston, eds., *Geography and the Urban Environment*, Vol. II. New York: John Wiley, 83–124.

Park, R. E., Burgess, E. W. and McKenzie, R. D. 1925. *The City*. Chicago: University of Chicago Press.

Pawley, M. 1978. *Home Ownership*. London: Architectural Press.

P.E.P. 1965. *Housing in Britain, France and Western Germany*. London: P.E.P.

Pennance, F. G., Hamilton, S. W. and Baxter, D. 1976. *Housing: It's Your Move*. Vancouver: Faculty of Commerce, University of British Columbia.

Peterson, G. E. et al. 1973. *Property Taxes, Housing and the Cities*. Lexington, Mass.: D. C. Heath.

Peterson, G. L. 1967. "A Model of Preference; Qualitative Analysis of the Perception of the Visual Appearance of Residential Neighborhoods," *Journal of Regional Science*, 7:19–32.

Phares, D., ed. 1978. *A Decent Home and Environment: Housing Urban America.* Cambridge, Mass.: Ballinger.

Pickvance, C. G. 1976. "Housing, Reproduction of Capital and Reproduction of Labor Power: Some Recent French Work," *Antipode*, 8, 1:58–68.

Pines, D. 1975. "On the Spatial Distribution of Households According to Income," *Economic Geography*, 51, 2:142–149.

Prichard, R. M. 1976. *Housing and the Spatial Structure of the City.* Cambridge: Cambridge University Press.

Putnam, S. H. and Ducca, F. W. 1978. "Calibrating Urban Residential Location Models, 1 Procedures and Strategies, *Environment and Planning A*, 10:633–650.

Pynoos, G. et al., eds. 1973. *Housing Urban America.* Chicago: Aldine.

Quigley, J. M. 1978. "Housing Markets and Housing Demand: Analytical Approaches," in L. S. Bourne and J. R. Hitchcock, eds., *Urban Housing Markets.* Toronto: University of Toronto Press, 23–44.

Rapkin, C., Winnick, L. and Blank, D. M. 1953. *Housing Market Analysis: A Study of Theory and Methods.* Washington: Housing and Home Finance Agency.

Ratcliff, R. U. 1949. *Urban Land Economics.* New York: McGraw-Hill.

Reid, M. 1962. *Housing and Income.* Chicago: University of Chicago Press.

Rex, J. 1971. "The Concept of Housing Class and the Sociology of Race Relations," *Race*, 12, 3:293–301.

Rex, J. and Moore, R. 1967. *Race, Community and Conflict.* London: Oxford University Press.

Richardson, H. W. 1977. *The New Urban Economics.* London: Pion.

Richardson, H. W., Vipond, J. and Furby, R. A. 1975. *Housing and Urban Spatial Structure.* Lexington, Mass.: D. C. Heath.

Robinson, R. 1979. *Housing Economics and Public Policy.* London: Macmillan.

Robson, B. 1975. *Urban Social Areas.* London: Oxford University Press.

_____. 1979. "Housing, Empiricism and the State," Chap. 5, in *Social Problems and the City: Geographical Perspectives.* London: Oxford University Press, 66–83.

Rodwin, L. 1950. "Theory of Residential Growth and Structure," *Appraisal Journal*, 18:295–317.

_____. 1961. *Housing and Economic Progress.* Cambridge, Mass.: Harvard University Press.

Rose, A. 1978. "The Impact of Recent Trends in Social Housing Policies," in L. S. Bourne and J. Hitchcock, eds., *Urban Housing Markets.* Toronto: University of Toronto Press, 261–278.

Rose, H. 1976. *Black Suburbanization.* Cambridge, Mass.: Ballinger.

Rosen, H. S. 1978. "Estimating Inter-City Differences in the Price of Housing Services," *Urban Studies*, 15-351–355.

Rossi, P. H. 1955. *Why Families Move: A Study in the Social Psychology of Urban Residential Mobility.* New York: Free Press.

Roweis, S. and Scott, A. J. 1978. "The Urban Land Question," reprinted in K. Cox, ed., *Urbanization and Conflict in Market Societies.* Chicago: Maaroufa Press, 38–75.

Sanders, R. A. 1976. "Bilevel Effects in Urban Residential Patterns," *Economic Geography*, 52, 1:61–70.

Sands, G. 1976. "Housing Turnover: Assessing its Relevance to Public Policy," *Journal of the American Institute of Planners.* 42:419–426.

Schafer, R. 1974. *The Suburbanization of Multi-Family Housing.* Lexington, Mass.: D. C. Heath.

Scheffman, D. 1978. "Some Evidence on the Recent Boom in Land and Housing Prices," in L. S. Bourne and J. R. Hitchcock, eds., *Urban Housing Markets*. Toronto: University of Toronto Press, 57–85.

Schnare, A. B. 1976. "Racial and Ethnic Price Differentials in an Urban Housing Market," *Urban Studies*, 13:107–120.

————. 1978. *The Persistence of Racial Segregation in Housing*. Washington, D.C.: The Urban Institute.

Schnare, A.B. and MacRae, C. D. 1978. "The Dynamics of Neighborhood Change," *Urban Studies*, 15:327–331.

Schnare, A. B. and Struyk, R. J. 1976. "Segmentation in Urban Housing Markets," *Journal of Urban Economics*, 3:146–166.

Seidel, S. R. 1978. *Housing Costs and Government Regulations*. New Brunswick, N.J.: Rutgers University.

Sharpe, C. A. 1978. "New Construction and Housing Turnover: Vacancy Chains in Toronto," *Canadian Geographer*, XXII, 2:130–144.

————. 1979. *Vacancy Chains and Housing Market Research: A Critical Evaluation*. Research Note 3, Department of Geography, Memorial University of Newfoundland, St. John's, Newfoundland.

Simmons, J. W. 1968. "Changing Residence in the City: A Review of Intra-urban Mobility," *Geographical Review*, 58:622–651.

————. 1974. "Household Movement Trends and Social Change," in L. S. Bourne et al., eds., *Urban Futures for Central Canada*. Toronto: University of Toronto Press, 199–217.

Smith, L.B. 1974. *The Post-war Canadian Housing and Residential Mortgage Markets*. Toronto: University of Toronto Press.

————. 1976. "Myths and Realities in Mortgage Finance and the Housing Crisis," *Canadian Public Policy*, 2, 2:240–248.

————. 1977. *Anatomy of a Crisis: Canadian Housing Policy in the Seventies*. Vancouver: The Fraser Institute.

Smith, Mary. 1977. *Guide to Housing*. London: The Housing Centre Trust.

Smith, V. K. 1977. "Residential Location and Environmental Amenities: A Review of the Evidence," *Regional Studies*, 11:47–61.

Smith, W. F. 1964. *Filtering and Neighborhood Change*. Chap. 3, Research Report 24, Center for Real Estate and Urban Economics, University of California, Berkeley.

————. 1970. *Housing: The Social and Economic Elements*. Berkeley: University of California Press.

Soloman, A. P. 1974. *Housing the Urban Poor*. Cambridge: M.I.T. Press.

Spurr, P. 1976. *Land and Urban Development*. Toronto: J. Lorimer.

Stafford, D. C. 1978. *The Economics of Housing Policy*. London: Croom Helm.

Starr, R. 1979. "An End to Rental Housing?" *The Public Interest*, **47**, Fall: 25–38.

Stegman, M. A. 1972. *Housing Investment in the Inner City: The Dynamics of Decline. A Study of Baltimore, Maryland, 1968–1970*. Cambridge, Mass.: M.I.T. Press.

Sternlieb, G. and Burchell, R. W. 1975. *Residential Abandonment: The Tenement Landlord Revisited*. New Brunswick, N.J.: Rutgers University.

Sternlieb, G. and Hughes, J. 1979. "The Post-Shelter Society," *The Public Interest*, **57**, Fall:48–68.

Stone, E. 1975. "The Housing Crisis, Mortgage Lending and Class Structure," *Antipode*, 7:22–37.

Straszheim, M. H. 1975. *An Econometric Analysis of the Urban Housing Market*. New York: National Bureau of Economic Research.

Stretton, H. 1979. "Housing Policy," Chap. 7 in P. Scott, ed., *Austrialian Cities and Public Policy*. Melbourne: Georgian House, 107–122.

Struyk, R. J. 1976. *Urban Homeownership*. Lexington, Mass.: Lexington Books.

———. 1977. "Housing Situation of Elderly Americans," *The Gerontologist*, 17:130–139.

Struyk, R. J. et al. 1979. *Housing Policies for the Poor*. Washington, D.C.: The Urban Institute.

Sumka, H. J. 1977. "Price Discrimination in a Racially Stable Housing Market," *Environment and Planning A*, 9:905–915.

Sutcliffe, A., ed. 1974. *Multi-Storey Living*. London: Croom Helm.

Taylor, P. J. 1978. "Difficult to Let, Difficult to Live in and Sometimes Difficult to Get out of: An Essay on the Provision of Council Housing," *Discussion Paper No. 16*, Centre for Urban and Regional Development Studies, University of Newcastle-Upon-Tyne, U.K.

Thomas, B. 1973. *Migration and Economic Growth: A Study of Great Britain and the Atlantic Economy*. Cambridge: Cambridge University Press.

Trutko, J., Hetzel, O. and Yates, D. 1978. *A Comparison of the Experimental Housing Allowance Program and Great Britain's Rent Allowance Program*. Washington, D.C.: The Urban Institute.

Turner, J. F. C. 1973. *Housing by People*. New York: Pantheon.

Umraith, H. 1969. "European Approaches to Co-operative and Non-Profit Housing," in M. Wheeler, ed., *The Right to Housing*. Montreal: Harvest House.

U.K. Central Housing Advisory Committee. 1978. *Council Housing: Purposes, Procedures and Priorities*. Report of the Housing Management Sub-Committee. London: H.M.S.O.

U.K. Secretary of State for the Environment, 1977. *Housing Policy: A Consultative Document*, Cmnd. 6851. London: MMSO.

U.N., E.C.E., Committee on Housing Building and Planning. 1977. *Housing for Special Groups*. Proceedings of an International Seminar. Oxford: Pergamon Press.

U.S. Congress. Congressional Budget Office. 1978. *Federal Housing Policy: Current Programs and Recurring Issues*. Background Paper. Washington, D.C.: GPO.

U.S. Dept. of Commerce and Department of Urban Development, 1978. *Annual Housing Survey, 1976*, Series H-150-76 (six volumes). Washington, D.C.: U.S. GPO.

U.S. Dept. of Housing and Urban Development. 1973a. *Abandoned Housing Research: A Compendium*. Washington, D.C.: U.S. GPO.

U.S. Dept. of Housing and Urban Development. 1973b. *Housing in the Seventies*. Washington, D.C.: HUD.

U.S. Dept. of Housing and Urban Development. 1978a. *A Summary Report of Current Findings from the Experimental Housing Allowance Program*. Washington, D.C.: U.S. GPO.

U.S. Dept. of Housing and Urban Development. 1978b. *Report of the Task Force on Housing Costs*. Washington, D.C.: HUD.

U.S. Dept. of Housing and Urban Development. 1978c. *The President's 1978 National Urban Policy Report*. Washington, D.C.: HUD.

U.S. Dept. of Housing and Urban Development. 1978d. *Housing and Planning References*. Washington, D.C.: HUD.

Urban Institute, 1979. *EHAP Research Series* (eight papers). Washington, D.C.: The Urban Institute.

Urban Land Institute. 1977. *Private Market Housing Renovation in Older Urban Areas*. Washington, D.C.: ULI.

von Furstenberg, Harrison, B. and Horowitz, A., eds. 1974. *Patterns of Racial Discrimination Vol. 1, Housing*. Lexington, Mass.: D. C. Heath.

Watson, C. J. 1974. "Vacancy Chains, Filtering and the Public Sector," *Journal of the American Institute of Planners*, **40**, 5:346–352.

Weicher, J. 1978. "Urban Housing Policy," unpublished paper, Urban Institute, Washington, D.C.

Welfield, I. 1977. "American Housing Policy: Perverse Programs by Prudent People," *The Public Interest*, 48:128–144.

Westoff, C. E. 1978. "Marriage and Fertility in the Developed Countries," *Scientific American*, Dec., **238**, 6:35–41.

Wheaton, W. L. C. 1964. "Public and Private Agents of Change in Urban Expansion," in M. M. Webber et al., eds. *Explorations in Urban Structure*. Philadelphia: University of Pennsylvania Press, 154–196.

———. 1977. "Income and Urban Residence: An Analysis of Consumer Demand for Locations," *American Economic Review*, **67**, 4:630–641.

Wheaton, W. L. C., Milgram, G. and Meyerson, M. E., eds. 1966. *Urban Housing*. New York: The Free Press.

Wheeler, M., ed. 1969. *The Right to Housing*. Montreal: Harvest House.

Whitbread, M. and Bird, H. 1973. "Rent Surplus and the Evaluation of Residential Environments," *Regional Studies*, 7:191–213.

White, H. C. 1971. "Multipliers, Vacancy Chains and Filtering in Housing," *Journal of the American Institute of Planners*, **37**, 2:88–94.

Whitehand, J. W. R. 1972. "Building Cycles and the Spatial Pattern of Urban Growth," *Transactions, Institute of British Geographers*, 56:39–54.

Whitehead, C. M. E. 1974. *The U.K. Housing Market: An Econometric Model*. London: Saxon House.

Wilkinson, R. K. and Archer, C. A. 1973. "Measuring the Determinants of Relative House Prices," *Environment and Planning*, 5:357–367.

Williams, P. 1976. "The Role of Institutions in the Inner London Housing Market: The Case of Islington," *Transactions, Institute of British Geographers*, New Series, Vol. 1:72–81.

———. 1977. "Building Societies and the Inner City," *Working Paper No. 54*, University of Birmingham, Joint Centre for Regional and Urban Government Studies.

Willson, K. 1978. "Spatial Submarkets for Housing and the Composition of the Housing Stock in Metro Toronto," unpublished M.A. thesis, Department of Geography, University of Toronto.

Wohl. A. S. 1977. *The Eternal Slum: Housing and Social Policy in Victorian London*. London: Edward Arnold.

Wolfe, H. B. 1969. "Models for the Condition Aging of Residential Structures," *Journal of the American Institute of Planners*, **33**, 3:192–197.

Wolman, H. L. 1975. *Housing and Housing Policy in the U.S. and U.K.* Lexington, Mass.: D. C. Heath.

Wolpert, J. 1965. "Behavioral Aspects of the Decision to Migrate," *Papers of the Regional Science Association*, 15:159–169.

Wood, E. E. 1934. "Low Cost Housing and Slum Clearance," *Law and Contemporary Problems*, Vol. 1:137–147.

Yeates, M. 1972. "The Congruence Between Housing Space, Social Space and Community Space, and Some Experiments Concerning its Implications," *Environment and Planning*, 4:395–414.

Yeates, M. and Garner, B. 1976. *The North American City*. 2nd ed. New York: Harper and Row.

Yinger, J. 1978. "The Black-White Price Differential in Housing: Some Further Evidence," *Land Economics*, 55:187–206.

Yinger, J., Galster, G., Smith, B. and Eggers, F. 1978. *The Status of Research into Racial Discrimination and Segregation in American Housing Markets:* A Research Agenda for the Department of Housing and Urban Development: Washington, D.C.: HUD.

Young, K. and Kramer, J. 1978. *Strategy and Conflict in Metropolitan Housing: Suburbia vs. the Greater London Council*, 1965–75. London: Heinemann.

Index